Breaking the Silence

Second Edition

BREAKING THE SILENCE

Second Edition

**A Guide to Help Children with Complicated Grief—
Suicide, Homicide, AIDS, Violence, and Abuse**

Linda Goldman

Routledge
Taylor & Francis Group
New York London

BREAKING THE SILENCE, SECOND EDITION

2 3 4 5 6 7 8 9 0

Cover design by Rob Williams.

A CIP catalog record for this book is available from the British Library.
♾ The paper in this publication meets the requirements of the ANSI Standard Z39.48-1984 (Permanence of Paper).

Library of Congress Cataloging-in-Publication Data
Goldman, Linda, 1946–
     Breaking the silence : a guide to help children with complicated grief—suicide, homicide, AIDS, violence, and abuse / Linda Goldman.—2nd ed.
        p. cm.
     Includes bibliographical references and index.
     ISBN 1-58391-312-2 (pbk. : alk. paper)
     1. Grief in children. 2. Bereavement in children. 3. Grief therapy. 4. Abused children—Psychology. 5. Victims of crimes—Psychology. I. Title.

BF723.G75 G64 2002
155.9′37′083—dc20

                                                              2001043251

ISBN 1-58391-312-2 (paper)

To Katy, Andrew, Chet, and Luke,

I have grown to know and love you all through the loving eyes of your parents. I have grown to respect and admire your life's courage, as children and as human beings on this planet.

I have come to see that *who* you are is very separate from *how* and *why* you died. Thank you for teaching me this lesson.

Linda

Table of Contents

Part 1
Complicated Grief

C H A P T E R   1

Part II
Breaking the Silence

C H A P T E R   2

CHAPTER 3

Breaking the Silence on AIDS 47

CHAPTER 4

Breaking the Silence on Homicide and Other Violent Crimes 59

CHAPTER 5

Breaking the Silence on Abuse 73

CHAPTER 6

Breaking the Silence on Bullying. 91

Part III
Techniques

CHAPTER 10

Communities Grieve: Involvement with Children and Trauma 179

Part IV
Resources

CHAPTER 11

National Resources Bridge the Gap 215

CHAPTER 12

Materials to Explore and Annotated Bibliography: There Is Hope 229

About the Second Edition

Our children of the twenty-first century are all too often inundated with school shootings, violent rampages, horrific bullying, natural traumatic disasters, and acts of terrorism. This second edition of *Breaking the Silence* sheds new light on these complex and sensitive areas of traumatic grief so that our global community can more openly deal with them. Two new chapters have been added: "Breaking The Silence on Bullying" and "Communities Grieve: Involvement With Children and Trauma." All previous chapters from the first edition have been broadened and practical activities for working with bully–victim issues and traumatized youth have been included. Resources have been greatly expanded. Books, videos, CD-ROMs, websites, curriculums, and other national resources have been updated. The second edition of *Breaking the Silence* confronts today's traumatic grief issues with realistic and comprehensive approaches to the groundswell of everyday complicated grief experiences our children live with and are subjected to in their homes, at their schools, in their communities, and in their world.

Anecdotes that appear throughout this guide contain names and stories that have been modified to maintain privacy. The children, adults, animals, and scenery in the photographs may not specifically relate to the material on the page where they appear.

Preface

There are no throwaway people. Every person on the planet is recyclable. Every person is worthy of help. Sometimes we think *those* people are not good enough, *those* people don't count as much, *those* people have so many problems that no amount of energy we give them can help them find another way of experiencing life. *Those* people are us. Our interconnectedness grows daily to the point that a murder, a suicide, an AIDS victim, an airplane crash, a terrorist's bombing cannot help but spill over into our lives. So opening the door for others opens the doors for ourselves.

I'm reminded of a story I heard recently that touched my heart, and I hope will touch yours. . . .

One night a man was walking on the beach. He saw thousands of starfish washed to the shore. A little boy was picking them up one at a time and throwing them back into the ocean. The man walked up to him and asked him, "What are you doing?" "Why are you doing this?" and "What does it matter?" As the little boy picked up the next starfish, held it up to the moonlight, and got ready to throw it back into the ocean, he replied, "It matters to this one."

Foreword

Linda Goldman has boldly broken the silence. Children in America today (as well as in Ireland, Bosnia, Rwanda, etc.) are bombarded by violence. It is on the news, in the video arcades, and in the streets. That is not news. Children are suffering both immediate and long-term effects of that violence. That is not news either. They *all* need help and *can be* helped. This is the news Linda Goldman delivers in this book. This is a book for professionals, parents, and other caring adults who touch the lives of children caught up in the trauma of their existence.

Many of us, uncomfortable as we may be with the day-to-day psychological traumas of our young people, find it difficult to address complicated grief—grief that results from senseless violence, abuse, social stigma, homicide, and suicide. Exposed to a brief but overwhelming experience, a child will retreat behind an invisible wall erected to protect what remains of the psyche. Left to their own devices for a period of time, such traumatized children learn to function with little interference from the original disturbance. However, it is at a great psychological cost. Personality patterns that may be dysfunctional in some contexts become established and maintained because of the security they provide in avoiding the experience of trauma and its sequelae.

Alternatively, chronic psychic fatigue is more likely to develop in children who live in the war zones that many urban environments and suburban televisions have become; in children whose personal tragedies of parental suicide or homicide occur in a life impoverished by lack of financial and/or social support; or in children who are abused over a number of years. Chronic psychic fatigue is an absence of hope; a bleak future, if any; an expectation of early death; apathy; low aspirations; impulsivity, and an emphasis on immediate gratification often resulting in substance abuse. We see these children in schools, day care centers, doctors' offices and as clients in various social service programs (e.g., AFDC, protective services, juvenile services).

We see them, but we may ignore them or their grief. In some instances, we ignore them because they do not appear to be doing too badly considering what has happened in their young lives. In other instances, we ignore them because we do not know what to do for them—we do not know how to break the silence, to get beyond the wall and provide comfort and healing so that the child can move forward.

Linda Goldman has written this book for all people who work with children experiencing complicated grief. She helps us see that we should not assume that time will heal the child. She provides us with concrete guidelines by which to identify the problems of children suffering from complicated grief. Most of all, she provides a conceptually based and structured procedure, descriptions of a wealth of concrete therapeutic techniques, and sources for additional ones. For those who deal with children, especially those who deal with children chronically exposed to violence and death, and wish to help them, this book is an invaluable resource.

Alfred Lucco Ph.D.
Child and Family Therapist
Associate Professor, School of Social Work
University of Maryland at Baltimore (UMAB)

Acknowledgments

I would like to thank:

my husband, Michael, for his love and continuous support for my work;

my son, Jon, for his boundless creativity and encouragement;

my father, Jerry, for his positive attitude and innate sense of humor;

my friend Jim, for his kindness and light;

my friend Greg for his wise counseling;

my dog, Bart, for his devotion;

Dr. Ellen Zinner for her invaluable work in editing;

Dr. Beverly Celotta, Dr. Lori Wiener, Dr. Joan Leibermann, and Laura MacKenzie for their expertise;

Al Lucco, Ph. D., for the knowledge he has shared with me and his continuing guidance;

Dr. Sam Ny, Eric Chen, Chang-Jen Hsieh, Professor Jie-Fang Chi, Venerable Huei Kai, Pamela, Chang Su-Ling, Evelyn Chen, and all of my Taiwanese friends and extended family;

Judy Madden and the Montgomery County School System and Jean Burgess and the Montgomery County Crisis Center for sharing information;

Kinder-mourn and Chris Crawford, Kelli Haughey, and Lura McMurray and the Robinette Family for sharing Ben;

The Kids' Place and Danny Mize for their efforts in contributing their story;

Lori, Keith, Kyle, Megan, Mark, Claire, and Andrew Benson and;

all of the children and adults throughout the world who bravely shared their experiences, materials, and photographs in order to help other children.

Complicated Grief

What is Children's Complicated Grief

TERRORISTS BLOW UP BUILDING AND MURDER KIDS AND ADULTS

MOM KILLS DAD • DAD KILLS MOM • BROTHER IS STABBED

OUTSIDE HOME • FRIEND HANGS HIMSELF • UNCLE MURDERED IN

DRIVE-BY SHOOTING • SISTER GETS AIDS • DRUNKEN DRIVER

KILLS TEACHER • GRANDMOTHER DIES OF SUDDEN HEART ATTACK

CHILDREN KIDNAPPED FROM HOME AND MURDERED

GRANDFATHER SHOOTS HIMSELF IN HEAD • TEACHER ARRESTED

FOR RAPE • MOM DROWNS TWO CHILDREN

BABYSITTER BEATS INFANT TO DEATH

A Look at Grief

My first book, *Life and Loss: A Guide to Help Grieving Children*, concentrates on normal grief work with children. The four tasks of normal grief—understanding, grieving, commemorating, and moving on—are presented and explained. The emphasis of *Life and Loss* is on recognizing and understanding the denial that so often accompanies loss and grief.

Death is viewed culturally as the enemy of life. Even though we know death cannot be avoided, we generally push it out of our minds and live in denial of its everyday presence. Consequently, we are unprepared to deal with death and become shocked and traumatized when we are forced to face it. Sooner or later, adults and children will be called upon to face the loss of a loved one. Our culture does not always provide the support and openness needed to accept normal grief, and the complications involved with issues of suicide, homicide, AIDS, abuse, and violence cry out for a new way of seeing in our society. If we, as a society, can see differently, so can our children.

The goal of *Breaking the Silence* is to provide a guide for caring adults to help children with these complicated issues. The scarcity of children's works on the topics of suicide, homicide, AIDS, violence, abuse, bullying, and terrorism only magnifies the need to create a resource that gives adults and children the words to break this prison of silence and denial that is so much a part of today's culture. This prison of silence and denial was not created by the children. They were born into it. A 12-year-old who refuses to tell her friend *that* her father died for fear she will have to tell her friend *how* her father died faces a prison of silence locked shut by society. An 8-year-old who continually runs away from school, shouting and screaming to teachers and administrators his desire to not live any longer, is told by the health care system that there is no hurry for him to be seen because he is just being manipulative. Couldn't suicide be the ultimate manipulation? And who would ultimately be responsible? We (society) would be. Let's get these kids help.

> We need to open a door and allow the children to breathe freely the fresh air of truth. By bringing these subjects into the light of day without fear and shame, we can create a healing environment for communicating loss and grief.

Hopefully, *Breaking the Silence* will help accomplish this goal. First, adults are given specific ideas, techniques, resources, and materials to use with children in each area of complicated grief. Second, adults are given the specific words to use with children and ways to initiate discussions of these anxiety-producing topics. Third, caring adults are given the information and tools to help them separate the child from the circumstances surrounding his or her loss and grief. These complications of grief must be recognized and dealt with before normal grief can be acknowledged and released.

Despite the complicated circumstances of suicide, homicide, AIDS, violence, and abuse, the underlying process of grief is universal and timeless. As horrendous as these circumstances are, they could happen to any one of us at any time.

<table>
<tr><td>〜</td><td>Photographs of nature, animals, and children are interwoven throughout this book to continually remind us that the cycle of life and death is ever present and ongoing. The death of someone or something we love is a normal and natural process of life that we all will experience.</td></tr>
</table>

The photographs in this book are intended to provide an ongoing reminder that suicide, homicide, AIDS, and other "unnatural events" exist in daily life and need to be addressed and dealt with openly. The "unnatural" has become a very common part of the world of today's children. By recognizing this, caring adults can break through the silent shame and stigma of complicated grief issues with children and help them reach the underlying feelings of loss and grief that everyone shares.

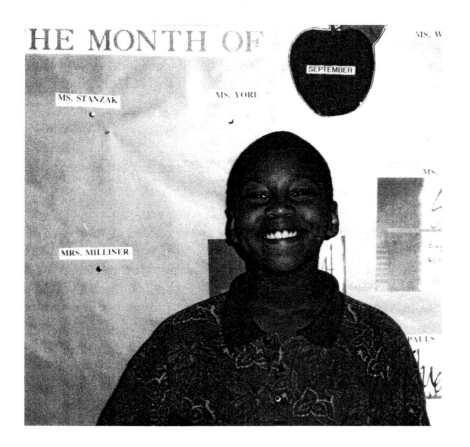

What is Normal Grief?

Grief is defined as a normal, internalized reaction to the loss of a person, thing, or idea. It is our emotional response to loss.

Bereavement is the state of having lost something, whether it is a significant other, significant things, or our own sense of will.

Mourning means taking the internal experience of grief and expressing it outside ourselves. It is the cultural expression of grief as seen in traditional or creative rituals. Traditional rituals are ones that are culturally sanctioned, such as funerals. Creative rituals can be writing a letter to the deceased and then destroying it.

Rituals are the behaviors we use to do grief work.

Goldman, Life and Loss (2000, p. 25)

These definitions are explained in my first book *Life and Loss: A Guide to Help Grieving Children* (2000). A brief overview of normal grief is important in order to differentiate between normal grief and the many complications that can occur. Sandra Fox, in her book *Good Grief* (1988, p. 21), defined the four psychological tasks of grief as:

Understanding
Grieving
Commemorating
Going On

The first task is *understanding*. Kids need to make sense of loss at whatever developmental stage they experience it. Children have different developmental perceptions of death. Young children feel death is reversible, and many times their magical thinking makes them feel that they may have caused the death. A cliche such as "your Mom is better off dead; she was suffering so much" can only inhibit the normal grief process of a child who misses his or her mom.

The second task is *grieving*. Children will experience physical, emotional, cognitive, and behavioral symptoms in normal grief. These normal grief signals range from stomach aches and nightmares to poor grades and hostility towards friends.

- Child continually *retells events* about the loved one and his or her death
- Child *feels the loved one is present* in some way and *speaks of him or her* in the present tense
- Child *dreams* about the loved one and *longs* to be with him or her
- Child *experiences nightmares* and *sleeplessness*
- Child *cannot concentrate* on schoolwork
- Child *appears* at times *to feel nothing*
- Child is *preoccupied* with death and excessively *worried* about health issues
- Child is *afraid* to be left alone
- Child *cries often* at unexpected times
- Child *wets the bed* or *loses appetite*
- Child *idealizes the loved one* and *assumes his or her mannerisms*
- Child becomes the *"class bully"* or *"class clown"*
- Child has *headaches* and *stomach aches*
- Child *rejects old friends, withdraws,* or *acts out*

The third task is *commemorating*. Children need to find concrete ways to make death and other losses meaningful. By lighting a candle, writing a poem, planting a flower, or sending a balloon into the air, grieving children can express their grief symbolically.

The fourth task is going on. By going on, we don't mean that the child will forget a brother that was murdered. Rather, the child will find an inner place for the love that lives for that brother and is carried throughout life. When a child is ready to revisit the playground where he and his brother played, he has moved to another level of grief work.

Grief is as unique as each individual child. Yet it is important to understand normal grief principles in order to recognize when a child may be unable to express feelings. The intensity, frequency, and duration of normal grief symptoms are good indicators of *underlying complications* leading to prolonged or unresolved grief. These complications may stem from competing or conflicting issues that inhibit the expression of normal grief. The child's grief process becomes frozen in time.

What is Complicated Grief?

| | When life issues are unexpressed or unacknowledged, they become locked in frozen blocks of time. |

Frozen blocks of time stop normal grief and deny the child the ability to grieve. For the child, it can feel as if life stops and time stands still. The natural flow of feelings is inhibited. There is no movement forward until the issues are resolved and the feelings are released. Suicide, homicide, AIDS, abuse, and violence are familiar examples of situations that lead to complicated grief because the child is unable to express what happened.

The grief process is normal and natural after a loss. When children become stuck in a frozen block of time, they are denied access to this normal and natural flowing process. Overwhelmed by frozen feelings, the grief process seems to be on hold or nonexistent. The child is either not in touch with his or her feelings of grief or those feelings are ambivalent and in conflict.

In complicated grief, it is as if an unexpressed or unresolved important life issue—a frozen block of time—has created a wall of ice between the child and his or her grief. Our job is to help melt that wall.

FACTORS THAT CONTRIBUTE TO COMPLICATED GRIEF

Sudden or Traumatic Death

Sudden or traumatic death can include murder, suicide, a fatal accident, terrorist attack, sudden fatal illness, or school shooting. Immediately an unstable environment is created in the child's home. Children feel confusion over these kinds of death. Desire for revenge is often experienced after a murder or fatal accident. Rage or guilt or both emerge against the person who has committed suicide. Terror of violence and death unfolds, and the child feels shock and disbelief that this death has suddenly occurred.

Social Stigma of Death

Social stigma and shame frequently accompany deaths related to AIDS, suicide, and homicide. Children, as well as adults, often feel too embarrassed to speak of these issues. They remain silent out of fear of being ridiculed or ostracized. These suppressed feelings get projected outwardly in the form of rage or inwardly in the form of self-hatred. Often times these kids feel lonely and isolated. They cannot grieve normally because they have not separated the loss of the deceased from the way the deceased died.

Multiple Losses

Multiple losses can produce a deep fear of abandonment and self-doubt in children. The death of a parent without a partner is a good example of a multiple loss. When the only parent of a child dies, the child can be forced to move from his or her home, the rest of the family, friends, school, and the community. The child is shocked at this sudden and complete change of lifestyle and surroundings and may withdraw or become terrified of future abandonment. Nightmares or bed wetting could appear.

Past Relationship to the Deceased

When a child has been abused, neglected, or abandoned by a loved one, there are often ambivalent feelings when the loved one's death occurs. A 5-year-old girl whose alcoholic father sexually abused her may feel great conflict when that parent dies. Part of her may feel relieved, even glad, to be rid of the abuse yet ashamed to say those feelings out loud. She may carry the secret of the abuse and become locked into that memory and be unable to grieve. Children often feel guilty, fearful, abandoned, or depressed if grief for a loved one is complicated by an unresolved past relationship.

Grief Process of the Surviving Parent or Caretaker

If the surviving parent is not able to mourn, there is no role model for the child. A closed environment stops the grief process. Many times the surviving parent finds it too difficult to watch his or her child grieve. The parent may be unable to grieve him- or herself or may be unwilling to recognize the child's pain. Feelings become denied and the expression of these feelings are withheld. The surviving parent may well become an absentee parent because of his or her own overwhelming grief, producing feelings of abandonment and isolation in the child. Children often fear something will happen to this parent or to themselves and, as a result, become overprotective of the parent and other loved ones.

> The question we must ask ourselves is: How can we protect children from the barrage of complicated grief that fills today's world and lies waiting for them inside their homes and outside their doorsteps?

The children in this new millennium face a grief seemingly far more horrifying than we did as children. They face the loss of the protection of the adult world—the loss of a future—the loss of safety and protection. Whether children ever really enjoyed the protection of the adults in their lives is a question we could debate, but the perception of that safety seemed to exist in previous generations. Although grief has always and will always exist as a part of life, today's kids are exposed to the news, the internet, their music and videos that constantly bombard them with images of school shootings, killings, violence and abuse. They are left with feelings of vulnerability and defenselessness. Whether by real circumstances or vicariously through media reports, children are disrupted from grieving normally by such issues as murder, suicide, AIDS, abuse, violence, bullying and terrorism.

All situations or circumstances that breed fear, shame, and terror cut off the grief process and result in children caught unexpectedly in frozen blocks of time.

FROZEN BLOCKS OF TIME

"Frozen blocks of time" is an important concept underlying complicated grief. Children experiencing complicated grief are usually unable to break free from overwhelming feelings experienced at the time of their trauma. They become imprisoned in these feelings if they are not given the freedom to work through their grief.

We, as caring adults, need to facilitate a "meltdown process" whereby children can be comfortable enough to reexperience all the overwhelming feelings they felt at the time of their loss. We can do this in four steps:

1. We can do this by seeing the child in the present and seeing his or her behaviors as cries for help. The frozen state of denial and endless searching for what was not available at the time of the loss must be replaced by trust in a process of remembering so that the child's pain is not carried into adulthood.

2. We can create a safe environment as a friend, an advocate for, or a guide to the child to walk him or her through grief work when ready.

3. When it feels safe for the child to remember the overwhelming feelings felt at the time of the loss, we can become a helper in remembering.

4. We can provide space to the child to reexperience the *denied feelings*. Each time a child can release the fears, tears, terror, rage, guilt, self-hatred, and love felt at the time of the loss, he or she is taking a step on the path toward healing. This is the essence of complicated grief work and the thread that binds everything discussed in this book.

THE MELTDOWN PROCESS

Too often children are given the following message: "Don't talk about it! Don't think about it! Don't feel about it! It makes me uncomfortable, and you, as a child, have a job to do—keep the adults in your life comfortable. We don't want to remember our own feelings or our own pain."

Often children are taught to put a bell jar over their feelings and live in a separate world of isolation to please adults. If children continue to avoid their own pain, they will again and again find themselves re-creating situations that attempt to access these hidden feelings. The following are three examples:

EXAMPLE 1: SANDY

Sandy was a young girl who came with her aunt and uncle to see me. Sandy's aunt and uncle were concerned that Sandy had not grieved the death of her mother. Sandy was withdrawn. She could not look at me and did not speak. Her guardians said she had not cried over her mother's death. Sandy was six years old when her mom died of a sudden heart attack. Sandy was taken away from her home, her friends, her family, her school, her community, and her day-to-day life as she knew it and brought to a new environment with which she was not familiar. As a result of these multiple losses she was reluctant to speak. It took several months to establish the trust to begin the meltdown process.

EXAMPLE 2: RACHEL

Rachel, a 29-year-old woman who began grief therapy because she had been overwhelmed by feelings of loss since childhood, appeared learning disabled, had suffered from depression for years, and relied on antidepressants. After exploring her childhood, it became clear that her mother's illness and death when Rachel was 11 was unresolved. Her feelings had not been heard or acknowledged. Her father remarried quickly and moved to another state with Rachel losing her friends, school, and safety as well as her mom all within one year. The painful feelings of loss as a child remained unresolved and plagued her in adulthood.

EXAMPLE 3: BONNIE

Bonnie came for grief therapy in her sixties. Her husband had died, and eventually she began to date. She came into my office one day terrified that her boyfriend was going to kill her cat. As we explored the facts, we saw that he had never shown evidence of violence towards her or her cat. We traveled back in time to her childhood and realized that she was terrorized at age 5 by a raging stepfather. She learned and feared that anger might be powerful enough to kill her, and that her anger could be powerful enough to kill someone else. When she began to see how her childhood trauma had been carried far into adulthood in an unconscious way, she began the meltdown process.

These examples illustrate that individuals ranging from 6 to 65 can be frozen in time in their childhoods. How much better might life have been had the complicated grief issues been resolved while they were still children? Each one of these individuals held stored fear and pain. This stored fear and pain can be projected inward and result in self-hatred or even suicide. It also can be projected onto others, resulting in violence, abuse, or homicide.

The meltdown process allows individuals who have become frozen in time by a deep trauma to re-experience their feelings in a way that they were not able to do at the time of their loss. For Sandy, a safe environment allowed her to feel secure enough to remember and reexperience the overwhelming sadness she felt at age six when her mom had a fatal heart attack. The meltdown process afforded Rachel a space to remember her mom's unbearable illness and death due to cancer when Rachel was 11. For Bonnie, it offered permission to feel the terror of a 5-year-old confronted by a raging alcoholic parent. No longer did these individuals feel the need to pretend or deny these childhood events. By bringing their own personal horrors into the light of day, the fear from being trapped in time was lifted.

FACILITATING MELTDOWN

We, as caring adults, need to achieve an openness about these previously closed topics by:

1. Stressing the need to separate the person who died from the way that person died to truly grieve the person's death.

2. Defining suicide, homicide, AIDS, violence, abuse, bullying, and terrorism to children in simple and direct language that eliminates judgment.

By separating and defining death, we can help the adult world re-create their concepts of the unspeakable. For example, children need to make sense of death and, even more, of suicide. If we define death for children as "when the body stops working," then we can define suicide for children as "when someone does/did something to their body (that made their) body stop working" (Sandra Fox, *Good Grief*, 1998, p. 11).

I have often found in my private practice as a grief therapist, that the adult caregiver's fear and shame are the major factors in noncommunication with children. A mom's terror about having to tell her 5-year-old daughter that an older brother got killed in a drive-by shooting locks her and her family into a hidden secret and their inability to express it. When the mother and I can role play that dialogue with her daughter, we can eliminate a great deal of the perceived terror she feels. She is then better able to communicate with her child.

Our inability to discuss these topics openly with kids creates an atmosphere of secrecy, loneliness, and isolation far more damaging than the actual death of someone close to them.

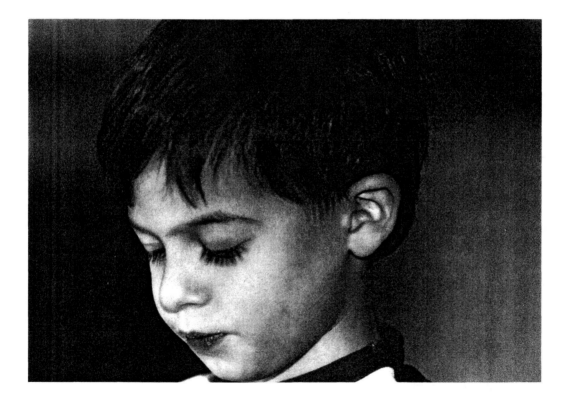

RESOURCES THAT FACILITATE THE MELTDOWN PROCESS

I Know I Made It Happen by Lynn Blackburn (1991) is a book that recognizes and addresses children's magical thinking and subsequent guilt that they are in some way responsible for the loss of a loved one. Children and adults can use this book as a resource with which to identify and relate. It is about the many things children feel they have caused.

As I read this book to kids experiencing a great loss in their lives, they often say that they can relate to the story. Robert explained, "It's my fault my dad died. If only I had not been playing at my baseball game and been with my dad at his baseball game when he had his heart attack, I know I could have saved him." "I killed my mother," insisted Margaret. "How?" I asked. "Well," she said knowingly, "she picked me up the night she had her heart attack and, if she hadn't done that, she wouldn't have died."

We were able then to talk about the *facts* of heart disease and separate these facts from the children's magical thinking. They began to melt down an important, frozen block of time. The unbearable responsibility of not saving their parent from death was brought out into the open, and the new understanding that it was not their fault that their mom or dad died was allowed to be created.

Aarvy Aardvark Finds Hope by Donna O'Toole (1988) is a story to be read aloud to young children. O'Toole uses animals as a vehicle for understanding the journey of grief and uses storytelling as a device to allow readers of any age to identify with their own pain and subsequent healing. Aarvy grieves over the sudden loss of his mother and brother who were suddenly taken away to the zoo. Aarvy had felt abandoned by his dad in the same way when he was a baby. These multiple losses and the shock of each loss creates a story of complicated grief that even a young child can understand and identify with. The *Aarvy Aardvark Video* by Donna O'Toole (1994) uses puppets and visual imagery to allow the story to come alive for young people. The pace of the film is designed to allow kids to feel a sense of the slow moving process of grief itself.

The Hurt, by Teddi Doleski (1983), is a sensitively written book that can open a discussion of painful feelings for children and adults. It is a wonderfully simple story with an underlying universal theme: *When we lock in our hurts, we become lonely, isolated, and scared.*

ACTIVITIES TO HELP YOUNG CHILDREN WITH COMPLICATED GRIEF

1. Read stories to children that allow them to project their feelings onto the story characters. This opens a dialogue with a child in a way that is not threatening.

2. Allow children to visualize their hurt, fear, or pain. They can then draw, use clay, or imagine these symbolic feelings being able to talk. If the hurt could talk, 8-year-old Nancy explained, it would say "Why me?" Nancy had experienced multiple losses, including the death of her younger sister. Feelings of having bad luck or being punished began to emerge.

3. Invite children to make a loss timeline, filling it in with people and dates in chronological order according to when they died. This loss timeline becomes a concrete representation of all the losses one has experienced.

4. Create with children a geneogram or family tree using a circle and square to represent people still living and people who have died in their life. Kids can see not only the extent of the losses they have had but also the support system of people that are still remaining.

> By helping children put their feelings outside of themselves we can facilitate their healing. Sharing their feelings can diminish their hurt.

TOMMY: A TOOL FOR TEENAGERS

The rock opera *Tommy* (The Who, music and lyrics by Pete Townshend, 1993, Kardana Productions) is an excellent medium to use in grief work with teenagers. The drama allows the audience to visualize and conceptualize through dance, music, and story the very poignant story of Tommy and his journey through complicated grief. The audience can experience Tommy's pain and actually see his frozen blocks of time appear, continue, and compound themselves through each of his life's traumas. Teenagers who may not relate to material geared to younger children may more easily accept *Tommy* and the rock music of Peter Townshend and The Who.

The story begins with 4-year-old Tommy witnessing an all too common occurrence in today's world. His father comes home and finds his wife with her new boyfriend. An argument erupts, and Tommy witnesses his father shooting and killing the boyfriend.

Realizing that Tommy witnessed this homicide, his parents immediately begin shouting at him over and over again: "You didn't see it, you didn't hear it. You didn't see it, you didn't hear it." As they continue to scream these words, the turmoil and confusion of the police investigation and trial whirl by him.

Tommy stops seeing, hearing, and speaking. He becomes frozen in time. The trauma of violence coupled with the prison of family secrets have stilled his being. Gazing at his reflection in the mirror is the only way that he can see the child within who remains suspended in time.

At age 10, Tommy is sexually abused by a drunken uncle. Tommy tells no one. Another frozen block of time is created, and he again sees its reflection in the mirror.

A few years later, Tommy is tormented by the neighborhood bully. Physically and verbally abused by him, Tommy again remains still in his silent world, except for the inner voice directing him towards the ever-present reflection of himself in the mirror. He sings to this reflection, "See me, feel me, touch me, heal me," throughout the play—his ongoing attempt to melt his own frozen blocks of time and be free.

His mother's frustration with Tommy's silence ultimately leads her to smash his mirror in a fit of rage. At this moment, the audience gets to see the 4-year-old, 10-year-old, and 17-year-old parts of Tommy, thus far held prisoner by trauma. The parts stand separately on stage. This visual representation displays the complicated grief Tommy held at various ages and how these parts needed to be brought together, out in the open, in order for Tommy to heal.

Tommy becomes a pin ball wizard and a rock star. His fame brings him many followers who look to him to find the way to their own happiness. His message is simple. They must look within themselves, for that's where the answers are buried deep.

Tommy's story is uplifting. We see his silent struggle with pain and his eventual breakthrough to become conscious of his tragedy. With his inner wisdom and insight, he demonstrates to teenagers a way to reframe their own private hurts and explore traumatic memories. This self-knowledge constitutes a right of passage with which young people can identify.

WHAT CAN WE DO FOR THE CHILDREN?

Journals

Fire in my Heart, Ice in my Veins by Enid Traisman (1992) is an excellent interactive journal for teenagers. It provides many resourceful ways for teens to put their thoughts and feelings on paper.

Manuals

Teen Age Grief (TAG) by Linda Cunningham (1990) is an excellent manual for initiating and facilitating grief support groups for teens. Kids explain how they grieve and provide practical ideas that may help them in their grief process.

Music

Music is a powerful form of communicating, especially for teenagers. Music can be an excellent vehicle for bringing feelings and memories to the surface, and it provides a way to help teens relax. Teenagers can be asked to share music that reminds them of their loved one to share or a favorite song that their loved one liked. If a teenager plays a musical instrument, he or she can play a musical selection. The following music may be highly effective with teenagers.

"The Way We Were" by Barbara Streisand
"I'll Be There" by The Escape Club
"Tears In Heaven" by Eric Clapton
"Fire and Rain" by James Taylor
"It's So Hard to Say Good-Bye to Yesterday"
by Boyz II Men
"Children Will Listen" by Barbara Streisand
"That's What Friends are For" by Whitney Houston
"Wind Beneath my Wings" by Bette Midler
"Between Heaven and Earth" by Cindy Bullens

Books

In *Death is Hard to Live With* by Janet Bode (1993), teenagers openly express how they have coped with the loss of someone they have loved. These losses include death by suicide and homicide.

Facing Change by Donna O'Toole (1995) provides an abundance of information and coping choices to assist teens with the grief process. Practical ways to help normalize grief are included.

Helping Teens Cope With Death by the Dougy Center (1999) is an excellent resource to help guide teens with death.

The C-Word by Elena Dorfman (1994), is a book for teenagers and their families coping with of cancer and the deaths it may cause.

The Grieving Teen by Helen Fitzgerald (2000) is a wonderful guide to living with grief for teenagers and their friends.

When A Friend Dies by Marilyn Gootman (1994) is a book for teens about grieving and healing. Gootman uses the words of teens, affirms their feelings, and presents positive ways of coping with these feelings.

Words

Abuse: When someone hurts someone else's body or feelings over and over again and usually does it on purpose. Sometimes someone can hurt us just one time and that can be abuse, too. The hurt can come from screaming, hitting, using mean words, or touching in a way that is uncomfortable or confusing.

Casket: A casket is a special box in which a body is buried.

Cemetery: A cemetery is a place where bodies in a casket are buried.

Cremation: Cremation changes a body into ashes. Some people say "the spirit leaves the body, something like when the butterfly leaves the cocoon. The butterfly flies out and the cocoon is left behind. When the person dies, their spirit leaves the body and goes to a safe place, and the body is left behind, like the cocoon. Some people choose to have the body cremated after the body has died. If that is their choice, the body is placed in a machine. The machine heats the body at a very high temperature until the body is changed to something called ashes or cremains" (Carney, *Our Special Garden: Understanding Cremation*, 1999).

Death: Death is when the body stops working (Fox, 1988, p. 11).

Depression: Depression is extreme feelings of sadness that last a long time.

Funeral: A funeral is a gathering of friends and family to remember a person who has died, to honor his or her life, and to say goodbye. Usually it is just before the body is buried.

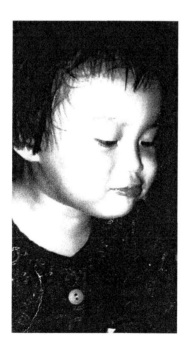

Grief: Grief is all the feelings we feel after someone close to us has died. We can feel sad, angry, frightened, or guilty.

Guilt: Guilt is a feeling that makes us think we are the cause of something and that we may have done something wrong.

Homicide: Homicide is the act of killing someone else so that his or her body stops working. Sometimes people kill out of anger or fear, or because they forget that every human being is important. There is always another way to work out our feelings without hurting someone else.

Mourning: Mourning is the way we take our feelings of grief and do something to remember the person close to us. It's how we show our sorrow.

Rage: Rage is a feeling of extreme anger.

Revenge: Revenge is an extreme feeling of wanting to get back at someone by hurting them in some way.

Shame: Shame is a feeling of extreme guilt.

Stigma: Stigma is a mark of shame of someone doing something wrong.

Suicide: Suicide is the act of killing yourself so that your body won't work anymore. People do this when they feel there is no other way to solve their problems, or they may feel at the moment that life is not worth living.

Terror: Terror is a feeling of extreme fear.

Breaking the Silence

C H A P T E R   2

Breaking the Silence on Suicide

SECRETS • SHAME • GUILT
ABANDONMENT

"Whoever preserves one life, it is as if he preserves an entire world."

Talmud

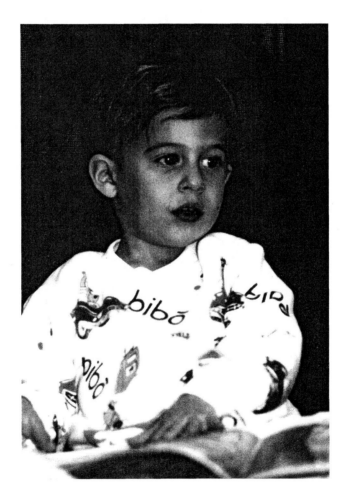

Facts about Suicide

Suicide is the third leading cause of death for young people between the ages of 15 to 24 (National Vital Statistic Reports, Vol. 47, No. 19, June 30, 1999).

More than 30,000 Americans die of suicide each year (*Washington Post*, September 26, 1999).

Between 1976–1997 the rate of suicide among young people ages 15–19 has increased 14% and the rate among children ages 10–14 has increased by 100% (*Washington Post*, September 26, 1999).

Teenagers polled in Washington, DC reported that 10% had attempted suicide within the past twelve months (*Washington Post*, September 3, 1998).

The Language of Suicide

Compassionate Friends has adopted new language to eliminate any negativity or judgment associated with suicide. They advise words such as "died by suicide" or "died of suicide" to replace the commonly used "completed suicide" or "committed suicide."

"Compassionate Friends" Moves to Change Suicide
Language,, Vol. 11, No. 3, Fall/Winter 1999–2000. Surviving Suicide/Published by the American Association of Suicidology

Complications of Suicide

Alice's husband, Matt, had died of suicide six years before she came to see me, when her son, Brian, was 4. Since then she had not dated and had no desire to be with a man. Her husband had left a suicide note blaming her for his death. Over and over she told stories of abandonment by friends and relatives who stopped calling or seeing her after her husband died. She felt totally rejected by her husband, and these feelings were compounded by rejection from the rest of her world.

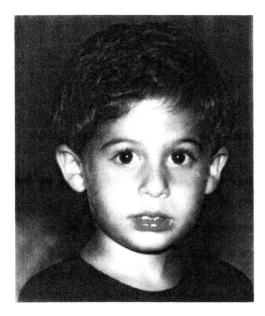

Why, she asked, did her family give so much attention to her sister, Page, whose husband died of cancer, and none to her and her son, Brian? No one ever mentioned her husband or his death. The loneliness of her mourning became greater than Matt's death. She could not grieve outwardly. No one would listen. The guilt and shame of his suicide grew. With no other adult to share it with, this guilt became her and Brian's unspoken family secret. Alice isolated herself and her son. She allowed no men into her life.

During Brian's routine 10-year-old checkup, the pediatrician suggested that Alice receive grief counseling. The doctor also stressed that Brian should begin to have some male figures in his life. Since his dad's death, Brian's mom and he had spent much of their time with each other, without any masculine role models for Brian to identify with. Sometimes children feel different if they don't have a dad around as they are growing up.

Shown here is a picture Brian drew. His Uncle John was the central figure. Alice was shocked because Brian rarely saw his uncle. For Brian, the primary problem seemed to be not having a man in his life to spend time with and look up to, and not his dad's death by suicide. The issue of how his dad had died had not emerged.

The complication of suicide left Brian without a dad. The complication of suicide left Alice with fear. Her fear was that speaking about or telling her son about suicide would destroy their lives even more. The terror that another man could destroy them both kept Alice and Brian isolated and alone. Suicide built a powerful wall around their physical and emotional home that no one could penetrate.

It is clear that adults suffer from complicated grief in the same way that children do. Therapy needs to involve both parent and child in order to be most effective. Adults are role models in the grief process. If adults are frozen in blocks of time by fear and secrecy, there is little or no permission for children to grieve.

Suicide—A Journey of Despair

As a certified grief counselor and death educator in private practice in Chevy Chase, Maryland, I am confronted with children that are suicide survivors and with children who consider suicide a possible solution to problems. In my search for literature for children on this topic, I found very little. This led me to create *Bart Speaks Out on Suicide,* an interactive storybook for young children. *Bart Speaks Out* provides words for adults and children to use to create open discussions about suicide. It invites children to write or draw their feelings and helps them learn to separate the person that died from the way that person died.

I have found projective techniques to be extremely effective in working with children and their thoughts and feelings of self-hatred and self-destruction. So often children cannot or will not verbalize their feelings directly. Sometimes their emotional environment reinforces silence. Often there are no role models to demonstrate feeling vocabulary and language. Children may be terrified of telling some deep family secret because of shame or personal threats. We need to help children acknowledge and express those feelings in therapy. Projective techniques such as storytelling, drawing, using toys to represent people and events, and working with clay can often open the locked doors to children's underlying and hidden grief.

> So often educators, therapists, and parents label a suicide attempt as a manipulation rather than a cry for help. We need to find out what's causing the manipulation. We need to understand what the children want and what they are asking for and not getting.

Complicated Grief: Suicide and Multiple Loss

Henry began grief therapy at age eight. His mom brought him to me because he was acting out in school and had been expelled several times. She relayed his patterns of sleep difficulty and occasional bed wetting. The school recommended that Henry get special help.

Henry had experienced multiple losses. Within the past six months, his dad had been murdered. Other losses included his parents' previous separation and divorce, his mom's serious illness, which often left him living with his grandmother, and his dad's moving away and subsequent death. Henry was an only child who had moved at least six times, often living with his grandmother and five other cousins. His mom, Carol, relayed that Henry had a history of being disruptive, had walked out of classrooms since he had been in kindergarten, and that his rage had grown since his dad's death.

His mom had a new boyfriend who was living with the family. Henry would not talk about him directly. Mom went to school at night, leaving Henry with his grandmother or sitters. He usually went to bed very late, and he had to be at the sitter's at 6 a.m. so Mom could go to work. His teachers reported poor attention in school and outbursts of aggressiveness and rage toward his teachers and classmates. He had difficulty concentrating and his grades were poor. Yet, he loved attention and could be a helpful and pleasant child.

Henry and I began by establishing rapport. We read stories and played games. We decided to make a contract about his behavior and what we would agree to do. Many times we role played. On one occasion, Henry wanted to take the part of his father. I was Henry. As he began to pretend he was his dad, Henry started screaming out, "I'll beat you with an electric cord. Call the cops! Put you in jail!" The next week Henry told me that if anyone talked about his dad he would get angry enough to "throw a desk out of the window and burn down the school."

Other times Henry came in and didn't speak. One day he began drawing pictures of a genie. I asked what he would wish for. His answer was, "I wish I was free."

- Bed wetting
- Difficulty sleeping
- Headaches
- Inability to concentrate
- Poor grades
- Outbursts of aggressiveness and rage
- Impulsivity in leaving classroom
- History of previous multiple losses
- Conflicted relationship with deceased
- Sudden death of father

THE MELTDOWN PROCESS: WORKING WITH ANGER

1. Draw or name the person the child is angry with or a feeling the child has toward that person and put it on a punching bag. Have the child use a punching bag, gloves, or foam bats to hit the bag.
2. Have the child tear up old magazines and throw pieces around the room.
3. Have the child punch a pillow.
4. Have the child scream into a tape recorder or paper bag.
5. Have the child write a furious letter. Let him or her rip it to pieces.
6. Have the child pound clay. With the child make a person the child is angry with and either create a dialogue or destroy the figure.
7. With the child use puppets to role play an angry scene.
8. Have the child use a disconnected telephone to tell the person he or she is angry with the child's feelings.
9. Have the child do physical exercise to release some of the angry energy (run, jump rope, play ball, etc.).
10. When possible, have the child tell the person directly when the child is angry. "I'm angry at you for yelling at me when I spilled my milk."

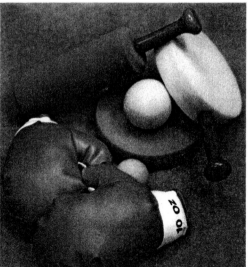

- Choose an activity such as karate or another form of exercise to help Henry work with some of his anger energy. He can also yell in the shower or go outside and shout if he needs to.
- Read the story *Don't Pop Your Cork On Monday* (Moser, 1988) with Henry to help learn some stress release techniques.
- Read the story *I'm Mad* (Crary, 1992) with Henry to find possible alternatives to hurting others with anger. Use ideas from *A Volcano in My Tummy–Helping Children to Handle Anger* (Whitehouse & Putney, 1996).
- Get a professional evaluation to determine if medication for depression, attention deficit, or both is needed, as if dosage needs changing.
- Suggest a team conference at Henry's school to request a complete evaluation and the possibility of special placement to meet his specific needs. Communicate with the teacher and the counselor often.

Henry continued to display extreme emotionality and an inability to control his feelings. Henry's walking out of the classroom and refusing to come back and his frequent emotional outbursts led to his expulsion from school. One day Henry left school and threatened to jump off the roof. School personnel immediately sent him to the hospital emergency room where he was evaluated: the medical staff urged a reevaluation of his antidepressant.

Carol called the therapist who was administering Henry's medication, relaying the seriousness of her son's behavior. She was told that Henry needed to wait three weeks to get an appointment. We both called and left messages urging an immediate appointment and received no return calls or replies. The days passed, and while we continued to call we still got no response.

Finally we spoke to Henry's doctor, who appeared angry that we were insistent on reevaluating the medication. "This child says he doesn't want to live," I reminded her. She responded that Henry was just being manipulative. "Isn't suicide the ultimate manipulation?" I asked. "You wouldn't want to be responsible for that, would you?" She made an appointment for him the next day.

From the time Henry expressed his suicidal feelings and the beginning of a satisfactory dosage level of his antidepressant, we openly talked about his suicidal feelings:

1. I asked Henry if he thought about killing himself. He said, "Yes, I don't want to live."
2. I asked Henry if he thought about how he would kill himself and what his plan was. He replied, "jump off a roof." We talked about how problems may seem so big that there does not seem to be a way out, but there always is.
3. We made a contract. Henry and I both signed it. Henry agreed not to hurt himself or anyone else until he saw me in a week. I gave him my telephone number as well as his teacher's and guidance counselor's phone numbers if his destructive feelings and thoughts reoccurred. School personnel were consulted and were in agreement with the contract.

HENRY'S CONTRACT

JANUARY 12, 2001

I will not hurt myself or threaten to hurt myself until I see Linda in one week. If I have these feelings I will call:

Linda	111-2222
My mom	222-3333
My teacher	333-4444
My counselor	444-5555

Signatures   Henry   Linda

I will tell my teacher when I begin to feel angry and frustrated in school and say that I need to see the guidance counselor.

Signatures   Henry   Linda

---

4. We decided on ways to get help at school. These included permission for Henry to call his Mom at work, to call me, or to leave class to talk to the guidance counselor.

A team conference was held with school personnel, Henry's mother, and myself. There was concern over his failing grades, his hostility toward others, and his continuing thoughts of not wanting to live. The team's recommendation was for a full battery of diagnostic tests and a careful monitoring of his antidepressant. We were to meet again when the tests were completed.

When Henry's antidepressant dosage increased, he became withdrawn and quiet. The dose was lessened, and he appeared calmer. Yet, he constantly relayed his inner need to be free. When the team met again, there was still great concern that the school was not meeting his needs. He was anxious, fearful, and still wished for a peaceful place. The school personnel felt he had stopped learning. When Henry met with failure, he would continue his pattern of shutting down, getting angry, and leaving. The psychologist reported during testing that Henry likened himself to a computer. "You're trying to take everything out of my mind," he explained. The counselor felt he was afraid of being hurt or hurting other people. His behaviors were a desperate cry reflecting his inner feelings of helplessness.

The decision of the team was to provide a resource teacher for Henry as well as home teaching to decrease his hours in school. The school initiated procedures for special placement services to meet Henry's academic and emotional needs. A small self-contained classroom, individual attention, and ongoing counseling were requested.

Henry entered a special school placement where he received daily counseling and a multitude of resources. There were eight children in his class, and his mom recently called to let me know he had earned the award for the best kid of the month. Henry is one of the lucky ones. He had support, love, and help in a system that could have easily buried his needs, his wants, and his underlying silent screams for help. The use of projective techniques were a valuable tool in beginning to unravel the knot of despair that lay twisted deep within Henry's soul.

Complicated Grief: Suicide and its Relationship to the Grief Process of the Surviving Parent

Nine-year-old Justin's mom had died of suicide when he was four. Justin's dad, Steve, decided to get help for his son because school personnel were complaining about Justin's continual fights on the playground. When questioned by his dad, Justin said it made him really angry when kids asked him how his mom died. He said he just wanted to hit them and run away. Steve never told his son the truth about how Justin's mom had died. Steve was unable to do that. Justin had been told that his mom died of a heart attack. Further details had been left out. A family secret lived in their house and grew as poisonous as any cancer.

> Kids know somewhere they are being lied to, and uncertainty and potential rage becomes an all-pervasive part of their lives.

We began to discuss what Steve could tell his son about the truth. At first, Steve refused to role play this dialogue with me. The terror of telling his son and the overwhelming shame of his wife's suicide had silenced his voice for seven years. After several weeks, he gained the courage to try the role play.

We then discussed the possibility of writing a letter to his son. Steve could send it, read it, or discuss it when he was ready. The possibility that Justin could learn about the suicide from someone else was brought out into the open. Asking Steve what would happen if Steve were to suddenly die in a car accident served as a motivator. Who would tell Justin the truth about his mom? What would he want Justin to know?

The letter was a written safeguard of Steve's truth. Writing a letter was the beginning for Steve to being able to externalize his secret. It brought him one step closer to the possibility of talking to Justin about Mom's death.

Dear Justin,

I've been waiting to tell you about Mom's death and how she died. I didn't know how to do it because it is such a difficult and painful subject, but I feel you need to know some things.

For a long time Mom was having problems keeping her thinking straight. She would get depressed and scared way beyond the normal way we all sometimes get depressed and scared. She went to a doctor, but he wasn't able to help her very much. The more depressed and scared she got, the more mixed up her thinking became. She was not able to organize her life. She would just not show up at work. She would do strange things like yell at the mailman one day and then the next day forget she ever did that.

When Mom wasn't feeling mixed up, she would like to be with you. She would read to you, sing to you, and love to rock you in her arms. She talked a lot about how much she loved you and how scared she was that she was not a good enough mother. I told her she was a good mother, but it didn't matter. Her thinking was very mixed up.

Eventually she got so mixed up that she began to think that we would be better off without her. The doctor and I told her that was not right, and she even acted like she believed us, but really she didn't believe us. For some reason we don't understand, she couldn't believe us. She just wasn't thinking straight.

One day she took a whole bottle of sleeping pills. We don't know if she was confused and only meant to take one or two pills or if she meant to take them all, knowing that it could make her body stop working and die. If this was her plan, I feel she did it thinking it was out of kindness and love for us. If so, that would have been the most mixed up thought she ever had!

We don't know all the reasons some people do this. Sometimes kids may worry that if a parent decides to end her own life, they might too. Suicide is not catching. It is not hereditary or genetic. Mom's depression and decision not to live belonged to her. You are separate and in no way caused or created it.

What we are sure of is that Mom made a mistake. Maybe she couldn't help it, but it was a mistake nevertheless. If her mind was working right she would have easily understood that her solution to her problems would create an even bigger problem. She would have understood that it would fix nothing to end her own life. She would have realized how much we would miss her because we love her so

much. And she would have looked harder for another way if only to save us so much sadness and pain. It makes me very angry because I miss her so very much.

Justin, Mommy made a very big mistake. She felt ending her own life was the solution to her problems. Nobody knows what the right solution might have been, but we would have continued to help her look for it if she would have just given us more time. There's always another way. It's as if Mom felt trapped in a room with no doors and no windows, except there is always a door, Justin. She just couldn't find the handle to open it.

Your mom and I love you very much,
    Dad

WAYS TO TALK ABOUT SUICIDE TO CHILDREN

- Define suicide as when "someone makes their body stop working."
- Give age-appropriate facts and explanations.
- Dispel myths of suicide.
- Retell good memories.
- Model feelings and thoughts for children.
- Emphasize suicide is a mistake because there is *always* another way out.

Writing can be easier than speaking, and speaking may be easier after writing. Steve felt great relief after he finished his letter. He still was not ready to tell Justin the facts but felt more prepared for when that time would come. When the adult survivor of a suicide is ready to tell a child the truth, usually the child is ready to hear it. Steve was frozen in time with the stigma of suicide. This first preparatory dialogue with Justin was the beginning of his meltdown process.

Parents are role models for children. Children learn much more from watching what their parents say and do than from what they tell them to say or do. The fears and terrors that stop parents from speaking the truth may seem protective but actually inhibit the freedom of children to grieve. Kids need to know the truth, and adults need the words to tell them. We, as caring adults, can help provide these words that free families from their prison of secrecy.

Complicated Grief:
Suicide and Shame (Stigma)

Jason was a fourth grader. He and his cousin were preparing to spend the summer vacation with his dad in Colorado. But his dad died of suicide on his birthday, a week before summer vacation. Jason stopped going to school, afraid to face his peers for fear they would question him about his dad's death. He was too embarrassed to talk about it. He was angry and bored, and much of his summer was spent fighting with his mom and friends. Jason rarely talked about his dad. Fearing he might need to acknowledge how his father died, he decided not to tell anyone that his father died.

Jason was frozen in time. He couldn't grieve for his dad because he wouldn't talk about his death. When school began that fall, Jason said he needed to make new friends and refused to call friends who didn't know of his dad's death. The fear of explaining *the way* his dad died kept him from explaining *that* his dad died. Remaining ashamed and silent, Jason experienced not only the loss of his dad but of friends as well. His need to separate who his father was from how he died was essential. We began by talking about suicide. Jason explained, "Suicide means not caring about yourself."

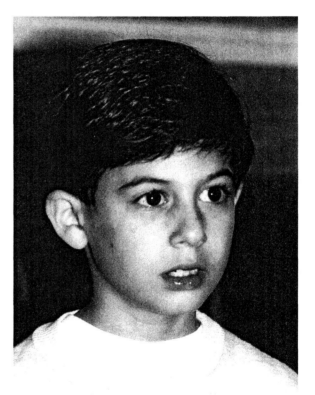

Another child, 12-year-old Dana, had experienced similar feelings about suicide. She revealed her ideas in the following explanation.

<u>Suicide</u>

The way I see it is that everyone who has died, exept for elders, committed suicide.

- <u>Examples</u> -

1. heart attack - overweight smoking (did nothing about it)

2. hit by car - didn't look both ways before crossing the street.

3. Murdered - Was probably involved with some people who were killers.

4. Cancer - Smoking - Never quit.

Defenition of Suicide -
Everyone does it sooner or later. (Hurt themsleves out or carelessness) Dan

Complicated Grief:
Suicide and Abuse

When Ashley was 10, her dad Peter died of suicide. Before his death, Peter had been emotionally abusive to Ashley and her mom. His behavior had been erratic and unpredictable, and Ashley and her mom lived in constant fear of his actions. When he died, Ashley secretly felt great relief. She also felt immense guilt about feeling that way. Her feelings of relief and safety could not be reconciled with her grief.

When kids have been abused by a parent, and then the parent dies, many ambivalent feelings surface. Once free from the fear of abuse, overriding guilt can appear. This guilt freezes the children in time and buries the normal grief feelings for the death of the abusive parent.

A seemingly unrelated incident became a trigger in releasing a frozen block of time for Ashley, a young girl whose father had died of suicide. Ashley had heard that a dog that had gotten killed at school. She came home furious at her dad for giving her dog, Misty, away when Ashley was five years old. She remembered the day well. Her father had decided for no apparent or logical reason that he didn't want Misty because she had begun to bark. He put the dog on a leash, took her in the car, came back without her, and never mentioned Misty again.

No one ever saw Misty again. This action sent a powerful message to Ashley. If Dad didn't like something she did, what would he do to her? Dad's suicide felt like Misty's story of abandonment. Dad left one day, for no apparent or logical reason to her, and never came back. He took his life and didn't say why.

Remembering and acknowledging Misty's abandonment put Ashley in touch with her rage about it. Only then could she begin to grieve for her dad. She felt validated by caring adults who gave her permission to express her anger at her father and to express the terror she inwardly held that she, too, could be abandoned. Knowing that it was okay to have those feelings, which were very natural under the circumstances, enabled a healthier part of Ashley to emerge.

Often adults admonish children by stressing, "You shouldn't feel like that. Your dad is dead. Don't talk about the dead." Sometimes kids internalize the suicide, homicide, violence, or abuse and feel that they are that act. They carry inside of them the shame of how the person died or how they themselves were mistreated. Children can begin to feel free when they realize they are not responsible for any suicidal act of their parent or loved one.

Suicide and Denial

Often educators, parents, and mental health professionals have difficulty finding the words to create open discussions with young people about suicide. They often remain silent or give false reasons why a person died. One school system asked me to work with a class of first graders, grieving over the death of their teacher by suicide. This school system phrased their request this way: *"We have decided not to tell the children the truth about their teacher's suicide. Can you help us work with their grief?"*

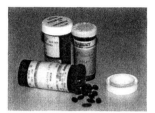

After explaining that the children may have the secondary loss of the trust of their emotional environment by not being told the truth, and that they may well hear about the way this teacher died from parents, older siblings, or the media, the school bravely decided to work with me to tell the children the truth. Brian Mishara, in his article "Conceptions of Death and Suicide in Children ages 6–12 and their Implications for Suicide Prevention" (Mishara, 1999), presents research findings indicating that by third grade children have an elaborate understanding of suicide, and younger children generally understand what killing oneself means.

Sometimes children that are feeling hopeless are labeled manipulative. One aunt complained to me about her 9-year-old niece, Amy, whose dad had died by suicide. "She's always talking to my kids about her dad and his suicide. She is so manipulative. How do I stop her from talking?"

Charles was a 14-year-old who was in the house when his brother, Mark, shot himself with a gun. Charles and Dad stayed with Mark for hours in the emergency ward, and then he died. Charles, shocked and overwhelmed, told dad he couldn't go back to the house that night. Dad said, "You don't need to worry about that, I've already decided to put the house on the market to sell. We are not going back."

Suicide and Over-Responsibility and Guilt

Paul was a 10-year-old whose dad died of suicide after years of struggling with depression. Mr. Jones, his guidance counselor, read to him a book about a dad dying. When Paul saw a picture of a child smiling in the book he explained:

"I'm happy my dad killed himself. That's what he wanted to do, and if he's happy, I'm happy. But my dad makes me feel guilty. He said I should be sad, but I'm happy because my mom did what she wanted to do, and now she is happy."

Paul had told Mr. Jones throughout the year that he felt it was "his job to make his dad happy." This was a job he could never do well. Sometimes children may consciously or unconsciously feel relieved after carrying such a stressful burden and may feel much guilt about it.

Suicidal Thoughts in Children

- Sometimes kids have suicidal thoughts and ideas and are afraid to express them.

- Sometimes kids have suicidal thoughts and ideas, express them, and no one listens.

- Sometimes kids have suicidal thoughts and ideas and they are accused of being manipulative.

- Sometimes kids feel they don't want to live any more because they feel there is no way out of their problems.

- Sometimes we as caring adults can help by just providing a space where kids can say, "I feel I just don't want to live anymore."

The following drawings illustrate the emotional pain a child felt after experiencing the sudden death of his older brother Adam. Tony was 7 when Adam overdosed on drugs.

As hard as it is for us as caring adults to see and hear his feelings of agony, we can only imagine how much harder it would be for this child to live with these feelings in silence.

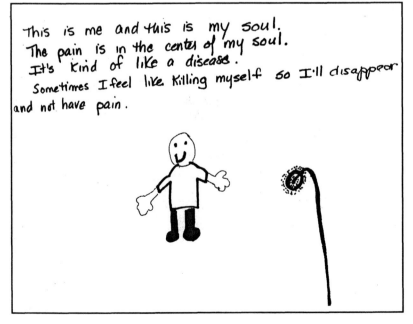

Tony was having suicidal thoughts that increased as the anger and frustration over his brother's death in his family grew. Tony's parents were enraged after Adam's death and arguments escalated between them. Tony felt he was in the middle.

Tony expresses his pain in his drawing. "I feel the walls are closing in on me. I can't stand it any more," he shouted as he drew his picture. "Who are the walls?" I asked. " My parents," he replied.

Signs of Suicidal Feelings

1. *Having depressing thoughts and feelings* over the loss of a loved one that cause prolonged grief. The child may wish to join a parent who has died.
   The child may say, "I wish I was dead, too."

2. *Hoping to punish the person* who died or making threats of getting even.
   The child may say, "Dad will be sorry he ever punished me. I'll show him."

3. *Attempting to regain power* or control.
   The child may say, "You can't leave me, I'm leaving you."

4. *Wishing to die to relieve tremendous guilt* of having done something very wrong.
   The child may say, "I can't forgive myself for Mom's death. I know I caused it. I was so mean to her the night before she died. I must die, too."

5. *Exhibiting self-anger and self-hatred*—angry feelings that cannot be expressed at an abusive parent.
   The child may say, "I hate myself. I don't deserve to live. I deserve to die."

6. *Crying out for help* as a desperate attempt to relieve overwhelming feelings of frustration and confusion over family conflicts or life events.
   The child may say, "I can't go on. I don't see a way out. It's hopeless."

7. *Flirting with death* as "a suicide game" can create a rewarding reaction from peers. (Mattson and colleagues, 1965).
   The child may say, "I dare you to drag race at 100 miles per hour."

8. *Losing touch with reality* and no longer being able to distinguish fact from fiction.
   The child may say, "I'm going to jump off this building and fly."

9. *Being preoccupied with death,* as with teenagers who plan their own funerals or begin giving belongings away.
   The child may say, "I'd like roses at my funeral. I'm giving all of my jewelry to my friend, Pam."

10. *Becoming socially isolated.* The child will not socialize and only wants to be alone for a sustained period of time.
    The child may say, "I have no friends. No one likes me or wants to be with me. What's the use?"

(Adapted from *Suicide in Children and Adolescents* by George MacLean, 1990)

WHAT CAN WE DO FOR THE CHILDREN?

Activities

1. Have the child make a memory book of the person who died. He or she should include the following:
   "Why did you take your life?
   I feel _____ about how you died."
   If I could do one thing over, what would it be?"
   Use specific memory book such as *Bart Speaks Out on Suicide.*

   Remind the children that the suicide was not their fault.

2. Have the child make a mural of (1) before death, (2) at the death, (3) at the funeral, (4) after death, and (5) now.

3. Have the child make a collage of healthy ways to work through painful and overwhelming feelings.

4. Use third person in language "Many people feel . . . " It's less threatening to kids and enables them to open up more easily.

5. Have the child participate in activities that involve writing, drawing, or talking about secrets.

"Secret Witchie" is a stuffed toy with an opening in her mouth in which kids can put their secrets.

Secret marker hides writing until it is written over with an encoding marker.

Painting messages with lemon juice creates secret messages until they are put under light.

Tape recorder talk lets children whisper their secrets into a tape recorder and play it back only if they choose to share the secrets with someone.

Computers are useful for storytelling and writing secrets. Children can create a secret file or contact computer programs such as Kid Works (1-800-556-6141). This storytelling program will allow the computer to read their story aloud once it is written.

6. Have the child write a letter to the person who has died by suicide, letting the person know how he or she feels about the suicide.

7. Provide a "worry box" where children can place any written or drawn worries about suicide.

8. Give the child a locked diary to privately write thoughts and feelings.

Books

Bart Speaks Out on Suicide by Linda Goldman (1998): This interactive memory and story book allows children to write and draw feelings as well as separate the person that died from the suicide.

But I Didn't Say Goodbye by Barbara Rubel (1999): This is a book for parents and professionals who want to help child suicide survivors.

Hurting Yourself by Jeanne Harper (1993): A pamphlet for teenagers and young adults who have attempted suicide or intentionally injured themselves.

I Wish I Was In A Lonely Meadow by The Dougy Center (1990): A compilation of children's feelings and experiences after having suicide affect their lives.

Words

Death: Death is when a person's body stops working.

Depression: Extreme feelings of sadness and hopelessness that last a long time.

Guilt: A feeling that makes us think we are the cause of something and that we may have done something wrong.

Grief: The feelings we feel after someone close to us has died. We can feel sad, angry, frightened, guilty or all of these feelings.

Suicide: The act of killing yourself so that your body won't work anymore. People may do this when they feel there is no other way to solve their problems or to escape their pain, or they may feel that life is not worth living at the moment. People can get help, but people who die by suicide don't realize this.

Other Resources

American Association of Suicidology (AAS)
4201 Connecticut Ave., Suite 310
Washington, DC 20008
(202) 237-2280

Suicide Information and Education Center (SIEC)
201, 1615 - 10th Ave. SW
Calgary, Alberta T3C OJ7
(403) 245-3900

Suicide Prevention Center, Inc.
PO Box 1393
Dayton, Ohio 45401-1393
(513) 297-9096

Suicide Hotline
1-800-621-4000

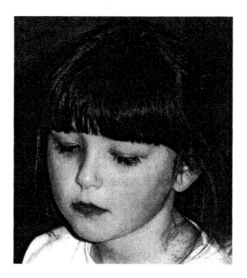

Suicide is a permanent and final solution to a temporary problem filled with over-whelming feelings. These feelings seem unsolvable at the time, but there is always another way.

A Suicide Summary

Tell kids to . . .

Talk about it. Tell someone. If that person doesn't listen, have the child tell someone else.

Write, draw, or create ways to take thoughts and feelings and get them outside themselves.

Get help! Go to parents, teachers, counselors, or a trusted adult friend.

Tell caring adults to . . .

Ask the child if he or she has suicidal thoughts. "Are you thinking of killing yourself?"

Ask the child if he or she has thought of a plan to kill himself or herself. "What is your plan?"

Ask the child if they have a way to kill themselves. "Do you have a weapon?"

Take the thoughts and feelings of the child seriously.

Ask the child to sign a contract with an adult, saying that the child will not hurt himself or herself. Provide names and numbers of people the child can call.

Get professional help to meet the child's needs.

Remember that kids that threaten to kill themselves often do.

The American Foundation for Suicide Prevention states that 75% of all people who try to kill themselves give prior warning of their intentions. (Suicide Information & Education Center, SIEC Alert, Alberta Canada, July, 2001, #45.)

Breaking the Silence on AIDS

WORRY • FEAR • SHAME • SECRECY
ISOLATION • REJECTION • DEATH

Be careful what you say,

children will listen.

Be careful what you do,

children will see and learn.

Stephen Sondheim

(From *Into The Woods*, music and lyrics by Stephen Sondheim,
© 1987 by Ritling Music, Inc. All rights reserved. Reprinted
by permission of Theatre Communications Group.)

Facts about AIDS

In the United States 1,500–2,000 children who have been infected with HIV are born each year (Lori Wiener, Cindy Fair, and Philip A. Pizzo, "Care for the Child with HIV Infection and AIDS," 1993, Hospice Care for Children, see page 85).

"As of December 1994, over 5,700 children under age 13 and over 1,700 adolescents in this country had been diagnosed as having AIDS" (Center for Disease Control and Prevention (1994). HIV/AIDS Surveillance Report, 6 (1)).

Forty-two percent of youths between the ages of 9–17 polled reported that their greatest worry about their future was contracting the AIDS virus (Yankelovich Youth Monitor, "Growing Up Scared," *Newsweek*, Jan. 1994, p. 50).

Estimates are that by the year 2010, 41.6 million children in 23 developing nations will have lost one or both parents as a result of the HIV/AIDS pandemic (U.S. Agency for International Development/research compiled by U.S. Census Bureau/ "Orphans of Worldwide AIDS," *Washington Post*, November 21, 1997).

Define AIDS for Children

**AIDS stands for Acquired
Immune Deficiency Syndrome**

David Fassler, in his book *What's A Virus Anyway?* (1990, p. 29), defines AIDS as follows:

> *Acquired* means the disease was caught after the person was exposed to the virus.
>
> *Immune Deficiency* means that the person doesn't have enough white blood cells to fight off infections.
>
> *Syndrome* means a person who has AIDS has a lot of sick feelings and symptoms.

Talk to kids about AIDS in simple and clear language. Explain that AIDS is a very serious illness and that it is hard for people to get AIDS unless they are having sex or using intravenous drugs. Begin by discussing viruses. Explain that AIDS is caused by the HIV virus and that lots of different people can get AIDS. Help children understand that there is much *fear and shame* surrounding this disease.

If I needed to talk to a child about AIDS, the following are the words I might use:

A virus is a germ that can make you sick because it can attack healthy cells in your body. A cold virus can make you sneeze, and a stomach virus can make you nauseous. Most of the time our white blood cells can fight off these viruses and keep us healthy. AIDS is caused by the HIV virus. You can't *catch* HIV. You *acquire* it through blood or other bodily fluids. The HIV virus attacks white blood cells and kills them. Once this happens a person can get very sick and die.

All different kinds of people get AIDS. Moms and dads, teachers, drug users, kids, and even babies. When people have AIDS, they often feel sick. They may feel sad and angry about being sick and having AIDS. It's hard for them because sometimes they worry if people will be afraid of them and not want to be their friends. This is too bad because people shouldn't treat a person with AIDS this way. People who have AIDS used to get fired from their jobs and kids with AIDS used to get kicked out of school, but as people learn more about the disease, this happens much less. Doctors are working to find a cure for AIDS. So far they haven't found one. They do have medicines that may help people with AIDS live longer.

People can get AIDS from having sex with someone who has the HIV virus, by taking drugs and sharing needles, and when getting blood from a person who has the HIV virus. If moms have AIDS, sometimes their babies get AIDS, too."

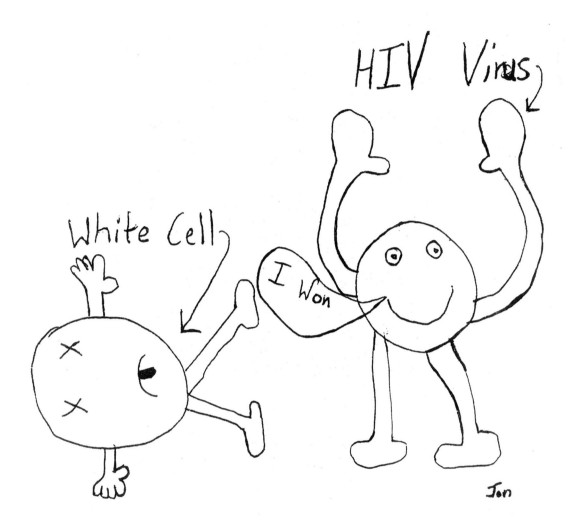

The TV show *60 Minutes* had a recent segment on a summer camp especially designed for and used by children with AIDS and their families. The director of this camp hoped to create an environment that was "not as terrified or angry" as the world from which most of these AIDS patients have come. A little girl at the camp was interviewed and asked the following question: "Are any kids afraid of you at your school because you have AIDS?" "They don't know," she replied. "Do you feel like you have a secret?" the interviewer asked. "I've always had a secret," she responded, "because my friends would say 'I won't touch you' if they knew I had AIDS."

Children Worry about AIDS

Melissa worries about her family. Her mom and sister have AIDS, and Melissa wonders what will happen to her family. She also regrets the need to lie about the disease and wishes she could tell the truth. The lies about AIDS feel like "a monkey" on her back. The following is her way of expressing these feelings. After Melissa wrote this story, her sister died.

Melissa, age 13

The Monkey on My Back

I often wonder what will happen to my family because of AIDS. I wish my sister would be all right but I know she may not be. I wish my mother would start relaxing and not jump to conclusions about my sister so quickly. I also wish my mother will continue to feel well.

I also wish I did not have to lie about my sister's and mother's health. Lying is hard to keep straight and I wish I could just tell the truth and get the monkey off my back.

Beth worries too. She worries about dying because she has AIDS, and she worries about when and where she will die. She also worries about parents and friends crying all the time, and what will happen to everything she owns. She's glad she can talk about these things, knowing how hard it is for other people to listen. Here is what she has to say.

Living with Knowing You Can Die

Everyone knows that you can die from HIV, but no one knows when. Also, no one knows how difficult this is to live with unless you actually have HIV yourself or you love someone with HIV. Living with HIV and knowing that you can die from it is scary. Knowing that you can die is very frightening. I think it is hardest in this order:

Not knowing when this will happen.

Not knowing where it will happen. (I would rather die at home.)

Worrying about my family. For example, will my mother and father ever stop crying? (I don't want them to cry but always remember me riding my pony and being happy.)

What will happen to my stuff and my room? (Casey will probably get most of it but making a museum would not be such a bad idea.)

Thinking about what my friends will think.

Thinking about dying is hard, but it is good to do because you think about it anyway. Most people don't want to talk about this because it makes them sad, but once you do, you can talk about it more easily the next time. Then you can go on LIVING!

Beth, age 12

(Essays by Beth and Melissa are from *Be a Friend: Children Who Live with HIV Speak*, compiled by Lori S. Wiener, Ph.D., Aprille Best, & Phillip A. Pizzo, M.D. © 1994 by Albert Whitman & Company. All rights reserved. Used by permission.)

Siblings Worry about AIDS

Siblings worry, too. Kevin was a 2 1/2-year-old child who died of AIDS. His older sisters, Miriam and Amber-Naomi, worried about him during his illness, his dying, and even after his death. He died in his mother's arms, surrounded by his favorite stuffed animals with a lullaby tape in the background.

Kevin's mom, Alex, said his 4 1/2-year-old sister, Miriam, often worried that she would forget Kevin, and that frightened her. Memories were kept alive through photographs, sharing times spent together, and engaging children in art activities to help remember. Collages about Kevin were made with pictures that told all the special things about him. Miriam also wondered where Kevin went after he died. Alex asked her to draw where she thought Kevin was. She drew the following picture. She said it was Kevin meeting God and the angels. Miriam explained, "I'm really sad, but God is happy because he has medicine for Kevin. He doesn't have to suffer anymore."

YOU CAN'T GET AIDS OR HIV FROM . . .

- Touching or hugging
- Toilet seats
- Mosquito bites
- Hair cuts
- Coughing or sneezing
- Sleeping, sitting next to someone, or touching clothes
- Being a friend
- Shaking hands or holding hands
- Donating blood
- Taking care of pets
- Eating or drinking
- Swimming in the same pool as someone with HIV/AIDS
- Needles at the doctor's office
- Playing with someone with HIV/AIDS or sharing toys

WHAT CAN WE DO FOR THE CHILDREN?

Activities

Make an *AIDS Feeling Book* with children about their person with AIDS. Here are some ideas:

1. Have the child write and draw about the five most special things you love about the person that has AIDS. What would you like to do to help that person?

   Sometimes kids feel helpless when someone they love has AIDS. It helps to draw or write what they love about the person and how they would like to help.

2. Have the child write about what worries him or her most about AIDS.

   Some kids worry about getting AIDS or if someone they love has AIDS. If they write down their worries, they usually don't seem so big and scary.

3. Ask the child if he or she has any secrets about AIDS. Have the child draw a picture about them.

   Sometimes kids have secrets about AIDS. Writing or drawing helps gets them into the open. Put secrets in a secret jar and have the children share only if they want.

Help the child make an AIDS quilt, go with the child to see an AIDS quilt, or encourage the child to be a part of an AIDS march.

"In the future, when you look at the history books that will be written about AIDS you will find that one of the highlights of the book will be a chapter on one of the good results of the disease—that is—humanity became more compassionate. From that compassion, the world became a better place."
   from the AIDS quilt

Books

Be a Friend (1994) by Lori S. Wiener, Aprille Best, and Philip Pizzo: This is a wonderful book of writings and drawings by both children with HIV infection and their non-infected siblings. They tell how it feels to live with this disease and how important it is to be a friend.

Daddy and Me (1993) by Jeanne Moutossamy-Ashe: This book is a photo story of Arthur Ashe and his daughter, Camera. It tells of their journey together with his AIDS illness.

What's A Virus Anyway? (1990) by David Fassler: This is a kid's book about AIDS. It's especially good for explaining to young children how AIDS is a virus.

Come Sit by Me (1990) by Margaret Merrifield: This is a book for young children that emphasizes the concerns kids have about AIDS.

HIV Positive (1977) by Bernard Wolf. This is a book for middle school children with pictures and information about a 29-year-old man with two children who has the disease.

Teens with AIDS Speak Out (1997) by Mary Kittredge. This book presents how teens feel living with this disease.

Resources

Resources include physicians, local public health units, and AIDS hotlines/committees.

National AIDS Hotline (USA)
1-800-342-AIDS

Words

Acquired: Acquired means that the disease was caught after a person was exposed to the AIDS virus.

AIDS: AIDS stands for Acquired Immune Deficiency Syndrome. It is caused by a virus called HIV. AIDS is really the last stage of the HIV infection when a person becomes very sick. Before that, there may be few symptoms.

Disease: A disease is an illness that can be caused by an infection.

HIV: HIV stands for Human Immunodeficiency Virus. It is the virus people get with the illness AIDS.

Immune Deficiency: A person who has an immune deficiency does not have enough white blood cells to fight infections.

Immune System: The body's healthy protection against illness—our body's army to fight sickness.

Infection: Infection is a disease caused by germs.

Syndrome: The syndrome is the sick feelings and symptoms people have with AIDS and other diseases.

White Blood Cells: White blood cells are the healthy cells in our body that fight viruses.

Virus: A virus is a tiny germ that can make you sick because it can attack healthy cells in your body.

CHAPTER 4

Breaking the Silence on Homicide and Other Violent Crimes

TERROR • SHOCK • RAGE • REVENGE • STIGMA

Life is not the way it's supposed to be. It's the way it is. The way you cope with it is what makes the difference.

Virginia Satir

Campbell, 1991

Violence and the Media: The Effect on Children

The violence that children face today would have been unfathomable to children of past generations. The media bombard our homes with this violence and have become surrogate parents and an extended family to our children—influencing them daily.

When children hear and see an ongoing saga of the search for two missing children and the futility of a mother's painful cries for help, they become involved participants in the nation's vigil. Each day they see and hear on the news the latest report on the whereabouts of the missing children. One morning, the kids wake up and hear on TV that finally the children have been found. They are dead. They've been drowned, murdered by their mother. Susan Smith (1994) Union, SC, put her children in a car, seat belted them in, and let the car roll into a lake. "How could this be?" was the nation's response. She was their mother.

> Not only did this woman fool the media and the adults of this nation, she fooled the children as well. She did the unimaginable—this mother murdered her children.

Soon after this story, my son, Jonathan, was doing his homework. He stopped and looked at me. "Mom," he asked, "would you ever murder me?" A new fear and insecurity were now a part of his psyche. I could not control it or change it. It was now a part of his world and the world of other children.

His friend, Josh, asked his mom the next day another poignant question: "What did these kids do so wrong for the mom to kill them?" He naturally presumed that the kids must have done something very bad for their mom to have killed them. "The children didn't do anything wrong," his Mom explained. I wonder if Josh and all the children in the nation really believe that. Violence in families is scary and ongoing, and kids usually feel they are in some way responsible.

Facts about Children and Violence

The FBI'S most recent statistics indicate that in 1992, 662 children under the age of five were murdered. Ernest Allen, president of the National Center for Missing and Exploited Children, estimates that about two-thirds of those victims were killed by one or both of their parents ("Parents who Kill," by David Van Biema, *Time*, November, 1994).

Jerry Adler (*Newsweek*, Jan. 1994, p. 44) in his article, "Kids Growing Up Scared" discussed outside influences affecting children and violence. The following are statistics Adler reported:

Television Violence: The average child has watched 8,000 television murders and 100,000 acts of violence before finishing elementary school (American Psychological Association).

Real Violence: One in six youths between the ages of 10–17 has seen or knows someone who has been shot (*Newsweek*, Children's Defense Fund Poll).

Violent Crime: Children under 18 are 244% more likely to be killed by guns then they were in 1996 (FBI Uniform Crime Report).

Violence has become a consistent theme in the life of American children, and its prevalence in the United States is growing. Randi Henderson, in his article "Caught in the Crossfire" (*Common Boundary*, Feb., 1995), reports the following startling statistics:

- A dozen American children a day die of gunshot wounds, according to the Children's Defense Fund. Between 1984 and 1990, the rate of firearm deaths among black males aged 15–19 increased by 300%. The increase among white males that age was 50%.

- A survey of 1,000 elementary and high school students in Chicago found that more than 25% had witnessed a homicide, 40% had seen a shooting, and more than 33% had seen a stabbing.

- The *1994 Kids Count Data Book*, a national and state-by-state effort to track the status of children, shows the juvenile violent crime arrest rate increased by 50% between 1985 and 1991.

- According to the National Center for Juvenile Justice, teenagers in this country are more than twice as likely to be victims of violent crime as adults.

- In a recent Harris poll of 2,500 students, 15% of middle and high school students said they carried guns themselves, 11% said they had been shot at, and 59% said they knew where to get a gun.

A friend told me that in her son's high school there was a boy who had a gun with a "hit list" to kill other students at the school. The students on the "hit list" were told to stay home from school. Henderson (1995, p. 31) quotes Thomas Blagburn as saying:

"I don't know of any society in history that had children arming themselves, killing and being killed."

Children are dying at the rate of about one child every two hours in gun violence in this nation. Between 1970 and 1991, about 50,000 of our children were killed by guns. This year we will lose 5000 more (Marian Edelman, Children's Defense Fund, *Washington Post*, Oct. 1994).

Firearms killed 4,205 children age 19 and under in 1997. Of these, 2,562 were murdered, 1,262 died of suicide, and 306 were victims of accidental shootings (*Key Facts on Youth, Crime, and Violence*, Children's Defense Fund, Feb. 2001, http://www.childrensdefense.org/youthviolence/keyfacts_youthcrime.htm).

A kindergarten student in Washington, DC, went to school with a loaded semiautomatic pistol to show his classmates. The mother was arrested and charged with a misdemeanor for giving access to firearms to a minor. The possible danger of a gun in the hands of a preschooler is enormous and frightening. The lack of safety for the children of America is growing daily.

The Center for Disease Control and Prevention predicts that by the year 2005 firearms will become the leading cause of injury-related death in the United States (*Morbidity & Mortality Weekly Report*, Aug. 26, 1994).

Homicide is the second leading cause of death in young people ages 15–24 in the United States (*National Vital Statistic Report*, Vol. 47, No. 19, June 30,1999).

A Child's Journey Through Violent Crime

The following information was explained to me in a workshop by The Dougy Center, in Portland Oregon. The Dougy Center is a nonprofit organization that works with grieving children.

When children experience the aftermath of a violent death, their basic belief system is questioned and often temporarily shattered. The world no longer appears to be a safe place, and the same question is asked over and over again: "How could this have happened to me?"

Often there is a tremendous strain on the family. Each person is feeling powerful grief emotions, making themselves unavailable for the children. Kids can then feel alone and isolated.

Children are usually in shock after a homicide and may miss the opportunity to say goodbye. Often there is no physical body. If there is a body which is mutilated and the children see it, this is their last vision. They need to continually re-create the act with words, actions, or projective techniques to take this vision outside of themselves and separate the act of violence from the person they loved.

Guilt and over-responsibility are often a part of the grief work involved with violent deaths. "It's all my fault! Why didn't I stay home? Why wasn't I there? Why didn't I know?" These thoughts plague children.

There is a stigma that usually exists with violent deaths. People sometimes associate murder happening to "criminals or people who are bad." Kids may distance themselves and cut off support systems or be cut off or ostracized due to the judgments of others, fear, or low self-worth. Ryan said his friend Adam wouldn't play with him anymore after his dad was shot because Adam wasn't "allowed to play with the son of a murdered dad." Sam went back to school after his dad was killed in a robbery. His friend Andy asked, "Did your dad really get blown up? Did you see it? How many pieces was he in?"

Law enforcement issues create a hidden complication. The story is repeated and repeated to the police but not to others. Families often put grief on hold until the legal process is completed. Not knowing what will happen to the murderer leaves an open wound too painful to touch. Sometimes publicity about murders is so invasive that families retreat and isolate themselves to avoid public scrutiny or sensationalism.

The last part of the legal journey is the sentencing of the perpetrator. No matter what the sentence is, it often doesn't seem to be enough. One of the questions that kids may demand an answer to is, "How dare those bad guys kill my sister?" Sometimes even the maximum sentence does nothing to undo the loss and pain. And, all too often, no perpetrator is ever identified.

The anger, rage, and revengeful thoughts and feelings that children have after an awful crime are often very scary. Children are taught: "We shouldn't think these thoughts and, if we do, we shouldn't say them to anyone." This locks the child into the secretiveness of thoughts and feelings as well as the shame of the event so that an additional conflict for the child is created. This must be brought out into the open if the child is going to separate the person who died from the traumatic event.

Normal Reponses to Homicide and Other Violent Crimes

I have often found that children show similar signs of grief when confronted with violent crimes. Terrified mothers and fathers question the normalcy of their children's thoughts and feelings after becoming victimized by such a crime. The following is an example of a situation that is all too common when a homicide occurs:

Mrs. Anderson telephoned for immediate grief counseling for her 16-year-old son, Brian. Brian's girlfriend, Annie, had been shot and killed by Annie's former friend who was angry that Annie had taken her boyfriend away. Brian was a good student and had no history of emotional problems. Now, explained Mrs. Anderson, he continually talks about death. He constantly tells the story of the murder, over and over again. He wonders if Annie suffered and tells his parents he is visualizing the murder constantly, over and over in his mind. Violent thoughts against the murderer plague his mind. Brian has recurring wishes to join Annie in death and is preoccupied with questions about the afterlife. Brian's mom felt horrible watching her child suffer this unbearable pain, and she was relieved to find out that these are all too common responses to tragic circumstances. Recurring wishes to be dead must be taken seriously and professional help must be obtained.

> The victim of a murder dies once. The survivors of the crime experience the violent act over and over in their minds.

CHILDREN'S COMMON RESPONSES TO VIOLENT CRIME

1. Concerns that the person suffered
2. Horror over repeatedly visualizing the crime in their minds
3. Constantly attempting to tell and retell the story of the crime
4. Needing to reenact the crime through play
5. Seeking revenge against the murderer
6. Yearning to join the loved one
7. Planning their own funeral (especially for teens)
8. Searching and questioning their beliefs in the afterlife

- Fear of death
- Fear of being left alone or sleeping alone
- Desire to leave school or call home
- A need to be with people that have been through the same experience
- A drop in grades
- Inability to concentrate
- Physical complaints (headaches or stomach)
- Clingy behavior
- Bed wetting
- Nightmares
- Fear of sleep

America's Killing Fields

Columbia Broadcasting System (CBS) presented a powerful documentary, *In The Killing Fields of America* (1995), with Dan Rather, illustrating the stories of children being killed in the United States. One story was about a 2-year-old girl who was abandoned by a system that lost the paperwork that would have placed her in her grandmother's care. Instead she was placed in a foster care home. Her foster mother kicked her to death.

A teenager was abandoned by his mother and father at a young age and left to survive on the streets. He was enrolled in a special school program and was about to graduate high school. Teachers and students loved him, felt he was a "really great guy," and thought it was amazing he remained a nice person given all the disadvantages he had experienced in his childhood. He was shot and killed by his girlfriend's jealous ex-boyfriend. In an interview the fall before his death, he was asked what he was thankful for. He responded, "I'm thankful I made it through the summer alive."

As the show ended, Rather left viewers with the following national dilemma: The children of America are suffering a great loss—the loss of a future. The horrors of living in these "killing fields" have left them unprotected by the adult world.

On American Broadcasting Company's (ABC's) Oprahy Winfrey Special, *There are No Children Here* (November 28, 1993, Harpo Productions), children living in America's battlefield were interviewed. One child was asked the following question: "What do you see yourself doing in the future?" The boy looked back at the camera, nodded, and replied, "I don't see a future."

WHAT CAN WE DO FOR THE CHILDREN?

Activities

1. Ask two questions:
   "How did you find out about the death?"
   "What do you think happened?"

2. Allow children to draw, paint, write, or use clay or toy figures and give them permission to tell and re-tell their story. They can then face the event in the open and see what their minds envision. Usually kids imagine far worse if they have no avenue to project imagined or real conditions. The following is an example of a child's perception of the way his dad was murdered as he was driving his delivery truck.

3. Suggest that children re-create their dreams or nightmares through drawing, using clay figures, or sand table play.

4. Have children write their worries and fears and put these inside a balloon. Blow up and pop the balloon. Children can choose to share their worries.

5. Use paper bag puppets or other kinds of puppets to act out what happened with a violent death and children's feelings towards the victim and murderer.

6. Have children write a letter to the person who was murdered or the murderer. Make sure children know the letters will not be mailed.

7. Have children draw in a memory book, "One Thing I Wish I Could Do Over." Guilt can create paralyzing secrets.

8. Suggest using clay to make someone or something that makes the child very angry. Ask "Why?"

9. Ask children to write or draw the answer to this question: "If a magic genie could give you one wish, what would it be for?"

10. Have the child make a memory wall or mural to commemorate and tell about the person and how he or she died.

11. Have the child use pictures from magazines to create a "feelings" collage or to create a story about the death.

Books

A Family That Fights (1991) by Sharon Bernstein is a book that offers words for children and parents to openly discuss domestic violence. It is a story about physical abuse in a family, and the author offers ways to cope with it and get help.

Children Are Survivors Too (1995) by Kathleen Aub is a guide book for young homicide survivors.

Hard Work Journal (1993) by Wanda Henry-Jenkins is a book for teenagers and young adults that defines the journey of survivors of murder victims and how it feels to be so deeply affected by murder.

Hear My Roar (1994) by Ty Hochban and Vladyana Krykorka is a story for young children about a father who becomes abusive to his wife and son. When Mom realizes the effect of this violence, she gets help towards ending the abuse.

Jessica and the Wolf (1990) by Ted Lobby is a story for young children who have bad dreams. This book provides a way to help parents when children have nightmares.

Just One Flick of the Finger (1996) by Marybeth Lorbiecki is a story about a young boy who takes a gun to school that then goes off in an argument.

Just One Tear (1992), by K. L. Mahon, is the diary of a 13-year-old who witnesses his father being shot and fatally wounded. His turbulent feelings of being the only witness to the crime and becoming an important person in his father's trial are clearly documented.

The Boy Who Sat By The Window (1997) by Chris Loftis is about a murdered boy and the cycle of violence surrounding his death.

We Don't Remember Them As A Blade of Grass (1991) by the Dougy Center, is a book by children who have had a loved one murdered.

Why Did It Happen? (1994) by Janice Cohen was written to help children cope with a violent world. Daniel witnesses a violent crime in the neighborhood and discusses how he feels about it.

Words

Court: Court is a place where a judge or jury decides on how people should be punished if they did something wrong.

Homicide: Homicide is the killing of one person by another person—someone choosing to make someone else's body stop working.

Judge: A judge is a person who helps decide in a court of law if someone is innocent or guilty of doing something wrong. If the person is guilty, the judge helps decide on his or her punishment.

Justice: Justice is when a person or court system gives a reward or punishment for something someone has done.

Jury: Jury is a group of people who meet in court to decide if someone is innocent or guilty of doing something wrong. If the person is guilty, a jury or a judge decide how this person should be punished.

Murder: Murder is when one person kills another person on purpose.

Sentence: A sentence is the amount of time a judge or jury says a criminal has to stay in jail.

Other Resources

National Hotline for Domestic Violence, 1-800-333-SAFE: Explain to the children that this number answers 24 hours a day. The people answering the phone will provide help right away, such as sending police or an ambulance. They may also give the children ideas of other ways to get help.

C H A P T E R   5

Breaking the Silence on Abuse

GUILT • ABANDONMENT • PAIN
SECRET • SHAME • SELF-HATRED

I never knew grief would feel so much like fear.

C. S. Lewis (Campbell, 1991)

Facts about Abuse

The estimated number of child abuse victims increased 40% between 1985 and 1991 (National Committee for the Prevention of Child Abuse, "Growing Up Scared," *Newsweek,* Jan., 1994).

In 1992, about 1,100 children died from abuse or neglect (U.S. Department of Human Health and Human Services, "Parents Who Kill," *Time,* November, 1994).

In the United States there were approximately 984,000 confirmed victims of maltreatment, including: physical abuse, neglect, medical neglect, sexual abuse, psychological abuse, and other abuses in 1997. Three-quarters of the perpetrators of child maltreatment were parents, and an additional tenth were other relatives (*Every Child Deserves A Safe Start,* Children's Defense Fund, Feb. 21, 2001, http://www.childrensdefense.org/youth/ keyfacts_youthcrime.htm).

An estimated three million children were reported to state child protective service agencies as suspected victims of child abuse and neglect (*Key Facts About Children and Families in Crisis,* Children's Defense Fund, Feb. 21, 2001, http://www.childrensdefense.org/youth/ keyfacts_family_crisis.htm).

In 1995, 3.1 million cases of child abuse and neglect were reported.

National Child Abuse Coalition www.casanet.org

One child is being abused or neglected on an average of every 10 seconds a day.

National Coalition for the Prevention of Child Abuse

11.8 out of every 1000 children are victims of abuse and neglect

US Department of Health and Human Services, Child Maltreatment, 1999

Most child abuse reports were made for children under the age of one. The average age of fatalities from child abuse is 2.6.

Child abuse is the leading killer of children under the age of 4.

At least 2,000 children die annually from child abuse; an average of five children die each day.

Child abuse leaves 18,000 children seriously disabled and another 141,000 children seriously injured each year.

Nation's Shame: Fatal Child Abuse and Neglect in US. U.S. Advisory Board on Child Abuse and Neglect, DC: April, 1995

In over 95% of abuse cases, the perpetrator is the child's parent, significant other, relative, friend of family, babysitter, sibling or someone else known to the child.

California Coalition for the Prevention of Child abuse, 1992

Abused children feel like ugly ducklings . . .

We can help them grow into beautiful swans.

Reporting Child Abuse

Child abuse is against the law. Abuse and suspected abuse needs to be reported by doctors, educators, therapists, and other caring adults in order to prevent and treat it. Kinds of abuse include physical injury, sexual assault, molestation, and severe emotional abuse. At least one of the following agencies exists in each state in the U.S.

- Department of Child Protective Services
- Department of Social Services
- Public Social Services Department
- Department of Protective Services
- Social and Rehabilitative Services
- Bureau of Children and Family Services

Emotional Abuse:
Words Hurt—The Story of Sammy

Sammy was a 9-year-old boy whose father died in a sudden fatal car crash. Sammy and his mom were feeling intense grief and sometimes this manifested itself in a rage over the helplessness of preventing this accident. Sammy often relayed stories of Mom's outbursts of anger since his dad's death. These misplaced feelings became targeted towards Sammy.

Sammy came into my office one day asking if he could draw. He began making a giant circle with the word "scream" printed boldly within it. Beneath scream was a series of numbers. The following is a representation of his work:

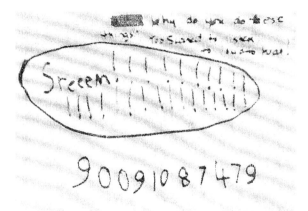

Sammy explained that the numbers represented his counting to himself while his mother was screaming at him. He said he would get into the corner of his bed and pull the covers over his head, waiting for the noise to stop.

> 'It feels like my mother hates me,' he said. 'I get scared and don't know what to do.'
> This is what she says: 'Why do you do these things?' she shouts over and over again.
> Sammy said he was 'too scared to listen, and the yelling was too loud to hear.'

Sammy and I took the following steps in addressing his grief.

1. I asked Sammy if we could share his drawings and feelings with Mom. He agreed.
2. In our next session, we openly discussed the terror Sammy experienced. We discussed the roots of this family anger and other ways to work with it.

3. Sammy's mom agreed to leave the room, go into another room, and close the door when she felt herself beginning to feel anger she might not be able to control.
4. Sammy and his mom would agree to meet at a designated time (15 minutes to 1 hour after the outburst) to discuss without screaming what she was angry about and how Sammy felt about it. Having more control over her anger enabled her to say what she thought and have her son hear her.
5. Sammy and his mom were encouraged to read together the book *Hear My Roar* (Hochban & Krykorka) and use it to create an open-ended discussion.

EXPLAIN VERBAL ABUSE TO CHILDREN

Help children understand what a verbal assault is and how adults teach them through their own behaviors. Adults are role models. On this page, Kevin is learning to model the behavior of his dad. Ask children, "When Dad shouts like this to Kevin, what is Kevin learning to do?"

"You are a stupid, bad child. I hate you!"

"You are a stupid bad dog. I hate you!"

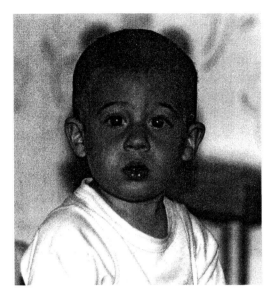

Ask the children how they think Kevin feels when his dad yells at him. Some reponses might be:

> small
> ashamed
> scared
> shivery

Ask the children how Kevin would feel if his dad said,

"Kevin, when your room is messy, I feel angry. I love and know you are capable of a good clean-up. I admire your abilities."

Sexual Abuse: The Loss of the Protection of the Adult World

Alice came to my office disturbed over the death of her father, the grandfather of her 6-year-old daughter. We began exploring relationships in her life and soon realized she missed her father so much because in her mind he had been her protector. Alice complained she felt unprotected by her husband and was scared to sleep without her daughter. She worried that they both needed protection.

After many months, we discovered Alice had been sexually molested at age 9 by an uncle. She blamed herself and told me it was her fault that it happened and that it was stupid of her to have created that situation. She was taken away in a car by this man, her mother's brother, and sexually abused by him. He told her it was her fault and that if she told anyone he would kill her. Alice remained silent until she was 40. After the incident, she became extremely shy and withdrawn, and terrified of being around strangers. She also acted out sexually with her brother, for which she was often punished. From that time on, she was afraid to go to sleep. She had frequent nightmares and fears throughout her childhood.

Alice suffered the loss of the innocence of childhood and loss of the protection of the adult world. She carried these losses with her through life with an underlying fear that she could never be protected against the outside world. Alice was frozen in time from a trauma that was so great that she remained silent for 31 years. Holding the childhood terror that she could lose her life if she spoke up about her abuse, she remained unable to relay to anyone what had happened to her. We, as caring adults, need to protect today's children so that other Alices, at age 9, can speak up and be heard.

SIGNS OF ALICE'S GRIEF

- Withdrawal
- Insomnia
- Nightmares
- Fear of strangers
- Acting out sexually
- Self-blame
- Loyalty to abuser
- Difficulty trusting adults
- Hidden or denied feelings

WAYS TO HELP CHILDREN WITH THE ISSUE OF SEXUAL ABUSE

1. Know that children cannot always verbalize an experience of sexual abuse. They may not know the words to use. Doris Sanford (1986), in her book *I Can't Talk About It*, cautions adults to "be aware of nonverbal cues such as nightmares, withdrawal, school or home behavioral problems, bedwetting, or unusual knowledge of sexuality matters." Some kids may show no physical or emotional signs of abuse.

2. Realize that children usually feel they are the cause of the abuse, and sometimes the abuser tells the child it is the child's fault.

3. Understand, as Sanford (1986) warned, that children may remain "an emotional prisoner" of the abuse because it becomes difficult to distinguish between sex and love. The abuse creates a blurring of the boundaries, especially when the abuser is a friend or family member.

4. Allow children the opportunity to tell their story over and over again. It is their way of putting it outside themselves.

5. Believe children when they tell you about abuse. Honor their confidence in you and don't repeat the story to someone else while children are present.

6. Tell the child you are sorry this has happened and that you will make every effort to protect him or her.

7. Allow the child to be angry without taking on his or her anger. Adult anger can inhibit a child's expression of feelings.

8. Offer to read books such as *Cat's Got Your Tongue* by Charles Schaefer, a book about stranger anxiety, or *I Can't Talk About It* by Doris Sanford, a book about sexual abuse. (Adapted from *I Can't Talk About It,* by Doris Sanford, 1986, Portland, OR: Multnomah Press)

Abandonment and Physical Abuse: Harold's Childhood

Harold was a 10-year-old boy who had continually watched his mom being physically abused by his stepfather, Dan. His biological father had abandoned the family when Harold was 2 and never contacted them again. Harold often talked about his stepfather's violent episodes.

One day Dan had dragged Harold's mother out of the car by her hair, kicked her, and left her by the street as Harold watched. Dan's outbursts of violent rage would erupt towards Harold and his mom, often appearing uncontrollable and unpredictable. Harold lived in terror that he and his mom could be badly hurt or killed.

One particular traumatic memory was of a Sunday afternoon when Dan became enraged for no apparent reason. He took the telephone cord and wrapped it around Harold's neck, trying to strangle him.

Because of many similar experiences, Harold often ran away, staying with friends or relatives, and constantly worrying about himself and his mom. He often felt this abuse was his fault and that in some way he was responsible. Sometimes he secretly wished he could kill his stepfather for hurting his mom. He was afraid to tell anyone.

BEING AROUND PHYSICAL ABUSE MADE HAROLD FEEL

- Dirty
- Powerless
- Like running away
- Unprotected

- Like it is his fault
- Worried
- Terrified

WHAT CAN HAROLD DO TO GET HELP?

HAROLD COULD HELP HIMSELF IN THE FOLLOWING WAYS:

1. Talk to Mom and tell her how terrible it feels when violence happens. Kids need to have people to talk to. Tell other trusted adults such as teachers, grandparents, adult friends, and neighbors.
2. Decide ahead of time on a safe place to go when the violence begins.
3. Ask his parents to get help through counseling or with clergy or doctors. Sometimes adults need help with controlling their anger.

4. Remember that the violence is not his fault. The adults are responsible.

5. Tell Mom to call 911 and get help. If she can't or won't, then Harold can call.

CARING ADULTS COULD MAKE THE FOLLOWING SUGGESTIONS:

1. Harold or his mom can call a hotline. Bernstein (1991) suggested calling the national hotline for domestic abuse. 1-800-333-SAFE. The person who answers the phone can help Harold and his mom think of ways to get help.

2. Harold and his mom can stay at a shelter or with a friend or relative. (Adapted from *A Family That Fights* by Sharon Bernstein, 1991, Morton Grove, IL: Albert Whitman & Co.)

WHAT CAN WE DO FOR THE CHILDREN?

Secrecy Work

Children feel helpless if they feel they have a secret they can't share. If they are holding family secrets that they feel or have been told they cannot talk about, they carry a great burden. This burden stops normal grief from occurring. The following words may be useful when said to children before beginning this work: *Some secrets are not meant to be kept. If someone has been hurt or is continuing to be hurt, we can decide together what to do.*

Here are some ways we can get the secret out.

1. Encourage children to whisper their secret to a favorite stuffed animal in the room. Explain that some secrets are meant not to be held or kept. Let's decide together if this is a secret to keep or not to keep.
"What is your secret?"
"How do you feel after you have told your secret?"
"Imagine what the stuffed animal might say about the secret?"

2. Provide a tape recorder or toy telephone that the children can talk into and tell their secret. If the children use a tape, they can keep it and share their secret when they are ready.

3. Read a story to help children recognize feelings and to show them that others feel like that too. *Once Upon A Time: Therapeutic Stories* by Nancy Davis (1990) is an excellent resource of projective stories to help kids free their feelings. Davis is a psychologist with expertise in working with abused children, their families, and the court system.

4. Use computers as a tool for confidentiality. Today's children are becoming very computer literate, and there are many programs they can use as a silent source of stored thoughts and feelings.

Kids can save their work and choose whether to keep it hidden or print it out to share or maintain as a journal. Good examples of computer programs for children are:

Kid Works
Davidson & Assoc. Inc.
P.O, Box 2961
Torrance, CA 90509

Psych-Pik Programs
No Secrets Anymore; Feeling Kids; People and Objects; Backdrops

The Center for Applied Psych, Inc.
P.O. Box 61586
King of Prussia, PA 19406

5. Artwork and poetry are valuable tools in accessing hidden thoughts and feelings. Children, teenagers, and adults can share present and past memories and perceptions using these vehicles to express their terror and despair.

This drawing is a statement about childhood sexual abuse that a little girl experienced from ages 3 through 9 by a family member. Her drawings relay her inability to get help, with blindfolds on the teachers, doctors, and family members she tried to tell. Only after she got away from the abusive situation could she begin to tell through her artwork and poetry about the painful ordeal she had kept inside.

THE BRAVEST LITTLE GIRL I KNOW

by Jill

A little girl played with her doll one day

The next, she hugged that doll and said goodbye

Her childhood of colors had faded into gray

And her little heart prayed with screams to die

In a moment she had been drafted into a war with shame

And her purity was lost to one that she cherished

He gave her life, yet for this death he was to blame

For while her body withstood, her innocence perished

An adult was then born, mechanically revived

But that child, has she refused to mature, to grow?

She has done both, more importantly, she has survived

She lives inside me—the bravest little girl I know

Books

A Terrible Thing Happened (2000) by Margaret Holmes is a story about a boy who sees something terrible and becomes anxious and angry. An adult helps him talk about his feelings.

Do You Have A Secret? by Pamala Russell and Beth Stone (1986) is a book that helps adults talk to children about sexual abuse. It offers important resources for kids who have been victimized.

Let's Talk About It by Dr. Michael Pall and Lois Blackburn Streit (1983) is a book written for kids from 8–14 that explains what child abuse and child neglect are in very simple, direct language.

Shiloh by Phyliss Reynolds Naylor (1991), is a Newbery Medal winning story about a dog that was abused and the boy who loved him.

In *The Words Hurt* by Chris Loftis (1995), Greg is a young boy whose dad says awful things to him. This verbal abuse makes him feel very sad. He finally expresses his feelings to his dad.

Words

Abuse: Abuse is when someone hurts someone else's body or feelings over and over again. Usually they know they are doing it. Sometimes someone can hurt someone else badly just one time, and that can be abuse, too. The hurt can come from someone screaming,

hitting, using mean words, or touching in a way that hurts, is uncomfortable, or feels confusing. Not being protected from an adult who is using a child's body in a way the child doesn't like or understand can cause bad feelings.

Bribe: A bribe is an offer to give a child something he or she wants so that the child will do something he or she doesn't want to do.

Guilt: Guilt is a feeling that makes us think we are the cause of something and that we may have done something wrong.

Protection: Protection is a way of being defended or taken care of so that we won't get hurt.

Rage: Rage is a feeling of extreme anger.

Shame: Shame is a feeling of extreme guilt.

Stigma: Stigma is a label put on someone because others feel he or she has done something wrong.

Terror: Terror is a feeling of extreme fear.

Violence: Violence is extreme force or energy in a physical or emotional way. It can be sudden and unwanted.

Other Resources

American Association for Protecting Children
c/o American Humane Association
63 Inverness Drive East
Englewood, CO 80112-5117
303-792-9900

Parents Anonymous, National Headquarters
22330 Hawthorne Boulevard, Suite 208
Torrance, CA 90505
1-800-421-0352

Childhelp IOS Foresters
National Child Abuse
P.O. Box 630
Hollywood, CA 90028

CHILD ABUSE HOTLINE
1-800-4ACHILD

TDD FOR HEARING IMPAIRED
1-800-2ACHILD

These are 24-hour hotlines, operating seven days a week in the United States and Canada.

CHAPTER 6

Breaking the Silence on Bullying

BULLYING AND VICTIMIZATION • GUNS • SCHOOL SHOOTINGS
INTIMIDATION • HARASSMENT • ISOLATION • RAGE

Bullying has become a national disease, an epidemic reaching record proportions from preschoolers to teens.

School Shootings:
Bullying as the Underlying Cause

The Santana School shooting in San Diego, California, 2001 shocked all of us. So often we see this kind of behavior as one person's cowardly act and delve no further. Too many of us have this perspective and too few see the relationship between juvenile homicide and suicide and repressed rage from years of bullying, taunting, intimidation, isolation, and abuse by classmates taking place within our schools in this country.

School shootings affect kids, parents, educators, communities, and nations. Youth violence terrifies the youth and the surrounding adults. Santana High is one of the many examples of a horrific shooting with bullying and victimization at its core. The lone gunman was a 15-year-old boy whose rampage killed two of his classmates and injured 13 others. It was reported that he had suffered verbal abuse and was constantly subjected to ridicule at school. He was called "gay," "skinny," and "a country boy."

Friends of this outraged boy have been ostracized and told not to come back to school for their own safety. Classmates were enraged at these friends' failure to take the warnings signs of the young gunman's boastings of future killings seriously. They did not tell authorities.

These friends experienced many secondary losses, including the death of classmates, the incarceration of a friend, the ostracizing from classmates and faculty, the loss of their school, and the guilt of knowing they could have done something to stop the violence and did not. This is compounded by a media that soulfully rapes these kids and other student witnesses and survivors by interviewing them immediately on national TV with their raw emotions for the country and the world to see over and over again.

Like the shooter's friends who heard his plans to kill classmates and kept silent, the adult who was told also did not tell. This adult said the troubled teen was just kidding about his threats and explained, "I never thought he would do that. I knew he was teased and taunted. I saw it happen myself."

Again and again we hear of students who resort to violent rampages after being victims of continuing harassment at school over long periods of time. No adult or peer stood up to stop their abuse. Victimized youth disown their confusion, sadness, and rage, and all too often project these attributes onto the world through guns, drugs, and shooting sprees. These kids are living in isolated, hate filled worlds, with no moral compass to help them navigate through their destructive feelings and thoughts.

Our western concept of a gun toting anti-hero only magnifies and glamorizes an angry youth's attraction to guns. Gun control is a timely argument to help stop the violence in our schools, and curb the aftermath of bullying and victimization.

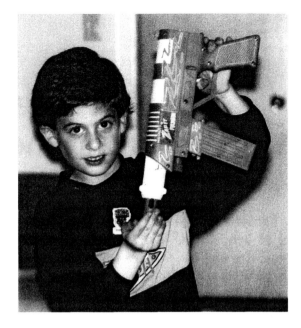

Clearly we must recognize the impulsivity of children and teens, and the allure and mystification surrounding guns in today's culture. Studies show that our brightest children, when left alone with a gun, act impulsively and will play dangerously with it. They seem to forget all of the adult warnings for that instant gratification of feeling all powerful. If they have no access to guns, they can not follow through by using them. Prime Time Live reported on March 8 that, "43% of American homes have guns," and explained that if kids do not have them in their own home, statistically, the kids in the house next door probably do.

In today's world our children can't stop bullying or violence without the guidance, modeling, and absolute support of the adult world. Zero tolerance of violent threats and actions is imperative. Schools must vigilantly create no-bullying policies and use no-bullying curriculums to teach children from kindergarten through twelfth grade to recognize bullying behaviors in themselves and others. It is important to define bullying for children, explain the difference between telling and tattling, and instill the concept that we help people and save lives by speaking out. Children need a clear policy for strategies to deal with bullying and accessibility to adults that will take charge. *It is impossible for children to solve bullying issues alone.*

Parents, educators, and other caring professionals are role models. Their behaviors and words can reflect nonviolent relationships and safe ways to express anger. Verbal abuse, physical threats, and sexual innuendoes cannot be tolerated. One six-year-old relayed a story of being picked on and called names for being overweight. She ran home to be comforted by her mom, tears streaming down her face. "Stop that crying," her mother demanded, as she slapped her hard on the face. Another third grader, Tony, was tormented on the playground by bullies. They constantly called him names and taunted him and his friends. Telling the teacher did him no good. The bullies and victims were punished together for creating a disturbance. In both instances the harassed kids were punished for telling adults.

> Over 70% of the kids polled in a Weekly Reader survey report that they have been bullied, and the bullying takes place on the playground, the halls, the cafeteria, and the busses of our schools. (April 28, 1998 Weekly Reader Survey)

Adults can spontaneously create teachable moments about bullying when watching the news with kids, teaching current events in the classroom, or even witnessing mistreatment at a shopping mall. Talk with children about what is acceptable and appropriate behavior. Teach children the guidelines to follow to report threats safely. Help them to see any bullying behaviors in themselves and implement boundaries to help them eliminate these behaviors.

Combining restrictive laws on guns, changing the mentality on bullying, and maintaining the capability of adults to be accessible to kids are solid beginnings to stopping school violence. Gun safety legislation can be followed with mental health legislation for our youth.

Compassion, kindness, and responsibility for oneself and others can be taught and learned. Intimidation and abuse can be branded and extinguished. Only then can we help children grow their hearts in order to grow their consciousness.

Bullying: Facts about Bullies and Victims

Thomas Brown, creator of the video, *A Broken Toy* (Summerhill Productions, 1993), gives the following facts about bullying.

- 90% of students feel that being a bully caused social, emotional, and academic problems.
- 60% of victims report boys bullied them and 40% report girls bullied them.
- 69% of students believe schools respond poorly to bullying and victimization.
- Each month, over 1/4 million students report being physically attacked.

Suellen Fried and Paula Fried present the following statistics in their book *Bullies and Victims* (1996).

- Young bullies carry a one in four chance of having a criminal record by age 30 (study by Leonard Eron and Rowell Huesmann).
- The National School Safety Center estimates that 525,000 "attacks, shakedowns, and robberies" occur in an average month in public secondary schools.

> It is estimated that 160,000 children miss school every day, due to fear of attack or intimidation by other students. (National Education Association). *Bullies and Victims*, Fried & Fried, 1996

Despite these sobering statistics, our society seems to live in a state of denial about the devastating existence and effects of bullying and victimization on our children's world, and the life-altering repercussions that kids may carry into adulthood. Too often children are told to resolve these offensives of abuse and destruction on their own, being given the strong message that this is normal and they can handle it.

Children cannot handle bullying alone. They must have adult modeling and support.

> Bullying takes an average of 30 seconds, and most of it is verbal. Adults don't know what is going on. Kids can hide it from us because they know we don't like it. Debra Peplar, "Expert on Bullying Tells How it can be Stopped." *The Province News*, October 22, 2000.

Alex was a fifth-grade boy who often complained to his mom of being teased at school. One day he came home saddened and scared after a hurtful incident with a bully. Alex and his friend Rob were sitting at the lunch table with Anthony and Henry. When Rob got up to get a drink, Anthony and Henry began destroying his lunch, squashing Rob's fries and dumping them back on his plate. Alex tried to stop them and they refused to listen. He went to the assistant principal for help. She punished Alex, Rob, and the other two boys for having an altercation. Alex went home feeling very defeated. He said he would be afraid to ever tell again because he would be punished for doing so. Anthony and Henry continued to harass Alex and Rob at lunch. Alex began to not want to do his homework. "Every time I sit down with school work, I think of what happens at lunch and get overwhelmed." He would stop doing his homework and turn on the TV.

Sam, a sixth-grade boy, expressed his deep frustration with bullying in the following journal:

In the sixth grade these days being bullied is not easy, especially if it is the teachers who are doing most of it. At school almost all kids go through being bullied by other kids, but at least when that happens you know that you have some sort of control over the situation.

However, when kids are treated unfairly by adults for no reason, you just can't do anything. At my school if any student so much as talks back to a teacher they get suspended. Because of this students can't even complain about being treated unfairly.

For example in my school a couple of kids knocked over my friend's lunch, and I mean they just dumped it. So when my friend called a teacher over to try and find out who had messed his lunch up I just had to tell (this is partly because these kids were doing jerky stuff like tipping kids lunches). When the teacher heard what I had to say, the other kids lied and said they had not done a thing.

The teacher decided that he would just punish both the nasty kids and me because he did not want to take the time to solve the problem. This is just one time out of many of similar examples of a teacher being the bully. Because of this a kid has no way to fight back. It makes you really mad to be treated unfairly.

Sam

> Educators, parents, and all caring professionals need to take action against the power structure inherent in bullying. Caring adults must become role models through language and action, creating strong boundaries of nontolerance of any verbal, physical, or sexual abuse of any kind.

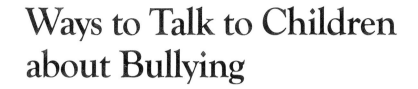

Ways to Talk to Children about Bullying

1. Define bullying for children. The following are words to use with children to create a dialogue about bullying:

   "A bully is someone who is intentionally mean to other children a lot of the time. The bully uses his power in a cruel or negative way. Sometimes he or she may be older, stronger or more 'street smart' than the kids being picked on. Boys and girls can both be bullies. Short or tall, fat or skinny, rich or poor, black or white—bullies come in all shapes, sizes, and colors. There is one thing they have in common—they all know how to be mean. Being a bully is not cool. It's cruel and cowardly!

   "Bullies aren't born, bullies are made into bullies. Bullies are very under confident and insecure, and pick on weaker people to make themselves feel stronger. They may appear strong, but inside they are always weak. Usually bullies have learned their behaviors from someone who has bullied them, like a brother or sister, a mom or dad, or a friend or classmate at school. Bullies may not even know why they are cruel. They just do to others what has been done to them. It's very sad and it's bad for everybody, both the bullies and the bullied.

   "Most of the time bullies harass other kids in secret, and teachers or other adults are not around to help. Although other kids may see or know of the bully and what he or she is doing, they often do not speak up because they are afraid too. Some kids say they don't feel safe on the bus, in the gym, in the halls, in the cafeteria, or even on the playground, because they are the places bullies can 'get you' when no one is watching. Remember, bullying happens when one kid hurts another kid over and over again. Since this behavior cannot be accepted from anyone that goes to school, we must work together to stop it. Together, we can stop bullying."

2. Help children look for bullying behaviors in others. The following is a list of common actions of bullies.

- Picking on other kids that are smaller than them or animals.
- Teasing or making fun of other kids.
- Ruining other people's things on purpose.
- Looking tough and mean on purpose.
- Being angry a lot.
- Taking revenge if someone hurts them.
- Blaming other people when something goes wrong for them.

- Needing to win at a game or sport; it doesn't matter to them if they play fair or not.
- Hating when good things happen to other kids and having to say or do bad things to these kids because the bullies are jealous.

Children Can Help Themselves with Bullying

Children can:

1. *Learn self-defense.* It's a good way to learn self-protection and enhance self-esteem.
2. *Stay safe from a bully.* Tell kids to stay safe and away from a bully. If a bully is scaring a child, the child should scream loudly "Stop!" or "Get away from me!" and then run away. If a bully threatens to hurt someone, a child should not bring a weapon to school for protection. Instead, he or she should get help.
3. *Tell someone they trust and report the loss of possessions and threats of violence.* If the bully continues to harass a child he or she needs to tell someone. Explain to children that there is a difference between telling and tattling. Telling is about helping to stop harm to them or someone they care about. Tattling is about hurting someone. If someone takes something away by force that is stealing and is illegal. If someone has a weapon or is threatening to harm someone, informing an adult can help save a life.
4. *Take a look at themselves.* Children need to recognize if they have any bullying behaviors, such as hurting or teasing someone. Hurting someone's body or things, hurting someone's feelings, or hurting someone's friendship is bullying. Help them see they need to stop it in themselves and recognize it in friends and classmates. Role-playing with bully–victim scenarios can help children develop compassion and empathy for victims. Remind children they have a choice in how they want to act and who they want to be friends with.
5. *Stay away from gangs.* Gangs are groups of bullies that often wind up in trouble. Emphasize that gangs may try to persuade kids that the gang is cool, but it is not cool to wind up a criminal or dead.
6. *Walk in groups on the playground, in the hall, and to and from school.* Explain to children that walking with other friends helps prevent bullying. Bullies tend to pick on kids who are alone. Remind children who are alone to walk confidently with their head up. Standing tall helps them keep alert and discourages anyone from bothering them.
7. *Report bullying.* Ignoring bullies will not make them go away. The problem won't go away until they know the bullies have to stop. Keeping bullying a secret compounds the fear and humiliation of being bullied with the isolation of not sharing it. Children should tell at least three trusted friends and three trusted adults.
8. *Defend classmates from bullying.* When a classmate is being mistreated by a bully, boys and girls should not stand by and watch or pretend they don't see. Instead, they should stay

in groups and tell the bully they don't like how he or she is threatening their friend. Children are more effective in speaking up against bullying in groups. These groups can increase their power. They can write a note to the principal, guidance counselor, or teacher about any incident. If they are afraid to sign their name, they can leave the bully's name and ask for help.

9. *Start a bully prevention program in school.* Students can ask teachers, counselors, and administrators to create an educational program to prevent bullying and request open discussions about this issue. Kids can ask educators and parents to use their adult power to stop bullying.

10. *Create a bully policy in school.* Children can urge school personnel to set up rules and consequences for kids about any physical, emotional, or sexual abuse. Parents of bullies and victims should be called and told of the incident. Educators and kids should know and adhere to uniform rules and consequences of breaking the rules. Boys and girls can request strong playground, bus, and cafeteria supervision.

Educators and Parents Can Help Children with Bullying

Adults can:

1. *Provide support and modeling.* Children cannot solve the problem of bullying without the firm support of their adult world. Educators and students must join together to eradicate bullying behaviors from their school environment. The old advice of ignoring tormentors doesn't work in today's world. Adults can no longer give children the message that they are capable of solving the bullying on their own. Teachers, counselors, administrators, and parents need to step in, stop the bullying, recognize the feelings involved with victimization, and teach alternative behaviors to bullying in solving problems.

2. *Maintain a no-bullying policy.* Educators and students need to create and adhere to a no-bullying policy at school. This policy does not allow physical, verbal, or sexual abuse inside or outside of school and is modeled by school staff. Mean spirited behaviors are unacceptable by everyone and are reported immediately with appropriate repercussions. This reporting policy must be clear and relayed effectively to the entire student body through assemblies, class meetings, and letters to parents. A sensible and rational code must be developed that clearly brands unacceptable behavior in ways kids can understand and relate.

3. *Teach the difference between telling and tattling.* Children need to understand that telling is a way to help a friend, not get him or her into trouble. Help children discover ways to break "a code of silence" that exists around bullying by emphasizing adult protection. Becoming tough with bullying behaviors can help all children feel more powerful and less victimized. Create a bully telephone hotline and give the number to kids.

4. *Find supportive research on bullying.* Rigby and Slee (1999) present research that involvement in bully-victim problems at school, especially for students with relatively little social support, was significantly related to degree of suicide ideation.

5. *Use resources and curriculums on bullying.* Bullying resources and curriculums can create safe schools. Educators need to use lessons and classroom discussions that brand bullying behaviors, define bullying, create compassion for victims through role playing, explore the feelings of bullies and victims, and present other ways to solve problems.

WHAT CAN WE DO FOR THE CHILDREN?: ACTIVITIES TO STOP BULLYING

1. Promote discussions on telling vs. tattling.
    Define telling and tattling. "Tattling is telling on someone to get them into trouble. Telling is reporting something to prevent trouble."

2. Create dialogue about bullying.
    Ask questions like. "What did you think when you see your friend be teased?"
    "If a friend told you he was going to do something scary, what would you do?"
    Share your experiences of bullying. "I had a friend in high school that got hit and teased so much at school he had to leave."

3. Insert teachable moments when school violence appears in the media.
    Give opportunities for students to express concerns, talk about violence, and participate as members of a global community to help one another.
    Some discussion questions are: "How did you feel when you saw the school shootings on TV?" "What do you worry about?" "Would you like to do anything to help?" Kids can write letters, draw pictures, collect money, and send these items to the troubled school.

4. Suggest bully-victim role plays with children.
    Allow children to feel what a bully and victim might by acting out short scenarios. Have each child play the bully and victim role. Underscore empathy and compassion for the victim and identify traits of a bully. Suggest solutions such as telling a trusted adult, asking friends for help, and using conflict resolution through peer mediation.

"Go back to where you came from!" shouted Andrew as he shoved Carlos onto the asphalt of the playground. "Ouch!" screamed Carlos. "Stop that! It hurts!" Carlos was a new boy from Chile who had just arrived at school. He was smaller than most of the kids and stayed by himself a lot. On this particular day, Joe and Henry heard Carlos scream. If you were Carlos what would you do? What should Joe and Henry do?

5. Brainstorm channels of communication to report bullying.

What is the school policy?
What kinds of issues would you report?
What might stop you from reporting something scary?
Who are the people you would go to?
If they didn't listen, what would you do?

Other Resources

FOR STUDENTS

Bullies are a Pain In the Brain (1997) by Trevor Romain is an easy to read book that talks to kids about bullies and ways to stop them.

Dealing with Bullying (1996) by Marrianne Johnston is a book that defines bullies, explains why bullies act the way they do, and discusses ways for change.

Getting Equipped To Stop Bullying (1998) by Becki Boatwright, Teresa Mathis, and Susan Smith (Rock Hill, SC: Educational Media Corporation) is a kid's survival kit for understanding and coping with violence in the schools.

*How to Handle Bullies, Teasers and other Meanies: A Book that takes the Nuisance Out of Name Calling and other Nonsense (*1995) by Kate Cohen-Posey is a book that gives ideas and healthy ways to respond to meanness, like name calling and insults.

How to Make Yourself Bully-Proof (Oct., 1998) by Linda Goldman is an article that is written for middle school children about bullying and practical ways to work with the problem.

Websites

WEBSITES FOR KIDS

Kidscape: http:/www.solnet.co.uk/kidscape/kids4.htm. This website contains a page "You Can Beat Bullying—A Guide for Young People." Kids share about being bullied and being a bully, with lots of ideas about solving problems.

WEBSITES FOR ADULTS

www.bullybeware.com and www.bullying.org are excellent websites that provide an abundance of information and resources on bullying.

Videos

Broken Toy: A Thomas Brown Film (1993) is a film for students that deals seriously with the danger of bullying for victims and bullies.

Bullying Curriculums

Bully Free Classroom by Allan Beane (1999) is a book that contains over 100 tips and strategies for teachers K–8.

Bully-Proofing your School by Carla Garrity, Kathryn Jens, William Porter, Nancy Sager, and Cam Short-Camilli (2000) is a comprehensive book of interventions against bullying for elementary schools.

No-Bullying Curriculum (1998) by STAR—Students Taking A Right Stand is a curriculum on bullying that gives classroom teachers the tools to deal with bully issues and involve all school personnel, students, and parents.

No-Bullying Program (1996) by James Bitney is a manual for preventing bully–victim violence in schools.

No Putdowns Character-Building Violence Prevention Curriculum (1998) is a school-based curriculum dealing with violence prevention and character building for educators.

The Peaceful Classroom by Charles Smith (1993) provides curriculum of many activities to teach preschoolers compassion and cooperation.

FOR ADULTS

Brohl, K. & Corder, C. *It Couldn't Happen Here.* (1999). Washington, DC: Child Welfare League of America. This book recognizes and discusses the needs of many of today's desperate children.

Fried, S. & Fried, P. *Bullies and Victims.* (1996). New York: M. Evans and Co. This book describes today's schoolyard as a battlefield with practical solutions to help children.

Lantieri, L. & Patti, J. *Waging Peace in Our Schools.* (1996). Boston, MA: Beacon Press. This book is a model of emotional intelligence to be used to resolve conflicts creatively in our schools.

Olweus, D. *Bullying at School.* (1993). Maiden, MA: Blackwell Pub. This book provides understandings about bullying at school and what can be done about it.

Rigby, K. & Slee, P. "Suicidal Ideation among Adolescent School Children, Involvement in Bully-Victim Problems, and Perceived Social Support." Summer (1999). Washington, DC: The American Association of Suicidology. *Suicide and Life Threatening Behavior*, 29(2), 119–130.

Ross, D. *Childhood Bullying and Teasing* (1996). Alexandria, VA: ACA. Suggestions about what school personnel and other caring adults can do about bullying.

P A R T   I I I

Techniques

C H A P T E R   7

Techniques for Complicated Grief

VISUALIZATION • DREAMS • SILENCE • PUPPETS
PHOTOGRAPHS • ARTWORK • CLAY • TOY FIGURES
PUNCHING BAGS • TAPE RECORDER
STORYTELLING

Create a Feeling of Normalcy

Create a feeling of normalcy by using reality checks when abnormal events and circumstances have happened.

Sharon was a teenager whose dad had been murdered in a drive-by shooting. After going to many therapists who told her on an initial interview that she was clinically depressed and needed medication, Sharon feared she was "crazy" because of her reactions to unbearable circumstances. "I think I'm going crazy; I'm so preoccupied with death. I'm constantly worried that I'm going to die." I suggested that she receive a medical checkup to help reassure her that she was okay and emphasized to her that children and adults often become overly worried about their health after being directly confronted with death.

Sharon relayed another preoccupation that was worrying her. "I'm terrified the world is going to come to an end." "Your world probably feels like it has come to an end after your dad's death," I responded. She nodded in agreement. Sharon said she felt helpless for not being there to save her dad. The randomness of her dad's killing was both overwhelming and terrifying. His death appeared to be a random act of fate. Understanding that her fears were directly related to her nightmarish experience was the first step in establishing rapport and making the intolerable normal.

WAYS TO HELP

Preoccupation with death is a common experience for young children and teenagers after a loved one has died. Kids question what death is, where their loved one has gone, and if something will happen to themselves or surviving loved ones. We can help them with worries and fears by providing "reality checks."

1. Provide a visit to the doctor for a checkup to help eliminate some concerns if children begin complaining of physical symptoms.

2. Allow children to call home at a designated time if they feel scared at school and fear for the safety or well-being of a surviving parent.

3. Become familiar with normal grief symptoms. Reassure children that their new fears of death are a normal part of grief and that these fears will eventually subside.

4. Respect the belief system of the child as a foundation for understanding their grief.

5. Invite young children to write about the person who died and any worries, fears, or longings they have toward their loved one. By getting these feelings into the open, we can begin to normalize them.

The following is a wonderful example of a loving letter by Amanda, a 15-year-old whose dad had recently died. Their extremely close relationship was a big factor in making this a more complicated grief.

"My Daddy"

My father was a stone cutter—one of those old mysterious trades I will never fully grasp. He was many things in his time. He was a decorator, a teacher, an artist, a painter, things I'll never be. He saw World War 2, blackouts, he was almost kidnapped once as a child for being half German. He saw California, he saw Florida, and best yet he saw New Orleans. He saw and did so many things I will never do. He was everything he could have possibly been in his years. He was a lot of things to a lot of people. Never an enemy though, never a tormentor. But most of all, the first thing on the very top of the list, he was mine, he was my Daddy.

I used to come home every day after school, and immediately rush down to the basement, where he would be sitting. Sometimes cutting a stone, or watching television, or drawing, or maybe writing a letter. I was always so glad to see him. I felt as though nothing bad was going to happen to me. I would always hug him, morning, noon, and night. I loved him so much, and made sure to tell him all of the time.

We always used to make special trips in his little blue car to places all over Maryland and DC. He couldn't walk well, but he could drive just fine. We always had so much fun on those trips. Going down the road with our music blaring over the radio, laughing and chattering about anything we could. We always had somewhere to go, something to do, and were always together.

To me my Daddy was like no other person in the world. He was bright and shining all of the time. He had fuzzy gray hair, and a fuzzy gray beard, and the most beautiful eyes. He smelled like goose feathered pillows and springtime. He loved me in a way that was mythical and as old as the beginning of time. And I loved him back. He watched out for me, and I watched out for him, every day, every second. We always had time for one another. As long as he was around, I had everything I'd ever need. The only thing he never included me in was his death. And honestly, I'm not so sure that pleases me.

Every day when I come home, I still go downstairs just to see if by some chance, some miracle, some grace of God, he's come back for me. . . . back for me so that we an make this final trip together. I want him to be waiting here for me one of these days when I come home, so he can hug me one last time, so I can feel what it's like to be loved again, so I can feel the roughness of his wool sweater against my face, so I could smell his springtime smell, and most of all so I could go with him this time. If someone were to ask me, do you want to stay here with us in this prison, or go and be free with your Daddy, the choice would be so easy to make. I would go with my Daddy, of course. Even if we had to go through the raging fires of Hell, I would go with him, because we'd be together.

But now there are no more stones to cut, there is no little blue car, there are no hugs, there are no hellos, there is no one here waiting for me after school, there is no one here for me to talk to. There is no more love, and there will never again be the feeling of his wool sweater against my face because I wear that sweater now. I wrap it tight around me as I'm waiting for my Daddy, as I'm here leaning against the window sill, I think about how it was all a beautiful dream I once had. So beautiful that I savored every moment of it. But it seems as though the death and destruction pounding on my door woke me up, quickly, without warning. The dream is gone now, and along with it went my Daddy.

Amanda Capps

Amanda's letter helped her to put into words her feelings of hopelessness and despair as well as her great love for her dad. We can feel the pull to join her dad in death, and we can encourage her to pull her dad's love for her into life. Sadness can be reframed into an inner vehicle to propel life. Amanda began to realize that children can carry their parent's love *with* them and in that way, their parent lives on *through* them.

Provide Symbolic Expressions of Commemorating

Provide symbolic concrete expressions of physical, emotional, and intellectual ways of commemorating.

Bonnie and Ken experienced the death of their 4-year-old daughter, Lisa, by a drunken driver. The total shock and unreality of never seeing Lisa again created a physical aching in Bonnie that could not be filled. The void was excruciating and, as the months went by, deep grief emerged. The grief was compounded by the lack of someone to nurture as Bonnie had been accustomed to doing on a daily basis. Winter had turned bitterly cold, and Bonnie was plagued by the fear that Lisa would be freezing in the ground and that Bonnie needed to do something to make her feel warm. Visualizing Lisa in a warm place with lots of caring around her was a first step. Bonnie's belief in an afterlife allowed her to picture her deceased dad (who had always helped keep her warm) being with Lisa.

As Bonnie began to explain her visualization, she said she only saw Lisa in shorts, a tee shirt, or bathing suit because she had died in the summer, and this clothing was the last visual memory. Ken remembered that all of Lisa's pictures displayed around the house were taken in the summer. He wisely suggested bringing out pictures of Lisa skiing, bundled up and protected in the winter snow. We then discussed taking one of Lisa's favorite stuffed animals and dressing it warmly for winter with socks and a warm blanket. Putting this stuffed animal on the sofa by a fire was a soft reminder of the warm love these parents carried for their child and a symbolic gesture of nurturing Lisa.

This symbolic way of continuing the love and nurturance of a child after death allowed the parents a way to express blocked energy. Although, Lisa can never be present again in her physical form, the ongoing quality of her parents' love can be continually recreated.

WAYS TO FACILITATE SYMBOLIC PROJECTION THROUGH USE OF CONCRETE OBJECTS

Eliana Gil, in her book *The Healing Power of Play* (1991, p. 64), suggests some of the following toys or techniques that work well to encourage children's verbal or play communication.

Puppet play: Children can use puppets to act out secrets or hidden feelings without identifying these thoughts and feelings as being their own. Having the children perform puppet work behind a barrier allows them to feel they are hidden and safe when they speak.

Telephones: Children can have private role-playing conversations on the telephone.

Nursing bottles, dishes, and utensils, dollhouses, and doll play: Children can use these concrete props to stimulate the expression of hidden thoughts and feelings in a safe way.

Feeling cards: Cards that have illustrations of faces expressing different feelings are useful tools to help a child project storytelling, the child's own feelings, or the feelings of those close to him.

Sand play: Children usually love to use sand. They like how it feels—it often produces a calming effect. Symbolic figures can be used in sand play to create a story, reenact a funeral or other event, or show perceptions of how a loved one died.

Sunglasses: Sunglasses can feel magical to children. Sometimes they believe that they can disappear when they are wearing glasses, and no one will be able to see them. If children feel shy or ashamed, sunglasses may help them feel they will go unnoticed and then they can communicate in an easier way.

Explore Dreams

Dreams can be used to help children release repressed feelings.

Michelle was a 7-year-old whose mom was killed instantly in a single car collision. Michelle, her dad, and her brother remained stunned by this unbelievable and unimaginable event. Mom would never come home again—this reality is so great and difficult to absorb for children and adults that it must begin to be bitten off one tiny piece at a time.

Michelle began grief therapy, sometimes talking of her mom, sometimes just needing the physical presence of mothering energy. She wanted to be read to and played with. The need to be nurtured in this way became an important part of our relationship.

> We can't expect or demand children to express their feelings directly. They often cannot verbalize their need for the care that had been taken away so traumatically.

Sometimes Michelle and I talked about dreams. One day, Michelle asked if she could write a story about her dream and draw a picture, too. After she finished she decided to share her dream work with her dad. Together they discovered new linking objects to Mom. Michelle and Dad could now use hot chocolate and a warm bath, Mom's loving ways in the dream, as symbolical nurturance from mom.

This dream allowed Michelle to receive the nurturing she needed from Mom at night, nurturing that seemed to be missing during the day.

The following is Michelle's dream:

Michelle's Dream

I had a dream that I was in the woods. A snake came next to me, so—I started to run. I was running and running. I came to the creek. I jumped over the creek and kept running. I ran into the woods and guess what I saw. A wolf! I got very scared. I started yelling. Guess who came. Mommy! She saved me.

So we went home. She asked me "Why did you go out there?" "I just felt like it." "I think you should go home and have a nice warm bath and some hot chocolate and then go to sleep. I'll sleep with you if you want," said Mom.

"Mom—you are the best Mom in the whole entire world. I love you."

The End

Michelle

WAYS TO WORK WITH DREAMS

1. Dreams can reflect feelings and problems that children may have a hard time sharing openly. Dr. B. J. Tongue, in his book *The International Book of Family Therapy* (1982), suggested presenting a picture with a girl or boy lying in bed with dialogue as another tool to facilitate dream work, for example: "Here is a picture of a girl named Sally. She is having a terrible nightmare. She could be a lot like you. Could you draw a picture of what Sally might be dreaming?"

Children can decide if they would like to share their work with a parent. This could be an invitation to involve the family in open feelings.

2. Children can retell their dreams in many ways. They can be asked to draw their entire dream or any part of the dream and write down any thoughts they have about it. Kids also can be invited to write down their dreams as if it were happening as the children are writing. This opens many discussions that can lead to discovering similarities between what is happening in the dream and what is happening in real life.

3. Children can be given the choice of changing the ending of the dream if they do not like it. Mary dreamed she was lost and couldn't find her way home. Every time she tried a new road, it led to a place she didn't know. She woke up frightened and sad. Mary wanted to change the end of the dream to one she liked. She decided to have her mom (who had died a short while ago) meet her on the road. Mary's new dream ended with her mom saying, "Don't worry. You are safe. Let's find the way home together."

4. Changing events within the dream offers children inner alternatives and solutions to perceived problems. For example, Peter dreamed he was being attacked by older boys and was running away and looking for a place to hide. He wanted to change the dream. This time he ran into his father. Together, they turned and faced the bullies, and the bullies ran away.

5. Give each person, animal, or thing in the dream a voice. Have the child write or say what they feel these different parts of the dream would say if the parts would talk. This helps the children see that everyone or everything in the dream can be a part of them and part of what they are thinking or feeling.

Use Drawings and Storytelling

Drawings and storytelling provide symbolic ways for children to safely project unrecognized feelings.

Michelle loved animals. Horseback riding was her special activity, and her dog, Harley, was one of the loves of her life. We decided to write a story about animals and have each animal talk about its feelings. Then Michelle drew a picture about the story. She allowed the animals to speak many of the thoughts and feelings she had kept inside after the death of her mom. The following is Michelle's story.

Mr. Squiggle and His Animals

The dogs are very scared *because he pays more attention to them. "Look at him, he pays more attention to his horse and cow, than us," they said.*

The cat loves *Mr. Squiggle because she gets to do things.*

The fish gets very scared *because where he lives there's a lot of thunder storms. He's afraid of the noise.*

The hermit crab is shocked *because he thinks Mr. Squiggle pays too much attention to the other animals.*

The cow is ashamed. *He did something so bad he's grounded for a month.*

The bunny is sad. *She thinks that Mr. Squiggle loves the other animals more than her.*

The chickens are happy *because they are taken care of. The horse feels like that, too.*

Michelle's dog, hermit crab, and bunny felt shocked, jealous, and sad that Mr. Squiggle might love some of the other animals more than them. I asked her if she felt that anyone in her life did that to her. "Well, my dad pays more attention to my brother then he does to me. I think he likes him better than me," she replied. "How does that make you feel?" I asked. "Jealous and sad," she replied. We invited Dad in and shared these feelings.

Michelle enjoyed using her imagination through story. One day she was waving the magic wand I have in my office and wishing she could create a magical place on earth. The following is her story about such a special place.

The Most Magical Place On Earth

Once there was a girl named Michelle. She came to a magical place where everything came true. She wanted a rainbow beside her every day. She wanted a house made with sticks and a sun with sunglasses. The rainbow would have a cloud and a pot of gold. The house was small on the outside and big on the inside. She hoped one day to live in a mansion bigger than any kingdom you've ever seen. She would live with her flowers. There are lots of animals.

Michelle

P.S. If I lived in a magical place I'd make nice people never die and bring a few people back from the dead. I'd like to meet God.

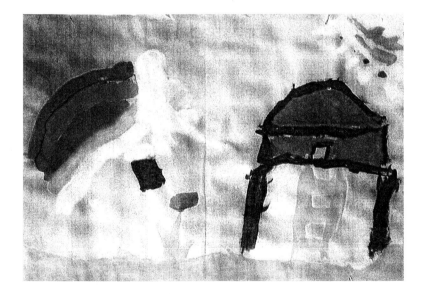

She began to explain that this place was where she pictured her mom to be. It was safe and beautiful and Michelle could visit it in her mind whenever she chooses.

WAYS TO HELP CHILDREN WITH STORYTELLING

1. *Use therapeutic stories.* These stories are a powerful method of reaching children's unconscious feelings and allowing them to identify safely with the figures in the story. Davis (1990) has written a superior group of therapeutic stories entitled *Once Upon a Time.* It includes a broad range of projective stories on very deep areas for children, including abuse and death. Harris and Dawson (1999) have created a grief dramatics adventure in their book *Death of the Forest Queen.*

2. *Make a story box.* In a decorative box, place objects such as:
   people—man, woman, children
   weapons—hammer, gun, ax
   animals—dog, cat, pig, wolf
   power figures—superman, monsters, dinosaurs

Children can pick one or several objects and create a story. The therapist and the child can take turns creating a continuous story.

3. *Make up a therapeutic story.* Therapeutic stories speak to children in a metaphorical way that is very powerful. They open the door to the unconscious by allowing the child to relate to the story without calling attention to his or her self.

We can create a story that speaks to the child about his or her particular issue without using the exact facts. If a 6-year-old girl was verbally abused by her dad, who later died of suicide, we can create a story about a 9-year-old girl whose Dad embarrassed her by screaming at her at baseball practice. Her dad later got arrested for robbery and put in prison. "How do you think she felt about her dad not being home anymore?"

Visualization Techniques

Visualization techniques allow children to use their imagination to re-create healthy thoughts and reduce anxiety.

Visualization techniques can be an effective method of working with grief. Children can visualize painful or disturbing feelings and then, through guiding their imagery, begin to substitute more positive visual memories and find inner resources for strength. We can combine imagination, fairy tales, and metaphor to create a powerful tool for change. Children can use their natural gift of imagination to reduce anxiety and establish helpful thoughts.

> When leading a child through visualizations, it is important to:
> * acknowledge feelings and thoughts,
> * emphasize positive affirmations,
> * incorporate all of the five senses, and
> * remind the child that he or she is in a safe place that he or she can return to whenever he or she wants.

Visualization or guided imagery can empower the child to create his or her own internal ways of dealing with fears, scary obstacles, distances, and absences. Children can experience this peaceful, magical place within their minds and realize they have the internal power to re-create it again and again.

PROCEDURE FOR VISUALIZATION

In order to facilitate visualization, make the following suggestions to the child.

Close your eyes. (Be sure kids are comfortable with closed eyes; some children don't like to do that.)

Begin a "tummy breath" by starting all the way down in the tummy and blowing out a big breath. Do this three or four times. (These yoga-like breathing exercises can be helpful to promote a relaxed state for some children.)

We are going to go on a little trip in our imagination. We can stop any time you want to. Just tell me. For now let's relax and enjoy ourselves.

Imagine a place in a natural setting. Try to see it in your mind. What does it look like? Look around you. What do you see? Where are you? Who is with you? What colors do you see? What is the weather? How does it smell? Can you feel the sand or soil. Does it feel smooth against your fingers, your feet? Does the wind blow against your face? Is it sunny? Can you feel the warm sun on your face? Can you hear the birds? What are they saying?"

The above painting is 11-year-old Jonathan's peaceful place to visualize.

Make sure to incorporate the five senses when guiding kids through visualizations.

Open your eyes and draw a picture about the place you imagined. (Remind children they can return to this safe place in their mind whenever they choose to.)

JOSHUA'S VISUALIZATION

Joshua is a 6-year-old boy who has talked about some scary thoughts associated with his mom's cancer. Josh says, "When I'm away from my mom and don't know how she is, I get scared that she might get sick and go back to the hospital." When he was asked to tell about his scary feelings he described them as big old dirty black spots. His mom created a summary visualization or "closed eye story" to help him transform his fears into a safe place. This technique can be adopted for children who have experienced a significant death, abandonment, or serious illness of a loved one.

This visualization (below) was effective in empowering Joshua to use his rich imagination to deal with his fears and anxieties. It is a technique that can be used well with such mentally sensitive children.

The story (Adapted from *The Search for the King)* takes place in a magical land with beautiful birds and a colored forest. There is a river separating the child from the loved one and a monster that guards it, not letting anyone across. The river is the barrier to the loved one and the monster represents the child's fears and scary thoughts. A magical white eagle comes to help the child cross over the river to be with Mom. The eagle symbolizes inner strength that can rise above fears. Together they create a giant rainbow of love and warmth that climbs over the river. The rainbow is faith in one's self.

This place of safety lives within the heart of the child. The beautiful eagle can be called at any time to again visit the magical land.

FOLLOW-UP ACTIVITIES

1. This visualization can be used for one session or used for several sessions as a continuous activity. A tape recording of the visualization can be made and given to the child to keep and use whenever he or she would like.
2. This visualization can be projected onto clay or sand table figures. Children can retell the story with emphasis on the affirmations of transcending fear through positive imagery within themselves.
3. Children can draw the magical land and the magical way it looks. "Draw how you felt before and after you crossed the river."
4. Children can make paper bag puppets of the characters. They can act out the story or role-play different parts.

Silence

Silence can be used to help children affirm their own feelings.

Jennifer was an 11-year-old client whose dad had died of a sudden heart attack. She burst into my office during the first week of school, enraged at her new teacher. She had bravely decided to tell this new teacher that her dad had just died. Her teacher never responded to her. She began punching the punching bag in the office and crying at the same time. "How could she not answer me?" she questioned. "Fear," I thought to myself. Later, when Jennifer had expressed and acted out some of her feelings, we discussed the idea that people's fears of not knowing what to say or of feeling bad themselves can create their silence. "What do you wish the teacher would have done?" I asked. "Given me a hug and said 'I'm sorry.'"

A seemingly unrelated incident with a 15-year-old client whose dad had suddenly died in a car crash surfaced about the same time. Debbie was deeply saddened by her father's sudden death. She had had an extremely close relationship with him, sharing life together intellectually, emotionally, and socially. Memories were painful. I usually invite the kids to bring in pictures of their loved one so we can share memories together. Debbie said she did not want to bring in a picture the first time I asked her. The next session I again mentioned she might bring in a picture of her dad.

She declined, stating that she didn't want to and when she was ready, she would let me know. We worked together many months. I remained silent about the picture, respecting Debbie's wisdom of knowing her own timing in her grief process.

Finally, we had decided it was time for Debbie to leave grief therapy. At our final meeting, I usually give the children a little goodbye gift. Debbie's was a picture frame. As she opened her gift, she handed me a wonderful picture of her dad that just happened to fit into the frame. Debbie taught me a great lesson—trust the inner wisdom of the grieving child.

Jennifer and Debbie's stories illustrate the power of silence. Silence given out of fear creates hurt, rage, and deep sadness. Silence given out of respect and love creates trust and inner strength. We, as caregivers, cannot fix the circumstances with which these children are faced. We can acknowledge and support them in their grief.

Memory Work

Use memory work with symbolic figures, drawings, and storytelling as a projective tool to release frozen feelings.

Jimmy, age 8, was a child whose father had been murdered. Before his death, Jimmy's dad moved out of the home but remained a strong disciplinarian. Jimmy's memories of his dad's frequent anger remained buried deep inside Jimmy.

Jimmy had great difficulty verbalizing his feelings. The use of projective tools became an important ingredient in our work together. The following is a picture Jimmy drew in a memory book showing life before his dad's death. Jimmy never drew real people, only cartoon characters. The picture shows Dad telling Jimmy, "Go to bed," and Jimmy saying, "Help."

During one session, Jimmy began making a story using symbolic figures (army men and power figures). In the story, the helplessness in the previous picture changed to powerfulness as he was encouraged to act out his fantasy with the objects. The following is the story he told:

"Once upon a time there was a dragon named Gonzilla. He was mean, hairy, and breathed fire. The people in the town were scared. They hired Jimmy, The Powerful, to protect them."

We took a photograph of Jimmy's figures and left it with his display for others to see. He asked many times what other kids had said about his story and was glad to hear they used his idea to make stories of their own.

Sometimes Jimmy would not or could not communicate. He would not speak at all or used only one word responses. One day we decided to make a scribble drawing. Jimmy began scribbling on a piece of paper furiously. When he finished, I asked him to think of a title for his work. "A Tornado" was his reply. "If the tornado could talk, what would it say?" I asked. "Help me," he sighed. The following is his drawing.

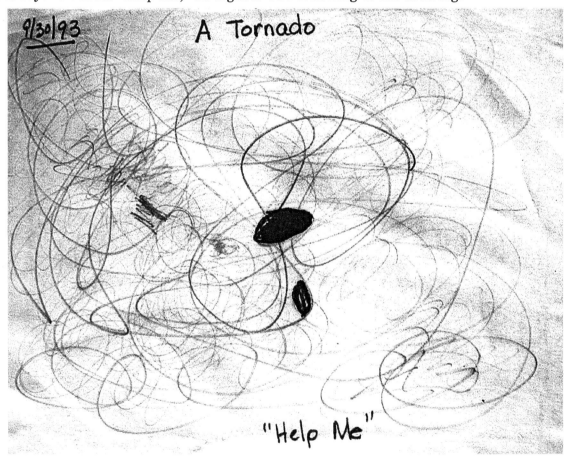

One day Jimmy came in filled with an anger he could barely control. He began punching the punching bag, saying nothing. Any attempt I made to engage in verbal communication was met with no response. I began to tell him a make believe story about a child who was very angry at his dad: "The Dad had left home to go to the war in Viet Nam. He used to punish his son a lot and make him clean his room. Now every time the boy walked by his Dad's picture, can you guess what he would say?"

Jimmy burst into a blast of words in a way I had never heard him do before or since. This was his response to the question:

"You get in my face, I'll knock you out!"

"Wish you were dead. Jump on cross. Knock you out—chop you up to a million pieces."

"Stab you! Stab you!"

"Belt"

"Touch you again. I'll crucify your butt!"

"Hate you for the rest of my life!"

"When I'm finished, I'll kick your butt. Hit you—hate you—crucify you till you die."

"If you touch me/Spirit come to my soul!"

"Hate you for the rest of my life!"

"You stink! You're and animal! Hate you dummy—you fool"

"Ass!"

The rage and violent thoughts that spewed out of Jimmy's lips filled the room. When he finished his forceful response, he became silent again.

Jimmy is one of millions of children on the planet whose complicated grief is getting in the way of his functioning as a normal child. By using the projective techniques of drawing, storytelling, and symbolic figures that allow him to begin to uncover the shame and terror he holds associated with his dad and his brutal death, Jimmy can begin the long journey of separating these circumstances from the actual death of his dad. Jimmy's hidden rage emerged behind his silence, bringing feelings into the open to be seen and witnessed. The first step to the meltdown process had begun.

TOOLS FOR MEMORY WORK WITH CHILDREN

Use *memory books*. Memory books are participatory workbooks that enable children to draw and write their feelings and thoughts in an interactive way. They can be purchased commercially or made to meet the specific needs of the child. The following is a story that accompanies a page from a memory book. The story and picture tell of how Danny's dad died and the way Danny remembers being told about the death.

How Dad Died

My dad, Michael, got killed. There was an accident. His car hit a tree. He's dead. He is in heaven.

My Mom told me on December 1st. When my mom told me I felt sad, but I didn't cry. I was shocked. The police had come and told my mother.

I said, "Why? What happened?" "He died," Mom said. "He died because there was ice. He slid into a tree."

Danny

P.S. I like to wear my Dad's shirt. It makes me feel good.

My Special Person died because...
there was a bad car accident.

COMMERCIAL MEMORY BOOKS FOR YOUNG CHILDREN:

Together We'll Get Through This! Learning to Cope with Loss and Transaction (Carney, 1997)
Memory Book for Bereaved Children (Braza. 1988)
A Child Remembers (Traisman, 1994)
Bart Speaks Out on Suicide (Goldman, 2000)
When Someone Very Special Dies (Heegaard, 1988)

COMMERCIAL MEMORY BOOKS FOR TEENAGERS:

Fire in My Heart, Ice in My Veins (Traisman, 1992)
Facing Change (O'Toole, 1995)

Use memory boxes or a memory table. We can help children create memory boxes or a memory table to provide places to store or share treasured items of their loved ones. Memory boxes house precious belongings and can be made from a shoe box that is painted and decorated. A memory table can be displayed in a child's room or special part of the house with pictures and things that are meaningful to the child.

Use *photos, videos, and tape recordings.* Photographs, videos, and tape recordings are concrete ways to stimulate visual and auditory memories of a loved one. Making a photo album of pictures and titling it "My Life" creates a clear picture of times and events shared and creates a motivation for the child to start a discussion. Videos and tape recordings of a loved one are very precious. Often kids feel they might forget how their person looked and sounded. These are wonderful ways to help children remember.

Have children make a list of the facts or *unanswered questions* they want to know about the death of a person who has been important in their lives. Help them *develop the resources* to find the answers through parents, relatives, counselors, books, and so forth.

Let children *tell how they were told* about an illness or death. Make a chart that explains when they felt included or left out. Have children draw to write about the ways they wish they had been told about or included in the illness or death of their loved one.

Linking objects are important memory tools for children. A loved one's key chain, sweater, drawing, and diary are concrete symbolic forms to help kids feel closer to the person who has died by providing tangible representations to hold and cherish.

Eleven-year-old Nancy felt her mom was with her every time she saw a butterfly. Her dad gave her a linking object, a necklace of a butterfly, for her to wear every day to help her feel Mom's presence.

Sally was a 6-year-old who became enraged when her Dad said he was selling the car her grandfather gave them before he died. Grandpa had said the car would always protect her and keep her safe. Selling the car triggered feelings of Grandpa's death. Sally and Dad discussed several linking objects such as a windshield wiper or armrest to help remember Grandpa. They eventually agreed upon Sally taking photos of the car, to create an ongoing reminder of her grandfather's love.

Summary of Ways to Help Children

1. Use *visualization techniques* to allow children to create positive images.

2. Use *concrete objects* to symbolically express feelings of nurturing and love that have suddenly been cut off.

3. Use *reality checks* such as medical checkups and phone calls home to provide sustained reassurance to someone in a very fragile state.

4. Use and respect the *belief system* of the child as a support and framework to assimilate and hold the experience of life and death.

5. Create *normalcy* whenever possible by emphasizing that overwhelming fears of death and worries of abandonment are absolutely okay and are a reasonable reaction in coping with the unreasonable.

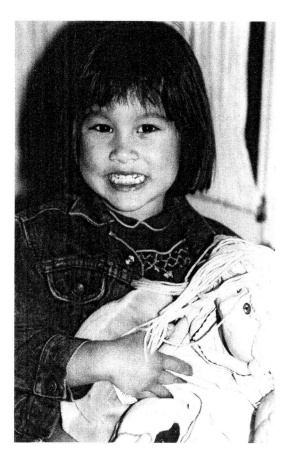

6. Use *role-playing techniques*. Children who experience a complicated grief usually have great difficulty. Shock, rage, and terror stemming from how the person died may block the flow of feelings. Plays, puppetry, clay figures, sand table stories, and doll houses are valuable tools that allow kids to project unresolved feelings in a more open way.

7. Use *dreams*. Dreams are a fertile ground to understand denied powerful emotions that can then be brought out into the open through stories and drawings.

8. Use *memory work*. Using photographs, newspaper articles, or treasured objects and belongings associated with loved ones who died will help solidify feelings and bring these feelings to the surface. Making memory books and memory boxes will help initiate discussions with children and provide a concrete form for valuable memories.

9. Use *projective tools* such as play figures, drawings, and storytelling to help release frozen feelings.

10. *Use silence.* Silence is a powerful tool for allowing a child to own his or her feelings rather than be told he or she should think and feel.

11. *Create rituals.* Children can create symbolic ways of sending love to a person who has died. Sending a balloon with an attached note, floating a note in a bottle in the ocean, ringing a special bell at a special time, eating at that person's favorite restaurant, or singing his or her favorite song can help create an inner bond of love that lives through time.

CHAPTER 8

Saying Goodbye:
Ways to Include Children
in a Funeral or Memorial

PLAY AREA FOR CHILDREN • BUBBLES

MEMORY BAGS • CHILDREN'S MUSIC

FREEDOM TO LEAVE / FREEDOM TO PARTICIPATE

TABLE FOR DRAWINGS AND STORIES

COMFORTABLE SEATING WITH FRIENDS AND FAMILY

Opening a Memorial Service to Children

Breaking the silence on funerals and memorial services by *including children* is an idea whose time has come. So many times parents call asking if children should come to a funeral or memorial service. Not only should they come, but the memorial service and funeral should become a shared family experience for them.

Andrew was a child who died suddenly of a rare virus on a family vacation in the Boston area. Friends and family were not prepared for this shocking and unexpected death. Andrew was 6 years old and had just completed kindergarten. The shock of his death needed to be recognized and processed before the overwhelming feeling of loss for Andrew could be honored. The memorial service was a vehicle for expressing this complicated grief.

The rest of this chapter explores how to include children in a funeral or memorial service by looking at how Andrew's friends and family did.

Preparing the Community

Andrew's parents carefully and consciously wrote the following letter (reprinted here with permission). It was sent to the parents of every child at Andrew's school before Andrew's parents returned home from Boston. Their letter tells the facts of Andrew's death and the events surrounding his illness.

Dear Friends,

Many of you have asked "What happened to Andrew?" We would like to share with you the last few weeks. We were vacationing. Andrew was happy and healthy, riding his bogey board on the ocean waves, fishing, and playing in the great out-of-doors. He had a slight fever for about a day and a half so we gave him Tylenol.

When Andrew went to bed Wednesday evening, August 10, he was energetic and feeling fine. During the night he complained of shoulder cramps, a stiff neck, and aching legs. Early in the morning, we took him to the hospital. He was tentatively diagnosed with spinal meningitis and medically evacuated by helicopter to another hospital in Boston. His father Doug rode with him.

The next days were a roller coaster ride; Andrew's condition quickly worsened and then appeared to stabilize. We hoped that, in time, the virus would pass through the body. We were with Andrew the entire time, talking, singing, caressing, reading to him. He was in no pain and knew that we were there. Andrew received excellent medical care, from loving physicians, nurses, and medical technicians. On the afternoon of Tuesday, August 16, Andrew passed away. His brain and his heart had been irreversibly damaged by an undetermined virus which caused meningoencephalomyelitis and myocarditis.

We know for sure that Andrew's illness was not contagious; no other family members or friends have been sick. Nor did Andrew have any predisposing medical conditions that contributed to his illness. It is possible that further medical tests will give us more information about the precise virus.

On August 20, we had a lovely funeral service for Andrew at a monastery chapel in Cambridge, Massachusetts. A small group of Andrew's family and friends joined us. On August 22, Andrew's ashes were interred at the cemetery, next to his paternal grandfather. Andrew had always loved the story of King Tut's mummy; we too, buried many gifts with Andrew, including favorite books, music tapes, family photos, toys, and shells, rocks, and sand from the beach. Later, in September or October, we will have a memorial service in the Washington, D.C. area. Friends of Andrew—of all ages—will be invited to celebrate Andrew's life and share their memories in drawings, poems, songs, and other joyful ways.

We grieve for our beautiful son; but we feel blessed that we had six wonderful years with him. A memorial fund will be established at Andrew's school to provide additional playground facilities. Also, a memorial fund will be established at a special hospital to establish an early childhood library in the pediatrics unit.

We are so grateful for your continued love and support.

Love,
Judy and Doug

 Parents and children need to know the facts about the loss. This letter tells the specifics about Andrew's illness and death, lessening fears and creating a foundation to grieve.

Preparing the School

Andrew's school included his parents' letter with this letter (reprinted here with permission) from the headmaster to all members of the school community. Additional written information and resources on children and grief were provided.

Dear Green Acres Parents:

Yesterday, I received this fax from Judy and Doug, parents of Andrew, who was a student in our kindergarten last year. Andrew passed away on August 16 after a brief illness. Because Judy and Doug have written such a lovely and moving letter, I would like their own words to tell you the story of what happened to Andrew.

I know that there will be many questions about how to talk to your children about Andrew's death. Many younger children may be fearful, and many parents may be uncomfortable addressing death with their children. I have talked with Linda Goldman, one of our parents and the co-director of The Center for Loss and Grief Therapy. She has passed along to me the attachments that offer some advice for talking about death with children. You might want to read her book: Life and Loss: A Guide To Help Grieving Children. *On the first day of school, a clinical social worker will be available to talk to children who are anxious or fearful or simply want to talk. A physician will be willing to answer medical questions for parents who may have them.*

Our community mourns the loss of Andrew. He was a vital, intelligent young fellow who loved the playground. Personally, I will miss him. He and I connected on a special level. I will not forget the afternoon of the Olympics when he and I watched the older children on the "Slip and Slide."

Judy and Doug will be back in the Washington area soon. I know that they will appreciate your caring and supportive wishes.

Sincerely,
Arnold S. C., Headmaster

Preparing the Parents

A meeting was held at Andrew's school for all interested parents and faculty. Information and appropriate resources were presented on how young children grieve. Feelings were shared about Andrew's death as it affected the children, and adults expressed their own feelings, fears, and vulnerabilities. Parents were given the following suggestions on how to prepare their children for the memorial service.

1. Tell the children the facts about Andrew's death.
2. Share your feelings of grief with your child.
3. Allow children to express feelings and commemorate through drawings and stories.
4. Emphasize children's need to be thoroughly prepared, with all of their senses, for what they will see, hear, smell, and feel when they go to calling hours, especially if there is a viewing.
5. Understand the psychological value of viewing as long as children are prepared and not forced to attend. It helps children recognize the reality of the loss.
6. Describe what will happen at the memorial service.
7. Invite the child to join you in coming to the service, but don't force him or her.
8. Explain that the children can participate if they feel like it by telling a story about Andrew or about something special they remember. They can share artwork or poetry. They do not have to participate if they do not feel like it.
9. Remind them they can participate in children's songs and art activities and that people they know will be at the service.
10. Tell the children that if they feel uncomfortable, they can leave (those adults who accompany the child to the service should be prepared to leave if the child wants to do so).
11. Explain that some people may be sad and cry, and that the child may be sad and cry. That's okay. However, also explain that the child may not feel sad and may not cry. That's okay, too.
12. Read children's resources such as *Life and Loss: A Guide To Help Grieving Children* (Goldman, 2000) and *About Dying* (Stein, 1994) to help prepare children and answer questions.

13. As much as possible, share what will happen ahead of time.
14. Encourage the children to ask questions.

Preparing the Memorial Service

Andrew's parents prepared a very child-oriented memorial service to celebrate Andrew's life as well as commemorate his death. Parents of Andrew's friends where told what the ceremony would be like. They, in turn, could tell their children what to expect. A notice was put in the school newspaper.

While Andrew's parents went through all of the normal pain, anguish, and stages of deep personal grief, this remarkable couple summoned their deep love for their son, Andrew, to create a loving tribute to his life. In so doing, their own grief process was enriched as was the grief process of all the others who were involved with the memorial service.

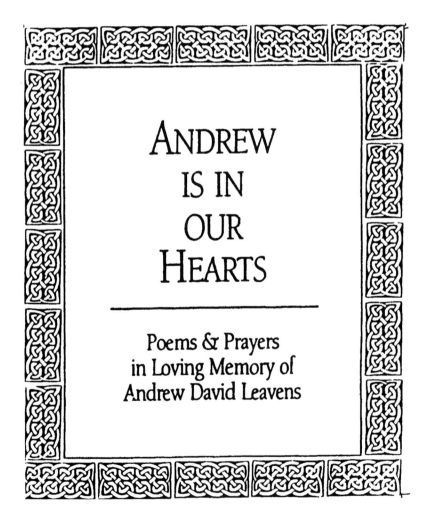

ANDREW
IS IN
OUR
HEARTS

Poems & Prayers
in Loving Memory of
Andrew David Leavens

Preparing the Children

Andrew's memorial service served as a model of what is possible when parents choose to commemorate and honor the dignity of their child's life with a true respect for all children. It was a celebration of Andrew's life as well as a commemoration of his death.

While there certainly was sadness, the service had a warmth and invited openness that allowed children of all ages, adult friends, family members, co-workers of Andrew's parents, school representatives, and Andrew's parents themselves to freely and spontaneously participate. Stories were told, songs were sung, and poetry was read that acknowledged the wonderful life that was Andrew's.

Children and adults sat on the floor. Chairs were also set up in the back of the room. Families were together. Children could lie down, stand up, or leave if they chose to do so. They *did not have to* participate, but they could if they wanted to. They could go outside and blow bubbles or play. The children made their own choices as long as the service was respected. A parent or caring adult was prepared to leave with each designated child. Children's artwork and stories were displayed on tables and walls. They told of memories and love and sorrow for their friend Andrew.

Sharing Memories

Andrew's parents made a booklet of favorite poems and prayers for each family to take home. The following are a few of the many loving remembrances shared.

We have selected these poems and prayers to capture the love and appreciation we have for Andrew. We celebrate his energy and curiosity, his joy in physical movement, his friendship, his ability to share and to help others share, his humor and love of nonsense, his understanding of good and evil and his trust in the potential for good, his respect for nature, his balance and grace, his daring, and his sense of the spiritual.

To see the world through the eyes of a child is truly a gift that opens our hearts.

Love,

Judy and Doug

The following was shared by Jillian, Andrew's sister:

Some people come into our lives and quickly go,
Some stay for awhile, leave footprints on our hearts,
 and we are never, ever the same.

> Andrew is in my heart.
>
> (written by Chris, age 7, Andrew's good friend)

Chris' mom was crying one night and Chris wanted to know why. "I'm crying because I'm sad that I will never be able to see Andrew," she said. "Don't worry," he replied. "I can see Andrew whenever I want, because he's always in my heart."

POEM [2]

I loved my friend
He went away from me
There's nothing more to say.
The poem ends,
Soft as it began—
I loved my friend.

(Langston Hughes)

From *Collected Poems* by
Langston Hughes. ©1994
by the Estate of Langston
Hughes, reprinted by permission
of Alfred. A. Knopf Inc.

The Memorial Service

Children and teenagers shared their thoughts, feelings, pictures, and stories. Their ages ranged from 5–16.

Some children shared their photo collection of special times with Andrew.

Some children cried. Some children did not want to participate. Some children felt they wanted to leave. That was all okay.

Some children and teenagers opened up their hearts and read poems they had written.

Some children and teenagers could not share. They were given a voice from a caring adult, such as Andrew's dad, who read their letters.

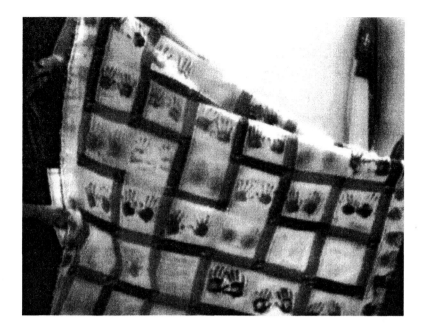

Andrew's adult friends and family shared their remembrances of Andrew's life.

Andrew's class shared their gift—each child's handprint on a quilt for Andrew's parents.

Community support was very meaningful. Andrew's school principal spoke of his memories of Andrew.

Andrew's parents shared their love for and experiences with Andrew. They told funny stories about their son.

Andrew's teachers and friends sang many of Andrew's favorite songs. They invited the children and their families to join in if they felt comfortable. Songs included: "The Earth is Mine," "When The Rain Comes Down," "I'm Being Eaten By a Boa Constrictor," and "The Garden Song." At the very end of the memorial service people held hands and sang "Friends, Friends."

After the Service

After the service the children were guided in making several hands-on commemorations of Andrew if they wanted. There was a crafts table where the children could draw pictures, write letters, or share stories about Andrew. Bubbles were provided for the children. They could take them outside to blow in remembrance of Andrew.

"Memory bags" were made for each child who attended. The bags were filled with treats like stickers and pieces of candy that Andrew's parents felt he would have liked to give his friends.

The room was filled with photos of Andrew, Andrew's own artwork, and the artwork and stories of Andrew's friends. The children could walk through the room freely and experience Andrew's life visually.

Favorite toys and books of Andrew's were on display as well as many photos of him, his family, and friends. Shown on the previous page is a picture that Andrew made at age 4 1/2.

Each family took home the booklet of poems and prayers prepared by Andrew's parents. Many families read selections as a way to remember Andrew. Classmates and friends read these poems at school or quiet times at home. One friend was inspired to create the remembrance shown here.

The children who attended Andrew's memorial service appeared to gain a great gift—the gift of inner strength. Knowing they could participate and be present with adults in a community remembrance of their friend gave them the awareness of how to honor Andrew's life. Knowing how to honor Andrew's life gives these children a way to value and respect their own lives. This undoubtedly will help them know and be prepared for the other life and death experiences they will face.

Commemorating After the Memorial Service or Funeral

Commemorating is one of the four psychological tasks of grieving (Goldman, 2000). We can help children accomplish this important task by enabling them to actively participate in the memorial service or funeral. We also can present rituals and other tangible ways to continue the commemoration process. The importance and effectiveness of offering children an ongoing concrete way to remember a loved one who has died cannot be emphasized enough.

Andrew's parents and school decided to continue remembering his life by creating a new playground in his memory. The site would be at the place where Andrew played the most. The project was designed to involve the community, families, and school children and personnel.

The school children would be asked for ideas and designs on how they would like the new playground to be. The parents would be asked to offer expertise and skills in the creation and production of the project. Families would be invited to come together in building the equipment. Teachers and school personnel were encouraged to join. Andrew will continue to be truly acknowledged and honored as children work on the playground, watch the new addition to the school being built, and play on this new source of fun for years to come. Many of the children will remember their experience of helping friends and family to create a living tribute to Andrew.

A Playground in Memory of Andrew

The following is an excerpt from Andrew's school newsletter. It describes the plan for a memorial playground for Andrew.

Plans are underway to build a playground structure in memory of Andrew. Manufacturers of playground equipment have been consulted, plus suggestions have been solicited from GAS faculty and K–Gr. 4 students. Frequently and enthusiastically mentioned ideas from children were mazes, monkey swings, forts, castles, haunted houses, climbing ropes, and ziplines. Some children even drew pictures of what they'd like to have on the playground.

Over the past few months, Andrew's parents have been meeting with the administration and development staff to find easy ways to translate these wonderful, imaginative ideas into reality. This week a working model of a playground maze was shown to the classes. The children were excited and suggested adding mirrors, banners, and tunnels. Over the summer, plans will be further developed. We hope that one weekend next fall, families can join together to help construct the new playground structure.

This memorial playground was completed in December 1995. Parents, children, faculty, and friends came together in sunshine and snow to complete this wonderful tribute to Andrew.

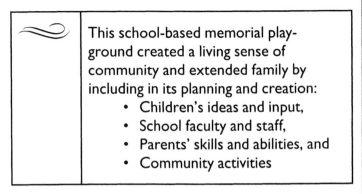

This school-based memorial playground created a living sense of community and extended family by including in its planning and creation:

- Children's ideas and input,
- School faculty and staff,
- Parents' skills and abilities, and
- Community activities

Remembering Special Days

Rituals are very powerful and are especially important when remembering loved ones on special days. Children's play incorporates the use of rituals as a physical way of providing a structure for the energy they wish to create. We can provide an opportunity for the children to continue to use concrete forms that hold the space that allows continued remembrance and honor of the people they have loved.

ANDREW'S BIRTHDAY REMEMBRANCE

Andrew's parents carefully prepared for the first birthday after his death. Much time, energy, remembering, and love went into the creation of this special day. His parents decided to include children in their commemoration and encouraged expression of the children's ideas about how to celebrate Andrew's birthday.

Several of Andrew's special friends had been talking about his upcoming birthday. Andrew's cousin Cristina reminisced about last year's birthday and remembered many of his favorite things.

She wished she could invent a machine that had a button she could press to bring Andrew back to life. Cristina wanted to make a cake with his favorite rainbow sprinkles on top. A neighborhood playmate wanted to get balloons. She said, "They must be green—Andrew's favorite color!"

His parents followed the lead of these children and, all together, they planned a birthday party. The children were invited to make a birthday cake for Andrew with his mom. Each friend participated in creating the cake and decorating in ways Andrew would have liked. Pictures were displayed from many of Andrew's earlier birthday parties. They remembered one of Andrew's favorite hiding games and played it.

Goody bags were provided, and balloons were launched by the children to symbolically send their love through time. The children made a circle around the balloons and began chanting spontaneously "We love Andrew, we love Andrew" as they sent them into the air. They then were allowed to choose plants to place in their own backyard as an ongoing remembrance that they could see and watch grow.

Ways Children Can Commemorate

- Plant a flower or tree.
- Blow bubbles.
- Send a balloon.
- Light a candle.
- Say a prayer.
- Write a poem, story, or song about the loved one who died. Send it to his or her family.
- Talk into a tape recorder or make a video of memories.
- Make cookies or cake and bring them to the family of the person who has died.
- Create a mural or collage about the life of the person who has died.

Summary of What a Child-Oriented Memorial Service or Funeral Should Include:

PREPARING THE CHILDREN

1. Give the child the facts about the death.
2. Invite the child to be included in the event.
3. Give the child the choice to participate in the service by sharing memories.
4. Allow the child to be a part of the decision making. What pictures or favorite memories would he or she like displayed?
5. Prepare the child for the service.
6. Prepare the child with all the senses—see, hear, smell, touch, taste.
   Describe how it will look.
   Describe what people will do.
   Allow children to ask questions.

7. Read resources such as *What About the Kids? Understanding their Needs in Funeral Planning and Services* (The Dougy Center, 1999) and *Honoring Our Loved Ones: Going to a Funeral* (Carney, 1997). These books contain ideas to help adults include children in the memorial services. Read *A Child's Book about Funerals and Cemetaries* (Grollman & Johnson, 2001) to children to inform them about death and funerals.
8. Remind children they can leave the service if they feel uncomfortable. Set up a plan ahead of time.
9. Emphasize that some people may feel sad and some may not. Either way is okay.

PREPARING THE SERVICE

1. Fill the room with memory tables that have the loved one's pictures and treasured items.
2. Display commemorative letters and drawings that others have made for and about the loved one.
3. Create a booklet of feelings about the person who died that includes children's work as well as adults'.
4. Arrange to include songs appropriate for children to sing in the ceremony.
5. Use a seating arrangement where people can sit on chairs and on the floor as a family.
6. Include spaces in the service for children to participate in sharing stories and drawings if they choose.
7. Provide an art table that children can go to after the service to draw or write letters.
8. Create memory bags to give to the children.
9. Provide bubbles or balloons for children to send off symbolically to their loved one.
10. Bring flowers as a way of remembering the continuing cycle of life.

Resources to Help Children with Funerals and Memorials

Pablo Remembers by George Ancona (1993) is a wonderful explanation of the Mexican custom of celebrating El Dia de Los Muertos, The Day of the Dead, by celebrating the life of a loved one over and over again.

A Candle for Grandma/A Guide to the Jewish Funeral for Children and Parents by David Techner and Judith Hirt-Manheimer (1993), helps to comfort children after the death of a loved one. The story tells of a Jewish funeral and burial practice in clear and meaningful ways.

Honoring Our Loved Ones: Going to a Funeral by Karen Carney (1997), gives children clear language and preparation for attending a funeral.

Barkley and Eve: Sitting Shiva by Karen Carney (2001) is a wonderful guide to describe the Jewish tradition of burial and mourning for childrent.

A Child's Book about Funerals and Cemetaries by Earl Grollman and Joy Johnson (2001) is an interactive book for young children to share their experience of funerals and cemetaries.

Thank You For Coming To Say Good Bye by Janice Roberts and Joy Johnson (1994) is an excellent source of information to help caring adults involve children in funeral services.

What About the Kids? Understanding Their Needs in Funeral Planning and Services by the Dougy Center (1999) is a very useful guide to help prepare children for funerals and services.

Educators Can Help: Let's Get Involved

RESOURCES AND SUPPORT FOR THE BEREAVED STUDENT

CRISIS INTERVENTION—COPING WITH A STUDENT DEATH

PROCEDURES FOR HOMICIDE AND OTHER VIOLENT DEATHS

SUICIDE PREVENTION, INTERVENTION, AND POSTVENTION

TEACH CHILDREN TO PREVENT ABUSE

IN-SERVICE STAFF TRAININGS ON CHILDREN AND LOSS

SCHOOL MEMORIAL COMMEMORATIONS

SCHOOL BASED LOSS AND GRIEF CURRICULUMS

MAINTAINING A NO-BULLYING POLICY

Resource and Support for the Bereaved Student

Margaret's dad died in a car accident. He was declared by the police to be a drunk driver, speeding at 60 mph in a 25-mile zone. A year later, Margaret was diagnosed with Attention Deficit Disorder (ADD) and told she must repeat fourth grade. She was an angry and disruptive child, not willing to socialize, and not wanting to do schoolwork. Margaret worried about her mom and wanted to be with her a lot. Her mom worried because Margaret had never cried over her dad's death. "Life's just not fair," Margaret would constantly say. "We're not a family without Dad." The following section shows what schools can do to help Margaret and other children like her.

WHAT CAN THE SCHOOL DO?

1. Teachers, counselors, and administrators can let Margaret know they care and are there for her if she needs them. Caring adults need to say words to the children without expecting or inviting a response. Reaching out lays the groundwork for future communication. Most importantly, educators need to listen, and the grieving child needs to feel heard.

2. Educators need to *prepare the class* for the grieving student's return, maintain contact with the family, and provide space for the grieving student and fellow classmates to express feelings and ask questions. Resources such as O'Toole's *Growing With Grief: A K–12 Curriculum to Help Young People Through All Kinds of Grief* (1989) is extremely helpful for ideas and insights.

Teachers can encourage classmates to maintain contact with the grieving child by calling, sending cards, making pictures or writing letters, baking cookies, or visiting the home. Classmates need to be given the facts and encouraged to express feelings and fears. Welcoming the grieving child and saying they are glad to see him or her means a lot to the grieving child. Encourage kids to listen and share and realize that *sadness is normal.*

3. Caring adults can provide resources such as school personnel, books, grief therapists, and community support groups to help facilitate the grieving process. A teacher may offer help to a bereaved student by suggesting there are many available people in the school and arranging time with them if needed. The school librarian has books on loss and grief. The school counselor has time and resources to offer. The school nurse can address medical questions.

4. School policy could allow Margaret special consideration if she becomes overwhelmed with thoughts and feelings. She may need reassurance more often than other children that family members are safe.

Margaret's teacher can express an awareness that it may be difficult for her to maintain her normal school routine and that she will help modify it by:

- Allowing her to leave the room if needed
- Allowing her to call home if necessary
- Scheduling visits to the school nurse and guidance counselor periodically
- Changing some work assignments
- Assigning a class helper
- Creating some private time in the day
- Giving more academic progress reports

A helpful resource for teachers is *Grief Comes to Class* by Majel Gliko-Bradon (1992).

5. Teachers need to be aware of important dates such as Margaret's dad's birth date and date of death. These are very difficult days for her and need to be acknowledged. Holidays such as Father's Day, Christmas, and Valentine's Day may create anxiety, anger, or sadness as it places her loss in the forefront. Invite Margaret to make a symbolic card, light a candle, or create a poem for her dad and join with other children in sharing memories.

6. School personnel need to be aware and accepting that children's grades usually drop after the loss of a loved one. This may be the time when impulsivity, distractibility, and hyperactivity emerge. Usually behavioral observations at home and school are the primary criteria for diagnosis of ADD. The following common grief responses are sometimes mistaken for signals of ADD:

- Restlessness in staying seated
- Calling out of turn
- Inability to wait to be responded to
- Incompletion of school work
- Difficulty in following directions
- Poor concentration around external stimuli
- Problems listening and staying on task
- Disorganization
- Reckless physical actions
- Being overly talkative

Without the awareness that grief in itself creates inattentiveness and an inability to sit still and concentrate, children can be misdiagnosed with some sort of learning disability. They can then begin the journey of labels and difficulties that make them viewed as unable or unwilling to learn. Rather, educators must maintain the necessary patience and respect needed for the grief process of children.

We, as caring adults, need to be educated in learning the signs of normal and complicated grief. Gaining a respect for and acceptance of the feelings of anxiety or depression that occur with normal grief can be a strong force in differentiating between grief and ADD.

7. Gather a comprehensive past history. The loss inventory in my first book, *Life and Loss: A Guide To Help Grieving Children* (Goldman, 2000) is an educational tool that takes a good look at a child's emotional, intellectual, academic, physical, social, and previous family loss history.

> Margaret's dad was a strong disciplinarian. He often spanked her, leaving marks on her skin, and screamed at her that she was stupid for not understanding her work. He had a history of alcoholism and financial debt. His sudden death may have created a complicated grief situation—the shock of her dad's death contrasted with the relief of not being yelled at or hit. Not crying for over a year was an indicator that something was blocking her from her feelings.

8. Educators need to *maintain as much consistency and continuity as possible* with the grieving child. Usually the death of a parent is the catalyst for a chain reaction of multiple losses. The surviving parent may temporarily not be present due to his or her own grief. Moves, remarriages, and financial changes often occur. The child needs an adult advocate at school to listen and relate when called upon.

9. The normal grieving process does not stop after a day, a week, a month, or a year. Complicated grief can be present for years. Caring adults need to remember that normal grief and

complicated grief symptoms can be present for an entire school year. The grief process is inhibited when kids are told they need to "move on with their life" or "it's been 6 months; you shouldn't be talking about your loved one so much."

Any attempt to acknowledge a parent or sibling who died by using his or her name or sharing a memory is a gift we can give the bereaved child.

The following is about how a school helped a student commemorate the anniversary of her father's death. A 7-year-old, Molly, was crying as she came into the office at school. It was the anniversary of her dad's death. He had been murdered, and she was feeling sad and wanted to talk to the guidance counselor. The counselor was not available, but the secretary, Mrs. King, volunteered to help. Molly explained her sadness. "I miss Daddy. I'll never be able to talk to him again," she sobbed.

Mrs. King remembered an idea that had helped her grandchildren when her son had died. She purchased several balloons, including one that said "I Love You." Molly wrote a note to her dad telling about her feelings and attached it to the balloon. Mrs. King took her outside, and together they sent the balloons off as a symbolic message to Dad. As they looked in the sky before they came in, they were surprised to see a giant rainbow, ending at the school playground. At the end of the day, Molly returned to the office to thank Mrs. King for her help. "I'm okay now. I think my dad got the message," she said, as she skipped down the hall.

10. Schools teachers, administrators, and other professional personnel need to establish and create ways to help students commemorate a death in the school.

WAYS SCHOOLS CAN COMMEMORATE

- Create a memory wall with stories and pictures of shared events.
- Have an assembly about the student.
- Plant a memory garden.
- Initiate a scholarship fund.
- Make a class book of memories and reproduce a copy for the family.
- Establish an ongoing school fundraiser such as a car wash or bake sale with proceeds going towards the family's designated charity.
- Place a memorial page and picture in the school yearbook or school newspaper.
- Send flowers to the grieving family.

WHAT CAN WE DO AS EDUCATORS?

Today's educators face a world where issues of abuse, violence, suicide, homicide, and AIDS must be presented and described to children in an open and clear way by

- Helping children understand each topic
- Creating an awareness that children are not responsible
- Allowing children the space to grieve their losses caused by complicated grief
- Teaching children strategies that empower them and maintain their safety
- Demonstrating nonviolent ways to resolve conflicts, pain, and anger

Children are resilient. Educators need to develop curriculums that include definitions of each type of complicated grief. These curriculums should include prevention, intervention, and postvention strategies and techniques for school systems. Examples of school-based curriculums are listed at the end of this chapter. Resources and pertinent school, community, and nationally-based supports must be made available for children and parents.

Signs of At-Risk Children

Complicated grief situations are all too common among today's youth. These situations can produce at-risk children. The following are signs to look for:

- Sudden and pronounced change in behavior
- Threat of suicide or preoccupation with or creation of artwork or writing indicating the child doesn't want to live
- Evidence of substance abuse—drugs, alcohol
- Sudden change in grades
- Avoidance or abandonment of friends
- Angry or tearful outbursts
- Self-destructive behavior
- Inability to sleep or eat
- Over-concern with own health or health of a loved one
- Creation of a will or giving away important possessions
- Sudden unexplained improvement
- Depression, isolation, or withdrawal

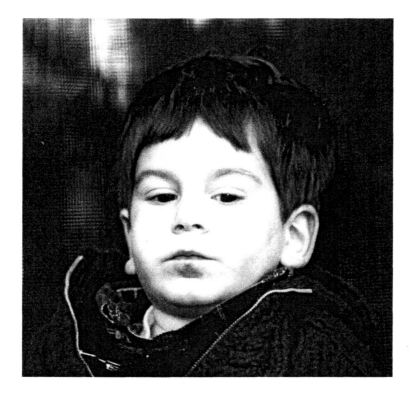

Identifying At-Risk Grieving Children

Teachers can create simple tools to help target children that are grieving and at-risk students. In the article "Searching for Suicidal Precursors in the Elementary School" (Celotta, B., Jacobs, G. & Keys, S., *Am. Mental Health Counselors Ass. Journal*, January, 1987), the authors found the two items at-risk children respond to 100% of the time are:

- "Do you feel hopeless?" and
- "Do you feel sad?"

	At-Risk Tool
Draw or write:	
What makes you the most sad?	What makes you the most angry?
What scares you the most?	What do you wish for the most?

This is a drawing a first grader, Eric, drew after his teacher gave the assignment to draw and write something about a pet. Eric drew the death of his cat and his feelings about how his cat died. This assignment helped identify Eric as a grieving child.

Self-Injurious Behaviors in Children and Teens

Self-injurious behaviors (SIB) in young people are becoming a more common phenomena in our country and our world. Children and teens who can find temporary "relief" from overwhelming emotional pain by self-injurious, self-mutilating, and self-abusive behaviors are youth that are difficult for most adults to understand. One child explained that "cutting herself temporarily eased her emotional distress." Some signs to look for are:

- Cutting, scratching, burning, pulling out hair
- Abusing drugs and alcohol
- Purging food or not eating
- Sexual promiscuity
- Risky behaviors

Dr. Annita Jones describes SIB feelings as having surgery without anesthesia, and having an overwhelming compulsion to do something about it. Dr. Jones defines an SIB reaction as "an individual's urgent need to take action against the pain." ("Self-Injurious Behavior in Children and Adolescents, Part 1: What is SIB?" *Healing Magazine*, Kidspeace, 1998. p. 35). Dr. Jones warns that SIB is often an effort to manage or avoid suicidal ideation "and may not necessarily be suicidal behavior." She suggests asking the child if he or she is thinking about suicide, and stresses the importance of addressing the underlying pain. The following is a poignant example of how a 12-year-old girl bravely and clearly articulated her underlying pain, her statement that something is wrong, and her cry for help.

I killed my monkey,
but it's back on my back.
I thought that it was gone,
untill I relapsed.
As I lay in my bed,
alone in the night.
Nothing is normal,
I'm not alright.
I thought I'd be okay,
but I realize I'm not,
Life is a lesson,
that cannot be taught.
And the bleeding lesson,
and the cuts got deeper.
And the hill I was on,
got a lot steeper.
I tried to cry out,
but I swallowed myself.

I needed it more,
than anything else.
~~started so~~ So I closed the door,
And turned off the lights.
I turned up my music
and pulled out my knife.

~~So~~ I started to cry,
and the pain was immense
But why did I do it?
It makes no sense.
I hate myself for it,
but need ~~anymore~~ for life.
But I can still do it,
without my knife.
My hands and arms
and feet are scarred.
And all that's inside
await to discharge.
~~And still.~~
As I lay in my bed
alone in the night.
Nothing is normal,
I'm not alright.

by Sara

This letter was an essay turned in as an in class assignment. The teacher felt this student could be an at-risk adolescent. She felt compelled to speak to the student, other school personnel, and the child's parents about it.

Identifying At-Risk Gay, Lesbian, and Bisexual Students

Gibson (1989) in the *Report of the Secretary's Task Force on Youth Suicide*, reported that gay and lesbian adolescents were two to three times more likely than peers to attempt suicide.

Gay, lesbian, and bisexual teenagers make up 1,500 of the 5,000 youths that have died by suicide each year. Risk factors to look for are low self-esteem, isolation, guilt, depression, and poor problem-solving skills (Capuzzi, 1994). This is compounded by the specific issues gay young people face. *The National Gay Task Force* (NGTR) surveyed 2,100 lesbians and gay men and found more than 90% reported being victims of verbal and physical assaults (NGTR, 1984). They often internalize a negative image of being bad or wrong or worthless based on societal stereotypes of homosexuality.

Schools need to educate students about homosexuality, allowing positive information and role models. So often gay and lesbian youths feel like "I am the only one." Schools can:

- Create and support Gay and Lesbian clubs to lessen social isolation and allow students to openly share their sexual orientation.
- Develop and implement comprehensive school programs that include a guidance curriculum presented by counselors or teachers about gay and lesbian issues.
- Encourage families with gay and lesbian members to become part of the school community.
- Invite guest speakers. One school asked a gay man to speak about the AIDS quilt.
- Motivate students to become involved with causes that support gay and lesbian issues.
- Implement responsive services that include individual and group counseling, and referrals.
- Provide information on successful gay and lesbian role models.

Suicide

SIGNS OF SUICIDAL INTENT

- Active planning of suicide
- Constant preoccupation with death
- Expression of thoughts of worthlessness and desires to end it all
- Giving away possessions
- Talking about one's own funeral
- Sudden unexplained improvement
- Inability to make changes and feelings that there is no way out

VERBAL SIGNALS

- "Life's not worth living."
- "I'm no good. I don't deserve to live!"
- "I can't see any way out."
- "I wish I was dead."
- "I want to kill myself."
- "What's the use?"

FRIENDS CAN HELP BY

- Listening
- Asking questions
- Staying calm
- Taking threats seriously
- Telling someone
- Offering suggestions and resources
- Talking about suicide
- Getting help

Important Concepts for Suicide Discussion

Most of us think about suicide at some time in our lives. It is very common. People think these thoughts because they are usually in a lot of emotional pain. People do not need to act upon these thoughts.

When a friend says "I can't take it any more, I wish I could die," what do you feel he or she is really asking for? Kids are crying out for help. They probably want help out of a problem or situation, and not necessarily out of life.

Children need to realize that emotional pain has a beginning, a middle, and an end. We can compare bad emotional pain to an awful toothache. The dentist can help reduce the physical pain. We can help children realize that intense emotional pain also can subside with help.

We look for reasons for suicide but can't always find them. We can focus on ways to prevent suicide by learning ways to help ourselves and others in emotional pain.

Suicide has different meanings at each developmental stage. We may need to retell and explain suicide at different ages.

DISCUSSION QUESTIONS AFTER A SUICIDE

- If you could see that person one more time, what would you say to him or her? What would you ask?
- How does this person's death make you feel?
- What did you lose when your friend died?
- What is your best memory/your only regret?
- Have you ever felt you didn't want to live? Do you think that is normal?
- If you would have known the person wanted to die, how could you have helped?

WHAT CAN EDUCATORS DO DURING A SUICIDE THREAT?

1. School staff must disclose any student's threat to harm himself or herself or another student and not keep it a secret.

2. School personnel must report any suicide threat to a designated school crisis team member or school counselor.

3. School personnel should contact the at-risk child. Acknowledge feelings and reinforce decision to share information.

4. The at-risk child must stay in school until all information has been processed. A member of the school faculty can stay with the child to assure his or her safety.

5. School personnel should listen and encourage talking from the at-risk child. Use the words "suicide" and "dead." Ask if the child is thinking about suicide. Ask if he or she has a plan or a method.

6. School personnel must report the suicide threat to the parents or guardians.

7. If the parents or guardians do not respond, protective services can be called. If it appears to be a medical emergency, notify the school nurse. If he or she is not there, call 911.

Violent Death

Violent death can make kids feel:

- Anxiety about being left alone or leaving remaining loved ones
- The need to relive the violent act over and over in their minds
- Tremendous terror of their own death or the death of those around them
- A strong desire not to stand out or be different
- A fear of going to sleep
- Revenge which can manifest in very aggressive behavior

Educators can help by:

1. Telling faculty, students, parents, and the extended community the facts about what happened. Everyone needs to know the truth as a way of dispelling fear that may be all-pervasive at these times. Thorough information is important even if it is violent. It provides a concrete base to work with the uncertainty of what has happened. If a uniform, clear picture is presented, it will help alleviate the hearsay and rumors to which children are exposed.

2. Acknowledging the tremendous fear associated with violent crimes. Adults and children become more fearful for their lives and the lives of loved ones after a violent crime. Anxiety is created about the inability to be protected by anyone in the adult world.

3. Suggesting ways to help reduce this fear and anxiety in the school and community environment to allow everyone to feel more secure, such as

   - Carpooling
   - Neighborhood watches
   - Extra security police
   - A buddy system for walking home or to the car
   - Whistles
   - Walkie-talkies on the playground

   (Suggested by The Dougy Center, Portland, OR)

4. Creating a school-based crisis team for added support for the extra responsibilities of media coverage and criminal prosecution.

Abuse

Important procedures in abuse prevention include stressing certain major points to children.

- It is not the child's fault.
- A child has the right to say no to anything or anyone that makes the child feel uncomfortable or scared.
- Children need to learn ways to tell others in their family or outside of the family what is happening to them.
- Children need practice in role playing potentially dangerous situations. Teach them to yell or use a whistle if necessary.
- Children need an adult advocate and confidant. Help them decide on two or three adults with whom they feel they can talk to. Help the child get these adults' telephone numbers.
- If something is happening to a child or a friend that seems scary or disgusting, the child should tell one of the trusted adults who can help stop it.

Educators can help by:

- Providing programs that give children the courage and tools to tell about abuse. These tools include recognizing of danger signals and enhancing of confidence.
- Creating school-based prevention programs that include parents. These programs can help parents talk to children about abuse and provide understandings of ways to help children prevent the abuse.
- Reporting suspected abuse to State Health and Rehabilitative Services or calling Childhelp USA at 1-800-422-4453.

WHAT CAN EDUCATORS DO ABOUT ABUSE?

1. Role-play with children: "What would you do if . . . ?" "How would you say no if . . . ?"

2. Create positive storytelling. Create a story about abuse and provide a safe and positive outcome.

3. Teach children their name, address, and telephone number. Teach them not to give this information to strangers.

4. Provide a preventive resource library. Include vocabulary books so that children can feel powerful and find positive solutions to abusive situations.

5. Encourage physical activity so that children gain confidence that they can protect themselves.

Resources Specifically for Educators

A Student Dies, a School Mourns by Ralph Klicker (2000) helps prepare educators for a death in the school community. It offers ways to assist the school in creating and implementing a crisis response plan.

Death and the Classroom by Kathleen Cassini and Jacqueline Rogers (1990) is a teacher's guide that provides practical suggestions for helping the bereaved student.

Death: In the School Community by Martha Oates (1993) is a handbook for counselors, teachers, and administrators to help provide the right words and actions to help students cope with death.

Good Grief by Barbara Ward (1993) is a manual that explores feelings, loss, and death for children under 11. It provides insight as to what to do when a child in school is bereaved.

Grief Comes to Class by Majel Gliko-Braden (1992) helps teachers work with bereaved children.

Growing Through Grief by Donna O'Toole (1989) is an excellent K–12 curriculum for helping children work through their loss and grief.

Helping the Grieving Student: A Guide for Teachers by The Dougy Center (1998) is a practical guide for dealing with death in the classroom.

Helping the Grieving Child in the School by Linda Goldman (2000) is an excellent resource for educators to help the grieving children.

Helping Teens Stop Violence by Allan Creighton (1992) is a practical guide for counselors and educators.

Managing Sudden Violent Loss in the Schools by Maureen Underwood and Karen Dunne-Maxim (1993) is a good resource on sudden violent death in school.

Suicide Prevention by Judie Smith (1989) presents a crisis intervention curriculum for teenagers, including attitudes about suicide, suicide information, warning signs, communicating skills, and crisis intervention, and community resources.

Suicide Prevention in the Schools by Antoon Leenaars and Susanne Wenckstern (1991) presents facts on suicide for children and adolescents and prevention, intervention, and postvention that can be used effectively in schools.

The Art of Healing Childhood Grief by Anne Black and Penelope Adams (1993) is a school based expressive arts program for the grieving child.

When Death Impacts your School: A Guide for Administrators by The Dougy Center (2000) is an excellent resource when death impacts a school.

OTHER RESOURCES

The Child Assault Prevention (CAP) Project is a comprehensive prevention program offering children's workshops, parents' workshops, and teacher/staff in-service workshops to help prevent verbal, physical, and sexual assaults on children.

CAP Project National Office
P.O. Box 02084
(614) 291-2540

The Children's Defense Fund: "The mission of the Children's Defense Fund is to leave no child behind and insure a healthy start, a head start, a fair start, and a moral start in life and successful passage to adulthood with the help of caring families and communities." www.childrensdefense.org/aboutus.htm

The Children's Defense Fund
25 E Street NW
Washington, DC 20001
(202) 628-8787

CHAPTER 10

Communities Grieve: Involvement with Children and Trauma

SUDDEN DEATH • EARTHQUAKES • TERRORISM
HURRICANES • WAR • TORNADOS

A child is like a blank piece of paper upon which every passer-by has the opportunity to leave a mark.

Chinese Proverb

A Community Dream

A dream of mine was quite inspiring. I clearly saw a huge amphitheatre where children, parents, educators, and mental health professionals were all gathered together to attend a workshop I was presenting on children and grief. This nocturnal vision allowed all the young people and adults to hear the same material at the same time. All could ask questions and share freely.

I awoke with the goal that this could and *should* be done in any community dealing with families and trauma. A few months later I was offering a public talk and found that my fantasy had become reality. Several children accompanied parents and professionals to this talk on children and grief. Adults and kids listened and shared, asked questions and responded, and the dream had become real. Information was presented with language appropriate for adults and children. Children's drawings, writings, and poetry stimulated dialogue and created new understandings.

The next day one of the moms at the lecture called to tell me of the profound impact the lecture had on her 7-year-old son, Keith, and her husband, Robert. She relayed the following conversation. "On his way home, Keith began talking to his dad. He asked questions about his younger brother Michael's death, questions he had never voiced before. 'How did he die' 'Why wasn't I there when he died?' and 'Where do you think he is now?'" The lecture had partially been about children's questions about death and their right to be answered. Robert felt strongly that had he not been a part of the workshop and received the information of children and grief with his son, he would not have felt comfortable enough to give honest answers.

Communities Grieve: Helping Traumatized Children

The automatic assumption of most adults is that our children are basically happy and carefree. The reality is that the majority of the world's children are grieving children. So many of our boys and girls are born into grief and loss issues that live inside their homes and lay waiting for them outside their doorsteps, on their streets, in their schoolyards, in their classrooms, and around their community. Increasingly, children are traumatized by prevailing social, societal, and natural loss issues in their families, their schools, their nation, and their world.

Children in the twenty-first century live with challenges that were unimaginable for their parents and teachers. Death related tragedies associated with natural disasters, accidents, suicide, homicide, and war and non-death related traumas such as abandonment and lack of protection, dislocation and loss of property, foster care, hopelessness, bullying, terrorism, and abuse and violence have left our children sitting alone in their homes, unfocused and unmotivated in their classrooms, and terrorized in their communities. They have become overwhelmed with their feelings and distracted by their thoughts.

Today's children are impacted directly and, too often, graphically, vicariously, viscerally, visually, and auditorally by the news media, film, music, video, and computer industries that act as surrogate communal parents and extended families to most of our children. Survivorship of trauma, whether first hand or through media input, creates for any child a loss of the world they assumed was filled with safety, protection, and predictability.

Children naturally assume their world will be filled with safety, kindness, and meaning as they attempt to answer the universal questions of who they are and why they are here. All too often these qualities seem to disappear into a nightmarish universe of randomness, isolation, and unpredictability when trauma strikes. This leaves many of today's young people immersed in a new assumption: There is no future. There is no safety. There is no connectedness or meaning to my life. By joining together as a global grief community, caring adults can co-create an assumptive world that again provides a child's birthright to presume love, generosity, and value will be integral parts of their lives.

Many children experience the trauma of natural disasters such as earthquakes, tornados, and hurricanes; sudden death such as car, train, and airplane accidents; and violent deaths and man's inhumanity to man in school shootings, terrorism, and war. These children become shocked, frozen, numbed, and terrified. The layers upon layers of loss and grief so quickly heaped upon their lives can be too overwhelming to consciously process and too great for one person or one resource to be effective.

Together, as a support team, communities can learn to really see children and hear their cry for help. Parents, educators, health professionals, and community leaders can learn the signs of grieving children, recognize their pleas for support and understanding, and create an environment that allows expression, respect, and patience for the grieving child.

Globally, a major percentage of children face the loss of the protection of the adult world, as grief issues infiltrate their inner and outer worlds. These children experience the shock of multiple losses coupled with disorientation and feelings of isolation. They too often become locked into a world of hurt and fear, in frozen states of trauma too painful to access. They shut down. They become numbed. They can't learn, they can't feel, they can't communicate.

Children need to grow their hearts in order to grow their consciousness. If they assume the world of love, support, and meaningfulness no longer exists, they may shut down their humanness and get lost in a new assumption of a terrifying, chaotic, random, unprotected universe, where the life they knew and the people they thought they were dissolve into a scary, unpredictable environment with an uncertain future . . . or no future at all.

The Continuum of Unexpressed Grief Feelings

When traumatic events devastate a community, children and families suffer multiple losses. Sudden death and trauma, destruction of property, relocation, and changed routines leave human beings feeling alone, abandoned, and overwhelmed. Our children and teens carry an enormous reservoir of unexpressed grief feelings after a trauma. All too often these feelings are projected outwardly—consciously or unconsciously—in the forms of bullying, violence, abuse and homicide, or projected inwardly—again, consciously or unconsciously—in the forms of self-hatred and victimization feelings, low self-esteem, depression, suicide ideation, suicide attempts, and death by suicide. The following continuum of unexpressed grief feelings is forever growing with suicide on one extreme and homicide on the other.

Bullying	Helplessness
Abuse	Victimized Feelings
Gangs	Self-Hatred
Violence	Suicide Ideation
Homicide	Suicide

(ARTWORK BY ROB WILLIAMS)

When our communities reach out to traumatized grieving children, we have a shared goal of bringing safety and protection back to families. By allowing children to share, express, and release their feelings in many ways we begin to release the trauma. This goal requires many to come together, for the job is too great for one person.

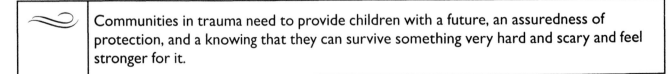

Communities in trauma need to provide children with a future, an assuredness of protection, and a knowing that they can survive something very hard and scary and feel stronger for it.

The Taiwan Earthquake:
A Community Trauma

The devastation and destruction of the Taiwan earthquake on September 21, 1999, has left permanent scars on its land and people. The quake-stricken images leave indelible imprints on the minds and psyches of children and adults. Although many of the visible signs of the earthquake will fade with rebuilding, the invisible trauma of loss of life, property, and security in one minute of sudden shock lives inside the children who experienced this catastrophe.

THE FEAR OF THE EXPERIENCE

1:47 a.m. "The heated dreams were interrupted by violent jolts. The post-war generation had never experienced, and for the first time, they felt fear as the earth shook. Such fear was new to them; some did not know how to deal with the fear so they just stayed in bed, while others ran out panic-stricken, driven out by instinct. Some kept on sleeping as they thought the shakes would soon be over, while others stayed lost in their heated dreams, never to wake up again" (p. 15, *Trauma of the Century* by Oliver, Lin Yun-ko).

Aftershocks forced many victims to sleep outside in the streets in tents rather than returning to their own houses. Many adults and children showed signs of posttraumatic stress with nightmares, flashbacks, shortness of breath, depression, disorientation, anger, and despair.

A MIRACLE CHILD

(PHOTOGRAPH BY KUO REI-CHENG, WITH PERMISSION)

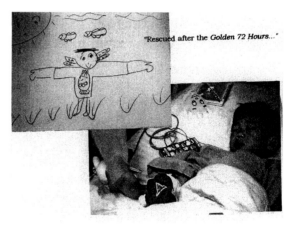

"Rescued after the *Golden 72 Hours...*"

After 87 hours of rescue attempts a small voice was heard under the rubble. After two hours of digging through the rubble, six-year-old Chang Ching-hung was discovered and rescued. He waved to rescuers and seemed alert and not seriously injured. He had survived the unimaginable . . . only to find that his father, mother, and two younger sisters had died. Chang Ching-hung was the sole survivor of his family. He was alone.

This is one of many of stories of the plight of the children. Orphaned by the quake, without home or family, many were placed in foster care and orphanages. With loss upon loss too great to speak of, children and adults began a new journey and a new life with unimaginable sorrow and terror.

CHILDREN'S VOICES

(WITH PERMISSION FROM *TRAUMA OF THE CENTURY* BY OLIVER, LIN YUN-KO)

"My daughter held me tightly, and with a look of panic in her eyes cried, 'I'm scared.' Actually, in my heart of hearts, I felt scared, too" (p. 187).

Four-year-old Wei-Hai pointed to the tangled lines he drew and said. "This is our home, our home has fallen down . . . " (p. 189).

"When morning came, some terrible news reached us. Li cin-han, my classmate, had been crushed to death when his home collapsed. I felt so sorry when I heard the news. I had not known that at 8 that night it was to be good-bye forever between him and me . . . " (by Yieh Ke-ro, a sixth-grader of Chung-ke Elementary School, p. 37).

Six-year-old Ho Zung-chi told his teachers on his return the day after the earthquake, "My brother has been flattened" (p. 45).

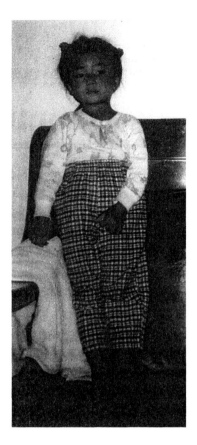

After the earthquake only 65 of 120 children returned to their day care center. This decreased number was not only due to death or injury, but shattered lives that were so chaotic parents did not return kids to the center and sometimes sent them to day care centers some distance away from the rubble.

The high school was destroyed by the earthquake. The elementary school across the road remained intact and untouched. The young elementary school children still go to their school, everyday viewing the destroyed high school that has now become a permanent memorial.

ALLOWING CHILDREN TO GRIEVE: CREATING SAFETY AND PROTECTION

As the children began their journey into the unknown world of grief and loss, the community came together to help bridge their deep feelings of grief with hope for a future in which safety and protection could be a part of their lives. The following picture is the track field of the high school that was demolished by the earthquake.

Although the high school was made into a permanent national memorial for remembering, the government built a new temporary school to house the grieving and shaken children of its country.

Children from other schools volunteered time and talent to draw murals on the temporary classrooms.

Students, teachers, and concerned citizens wrote letters of grief and made offers of help to the children and faculty of the destroyed high school. They were posted for all to read.

Parents and children worked together to plant gardens outside each temporary classroom. This served as a memorial for their grief and a tribute to rebuilding their lives.

Plant a Garden...

Write letters...

Students were brave enough to ask for help. Temporary schools did not have air conditioning. One student wrote a letter to the newspaper requesting help from citizens to purchase air conditioners for the school. Her requests were granted, and every classroom was given an air conditioner. The community gave power to this student for being her own advocate during this crisis.

Children practiced earthquake drills. This practice began to rebuild confidence that they again had some control over their lives. They were told what to do when an earthquake happens . . .

Practice Earthquake Drills...

- Take shelter.
- Turn off gas immediately and open the door.
- Hide behind a column or in the bathroom.
- Leave during the pause after the tremor hits.

(adapted from p. 68, *Trauma of the Century*)

HELP WITH GRIEF

Taiwanese educators, teachers, and counselors began exploring resources to work with children and grief. They purchased many books from other countries and translated them into Chinese to have the words to use with children and their multiple levels of trauma and grief. Extensive resource libraries were created. They also wrote and illustrated beautiful books for young children that spoke specifically of the earthquake in Taiwan—the devastation, terror, sadness, rebuilding, and bringing safety into the new life so many children were experiencing.

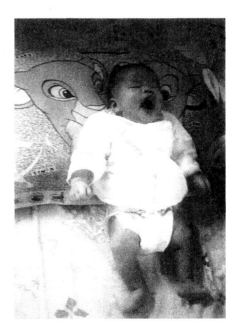

Memory work became a part of the work of caring adults with children. Memory books were created with counselors. Memory tables were used in the classrooms as shown in the following picture. Children were invited to create symbolic ways to work through their grief including using a big box to symbolize a casket with notes and pictures placed inside.

CONFERENCE ON GRIEVING CHILDREN

The educational community in Taiwan created a two-day training on "Children and Grief" as an important element for healing in their country. I was invited to share my work with 200 educators and mental health professionals in order to increase awareness and understanding of the grieving child. This was a direct byproduct of the earthquake with the underlying premise that children would be working through this experience for several years into the future.

> It is our greatest delight to announce that "The 2nd National Conference of Death Education" will be held in Changhua, Taiwan from October 20–21, 2000. A series of plenary and symposium sessions, workshops, and free paper presentations are expected under the Conference theme "Death Education for Children" (National Changhua University of Education).

College students, professors, and teachers earnestly shared, listened, and created new ways to work with the Taiwanese children who had been impacted by this catastrophe. Their goal was to create a life issues curriculum for their students that could experientially be a part of their school day and allow them to work through their thoughts and feelings. The day was sensitive, work-oriented, and dedicated to empowering grieving children and helping them survive a disaster.

A School Bus Accident:
Sudden Death and Trauma

Thirty-six elementary school children riding in their school bus on a rainy day experienced a devastating accident when their bus driver, Mr. King, was killed by an oncoming car. The children witnessed this fatal accident. All of the boys and girls survived. Some were okay. Some were injured. Some were shaken up emotionally and physically. When parents heard of the accident, they were traumatized. Approaching the bus with their kids inside, they could see blood and broken glass everywhere. The Montgomery County School System in Maryland partnered with the Montgomery County Crisis Center to meet the needs of their students and their community.

Since blood and glass were all over the bus, many children had strong and recurring visual imageries. The children were asked to reenact the accident on another bus by police immediately after the trauma. Some kids where able to do this, but for others it created further trauma. Many children felt that Mr. King deliberately saved their lives and sacrificed his own by swerving directly in front of the oncoming vehicle. He was the only one directly impacted. The next day counselors made sure that children that had questions and concerns would have an opportunity to address them. Grief counselors were present both in the school where the children in the bus attended, and in other schools where siblings of the youngsters on the bus attended class.

A discussion of grief, shock, and difficult visualizations was included in the debriefing of students. Training for providing a model of debriefing following crisis situations had been received by staff before the accident, with clear procedures for the responsibility of tasks. The primary role of the crisis team was to provide an opportunity for the children to discuss their thoughts and reactions regarding the accident and the death of their bus driver. Children and parents were notified when and where this meeting would be held. Two team members facilitated the debriefing and other team members and school personnel were on hand to observe and attend to any identifiable at-risk students. Using the Grief and Loss Inventory (*Life and Loss,* Goldman, 2000, pp. 125–129) can be valuable in recording behaviors, recommendations, and follow-up procedures by the school personnel for at-risk children. The crisis responders looked for the following reactions to trauma:

CHILDREN'S REACTIONS TO TRAUMA

- Confusion or disorientation
- Loss of appetite or overeating
- Flashbacks or preoccupation with accident
- Regressive behaviors such as clinging, bed wetting, thumb sucking
- Nightmares or an inability to sleep
- Overwhelming fears and anxieties

- Extreme actions of aggressiveness or withdrawal
- Inability to concentrate and low school performance

One facilitator guided the children through the model of debriefing, which includes a discussion of thoughts and reactions to the event, while simultaneously normalizing reactions and providing education and support to the children. This facilitator introduced himself and the other team members, discussed confidentiality, and reaffirmed support. The other facilitator scripted on a flipchart the remarks of the children. Children saw that a lot of their feelings were common reactions to trauma, and discussions helped to normalize their nightmarish experience. If anyone, overwhelmed with emotion, needed to leave the room, a team member would go with the child and support him or her individually and then encourage them to return to the group if possible.

A Post Traumatic Stress Quiz similar to the modified one below could be helpful for any child experiencing a traumatic event. When children complete this type of quiz, they may answer "yes" to many items. Realizing that many people feel that way after a trauma, children may feel less alone.

A Traumatic Stress Quiz

Answer yes or no:

_____I think about the accident more than I want to.
_____I dream about the accident.
_____I feel numb some of the time.
_____I have difficulty talking about my thoughts and feelings.
_____I get depressed easily, sometimes to the point of not wanting to live.
_____I find it hard to get close to friends, teachers, and family members.
_____I can't seem to make my friendships work.
_____I avoid things that remind me of the accident.
_____I hardly ever feel happy.
_____I feel guilty that I survived when others didn't.
_____I feel scared, nervous, and jumpy.
_____I look around a lot to see if something can hurt me.
_____I can't sleep.
_____I can't eat.
_____I have trouble remembering things.
_____I can't pay attention.
_____I get angry and frustrated a lot.
_____I worry I'll get too angry and hurt someone or something.
_____I can't figure out what's bothering me.
_____I feel hopeless and sad.

"If you feel that several of the items above apply to you, you are not alone. Thousands of people feel the same as you following a catastrophic or traumatic event. These reactions are a natural aftermath of a traumatic experience and are called Post-Traumatic Stress Disorder (PTSD)" (Through a collaborative partnership: Montgomery County Public Schools and the Montgomery County Crisis Center).

This quiz can be used to normalize scary thoughts and feelings for children. It also can be used as a tool to identifying at-risk children.

At the end of the session the scribing facilitator reviewed all the notes and emphasized the themes, creating teachable moments that added information about grief and trauma. Children chose what to do with the notes taken. Sometimes they decided to throw them away, other times a friend or relative wanted to keep them and take them home.

During the week of the accident the school system had the same bus and bus driver that picked the kids up from the crash continue for the entire week. This helped to reinstill safety and reduce fear. Parents were allowed to ride the bus with their children that week to help them feel protected, also.

Several dozen bus drivers were debriefed by the school system and the crisis center. They were very shaken. Many had never experienced a co-worker being killed. Some were fearful and even reluctant to drive their buses again.

AFTER THE CRISIS

Several safety patrol members were honored by the school board and county council for their invaluable help and level headedness in utilizing existing procedures with the involved school bus children. The patrol members were presented with plaques of acknowledgement.

The health education department of the school system notified educators in schools directly affected by the crash. They offered resources and curriculum lessons useful to teachers and counselors in helping students understand their grief process.

The entire community came together for the memorial and funeral of the bus driver. Children, parents, educators, friends, and family joined with bus drivers to honor his memory.

The bus driver's widow stayed in contact with the school community. She often came to school and gave kids candy. She addressed a PTA meeting about her family's grief. Trees were planted in memory of her husband and there was a memorial service. Food was collected and meals were sent to the family. The PTA started a fund that was contributed to from people throughout the country for the injured children and the bus driver's family.

Nine months after the incident, the counselor told of many kids who seemed to be going on with their lives, while others were still fearful. "One boy still won't ride the bus," she explained. "Some children have gone past it, some are still dealing with the crash. I am working with them now." The realization that traumatized grieving children may live with fears and sadness for quite some time is evident. The ongoing involvement of this school system manifests in its advocacy for their students.

A Student's Sudden Death:
A Community Outreach

In September of 1998, Ben Robinette, a freshman at South Mecklenburg High School in Charlotte, NC, was killed when struck by a car. He was running across a busy four-lane road in front of the school during cross-county practice. The accident was witnessed by several of his cross-country teammates, many of whom waited with Ben for the ambulance to arrive. This tragedy impacted a school, a family, and a community.

Kinder-Mourn, a nonprofit counseling agency for grieving parents and children in Charlotte, North Carolina, became involved in the aftermath of this tragedy in several different capacities. As a part of Kinder-Mourn's community outreach program, its counselors provided crisis interventions, educational trainings, and support groups for Ben's parents, friends, teammates, the parents of his friends and teammates, siblings, and the school community.

CRISIS SUPPORT GROUP FOR TEENS AND PARENTS OF CROSS-COUNTRY TEAM

Lura McMurray, a Kinder-Mourn counselor, and Carey Clarke, a counselor and basketball coach at South Mecklenburg High School, facilitated a crisis support group for members of the cross-country team who had witnessed the fatal accident. Some of the kids had witnessed Ben's death, others had run back to the school and called for help. One boy gave CPR to Ben. Many experienced difficult visual imageries of Ben's accident.

Within the confines of the group, the students were provided a safe place to talk about the accident, the aftermath, and their feelings, reactions, and fears. They were assured that they were experiencing normal grief reactions. They were offered options: listening to the 911 tape, seeing the EMT medical report, asking questions of the Emergency Room physician who pronounced Ben dead, and talking to Ben's mother.

The ER doctor who worked with Ben at the scene of the accident was invited to come to the group and share medical information and answer questions. Many of the kids wanted to know: "Did he die immediately?" "Did he suffer?" "Was there anything more anyone could have done?" The doctor explained Ben's injuries and answered questions. It seemed very important for the teens to be told by the doctor that nothing could have been done to save Ben's life, and that he probably died on impact. One boy said that while he was grateful the doctor helped so many teammates, his visualizations only became more intrusive for him.

Many of the teenagers showed signs of trauma. Two boys reported having feelings of panic and anxiety when crossing a street. Others spoke of recurring nightmares and waking visualizations. Many blamed themselves, God, the driver of the car, and even Ben. Some expressed anger at the media. Many of these young people felt invaded because the media had interviewed them at the scene of the accident while they were crying, sweating, and traumatized. Witnessing themselves on TV added trauma to trauma. One member shared concern for the grief of the driver of the car that hit Ben. Sharing their experiences, difficulties, pain, and questions helped these teenagers sense that what they were feeling was normal.

A month after the fatal accident, Ben's teammates ran in the Conference Tournament. They wanted to win the title for Ben, and by a very narrow margin they did. One of Ben's teammates clearly spoke these words into a megaphone after the team received their award. "We'd like to dedicate this race to Ben. He was a former runner of ours. He was here with us today" (*The Charlotte Observer,* 10/22/98).

Also impacted by Ben's death were the parents of the cross-country team who were left with grieving and traumatized teens. Kinder-Mourn created a support group to help these parents process their own grief and understand the special needs of grieving teenagers.

PARENT AND SIBLING SUPPORT

Ben's parents were involved in an weekly grieving parents support group, which takes place at the Kinder-Mourn home. Along with others grieving for their children, Ben's parents have been understood, accepted, and supported. In addition, Kinder-Mourn provided an educational workshop for the faculty and staff at the school where Mrs. Robinette taught. The staff wanted to talk about what happened and make sure their responses to Ben's mom were helpful and not harmful.

"How I Feel Inside"
Helping the Hurt Participant

Finally, Kinder-Mourn's "Helping the Hurt" outreach program provided a support group in the middle school that Ben's twin sisters attended. This nine week support group was for any student who had experienced the death of a family member or friend.

SUPPORT FOR FRIENDS

For three months after Ben's death, Kelli Haughey, another Kinder-Mourn counselor, facilitated a support group for 11 of Ben's childhood friends. When these young people began to feel comfortable, they shared (sometimes laughing and sometimes crying) memories about their beloved friend: "Ben's house was their favorite house to hang out at and play basketball."

With Kelli's help, Ben's friends decided to create and decorate stepping stones to give to the Robinettes for their back yard. Ben's parents provided snacks for kids while they talked and shared memories. Then they laid the stones together. Each teen who created a stone had the opportunity to explain his or her creation to Ben's mom and dad. Ben's parents were deeply touched. Ben's mom said one of her favorite stones was Ben on the 13th hole of a golf course throwing his golf clubs in the air.

BALLOON LETTER CEREMONY

Kelli asked group members to write a letter to Ben. She asked them to write about their life, about what they would have told Ben had they known he would die, or what they missed about him. At the next group meeting, Kelli gave each teen a helium filled balloon. Some students chose to read their letter to the group; some wanted to keep their letters private. Each young person attached their letter to a balloon and went outside.

The teenagers were given the choice of releasing the balloons individually or as a group. They chose to come together as a group and silently let the balloons go and watched them drift away. One of the boys had written an extra page to Ben, making his letter heavier on this windy day. When his balloon didn't fly as well as the others he joked that Ben was "playing with his balloon."

The kids in this group made copies of their notes and gave them as a gift to Ben's parents. Ben's mom says they are so special to her. She loves reading what Ben's friends wrote, like, "I love you Ben. I could never tell you that before."

A YEAR LATER

On the one-year anniversary of Ben's death the members of the cross-county team support group met together with Lura and Coach Clarke to talk about plans for remembering Ben. At this date, they decided to create a memorial at the site of the accident near the school.

Early in the morning on the anniversary of Ben's death, the group met at school and painted Ben's name on a memory rock in front of the building. The used the school colors—black, red, and white. Together with their group facilitators, they walked to where the accident occurred holding a red or black balloon. They tied their balloons close to where Ben had been killed. Some wrote notes and attached them to the balloons. They held a service of remembrance and love. Coach Clarke honored the courage of the survivors. Luri read several meaningful quotes including the Serenity Prayer: "Grant me the serenity to accept the things I cannot change, the courage to change the things I can, and the wisdom to know the difference."

Lura invited the group to speak to Ben. Some kids spoke. Some remained quiet. Everyone then walked back to school in silence, some with their arms around each other.

The following week Lura returned for a final session with the cross-country team support group. They enjoyed refreshments and assessed their experience together. The following are their descriptions of what had been helpful about the group experience.

The group experience was a safe place . . .

- to express feelings of guilt, anger, inadequacy, sadness, and anxiety
- to share what they had seen and heard
- to discuss their fears (crossing the street, facing other losses in their lives)
- to describe their nightmares and their waking intrusive images and thoughts
- to verbalize their frustrations with their parents' inability to offer the right support
- to begin to understand their guilt for blaming God, Ben, themselves, and their cross-country coach
- of encouragement to identify how they were different after the trauma of Ben's death; what they had gained and what they had lost
- of acceptance of their questions: Am I safe? Why couldn't the medical personnel save Ben? Where does God stand with me? Where do I stand with God?
- of support in deciding what to do about their "unfinished business": How is the driver of the car that hit Ben? How can I cope with conversations I want to have with Ben? How and when do I talk with Ben's parents?

The students agreed they would remember Ben whenever they ran. Lura shared what the group had meant to her, saying she would always admire their courage, openness, and strength. Now it was time for another goodbye.

TWO AND A HALF YEARS LATER

Mrs. Robinette continues to love talking with Ben's friends more than anything else. She feels the work of Kinder-Mourn in creating support groups for children and teens helped these young people be open to their feelings and subsequently to share them with her. "The teenagers helped me the most. The closest I can get to Ben is through them. All the hugs I could have given to Ben, I give to them." Two and one half years later, Ben's family received a letter from one of Ben's closest friends. She shared memories of Ben and still spoke of him as "a ray of sunshine." Ben's mom agreed.

The Oklahoma Bombing:
A Children's Grief Center Emerges

On April 19, 1995, 168 men, women, and children perished in the deadliest terrorist attack on United States soil. The explosion wreaked havoc on people and property and the visualizations of its destruction are forever daunting. Out of the rubble came the need for a place for traumatized children to grieve the myriad of losses incurred by the bombing. The Kids' Place for Grieving Children emerged, and six years later it is still a safe and supportive environment for the community to continue their grieving and memorializing of this unspeakable trauma.

Age-specific support groups for children and concurrent groups for their parents or guardians meet twice monthly. Activities include working with clay, drama, music, games, art and crafts, puppets, and recreation. Sharing times in groups emphasize discussions and peer interactions where freedom to express feelings or special memories is given. The following are examples of children's feelings expressed in these groups. The first drawing is by Andrew, age 10, a boy from a blended family of six children who had experienced multiple deaths in his family.

The second drawing is from Lafaye, age 11. She expressed her gratitude for all of the kindness and understanding she found in her group.

"To all my friends at the Kids' Place. We had fun times and sad times and hard times, But no matter what. You all cared about me. That is real Friends."

Love,

Lafaye

This drawing is on a card produced by In-Sight Books. In-Sight Books have pledged a donation for Kids' Place for every card purchased. To purchase these cards, call 800-658-9262.

When Kids' Place began their work with children after the bombing, many parents asked "How long will you stay open?" assuming they were in a temporary crisis. The community learned that just because the bombing was over, the need for dealing with the trauma for the children did not go away. Six years later this community children's grief program has grown and expanded, serving as a place for all grieving children in the area. However, it still meets the needs and ongoing grief and mourning of the survivors of the Oklahoma bombing. Child survivors still join in support groups. One of the adult survivors now acts as a grief facilitator to help others. Traumatic grief is ongoing—and the need to memorialize and commemorate is enduring.

Terrorism and Children: Attack on America

Trauma can shake the very foundation of our faith in safety and protection for children and adults. Americans witnessed this all too closely in the tragic terrorist events in New York and Washington, DC imprinted on our psyche and the world. On September 11, 2001 our nation deeply felt the loss of our assumptive world as a friendly place. Caring adults searched for words and meanings to give children comfort within the devastation, so accessible and graphically viewable. The following are suggestions for adults working with children and trauma using these terrorist attacks as a model.

(ARTWORK BY JON GOLDMAN, AGE 14)

1. *Define terrorism for children.* "Terrorism is an act or acts ov violence, abuse, murder, or devastation against unsuspecting people and countries by a person or group of people that beleive their cause is more important than human life or property. Their feeling of "being right" can be greater than their own life. Terrorist can be big or small, black, white, or any color, American or foreign. Their goal is to create fear, disruption, and vulnerability."

2. *Help children re-establish a sense of order.* Keep to the daily routine to re-create a sense of security. Create family activities that help reassure children. Read stories and have meals together. Place an American flag outside the house.

3. *Remember adults are role models.* Model for your children responsible ways to react to a disaster of this magnitude. Guide children to create ways to help. Emphasis contributing food, clothing, toys, and money. Include children in planning helpful activities and joining in carrying them out. Families may want to say a prayer or light a candle for victims and their families, and for world leaders to create peace.

4. *Monitor media coverage.* Consider how much children should be watching the unfolding media coverage, which can be very frightening. Restrict the time of disaster related viewing, allowing adults to help children process what they see and hear. Use this as a "teachable moment" to discuss violence and terrorism. Be aware that young children may perceive the video replay of the terrorist attach on TV as a new attack each time.

5. *Accept children's reactions.* They may range from playing to regression and clinginess, crying or fighting, and asking questions and needing to say their story repeatedly. Children's magical thinking can cause feelings of guilt and responsibility for the trauma. Reassure them it was not their fault and their reactions are normal. Symptoms of heightened anxiety and recurring fears (Stomach aches, nightmares, difficulty concentrating) may also occur. Encourage children to talk and share feelings using toys, puppets, clay, draw-

ing, and writing. Secondary reactions may emerge such as fear of riding on a plane, visiting Washington and New York, or riding the school bus.

6. *Affirm to children they have survived a traumatic experience.* The community, nation and world has come together to help. Support had come from people throughout the world through media reports, e-mails, and letters.

Activities for Traumatized Children

DRAWING AND WRITING

Eight-year-old Mary felt unprotected after sudden losses in her family. She was left alone a lot. Her drawing and writings share the very sudden loss of protection that engulfed her after her trauma.

I fell scared when I don't have protection.

WRITING STORIES

Megan was seven when her younger brother, Andrew, died suddenly. Megan and her three siblings were overwhelmed with grief. Two years later she decided to write a story about her brothers and sister, and included Andrew.

Once upon a time there was a family. A mom a dad and five kids.

'Everybody thought they had four kids only because one died his name was Andrew he was a twin his brother's name is Mark.

Children after a trauma usually have a need to tell their story over and over again in a variety of ways. Allowing them to draw or write about it is one way to begin to help them release it.

Telling My Loss Story

By_____

Draw or write:

I first heard about the death when . . . .

This is what happened . . . .

The very worst part was . . . .

What still sticks inside of me are . . .

Now I see myself as . . .

LOSS AND GAIN COLLAGE

Children can grow stronger by realizing they are survivors, and not just victims, of a traumatic experience. By recording their feelings of loss and gain after some time has passed, they may see that not all of their losses were bad and not all of their gains were good. They may also come to feel stronger and more prepared if another crisis occurs, and realize how far they have come from the initial trauma.

LIFE AND LOSS LINE

After a crisis children may feel scared of the future and be afraid to look forward. By creating a lifeline of past, present, and future life events, we can help traumatized kids again feel life is ongoing and has continuity.

SAMPLE LIFE LINE

Write or draw things you have done or would like to do by the time you die. Put in the age you think you will do your future important things (like driving, prom, school graduation, college, job, marriage, children, grandchildren, etc.) and the date you think you will die.

X_____X
Birth   Death

SAMPLE LOSS LINE

Write or draw all of the losses you have had on your loss line and how old you were when each one happened. Mark each one with an X. Write or draw all of the losses you think you will have until you die. Mark them on your timeline with Os.

X_____X
Birth   Death

A SCARY AND PEACEFUL PLACE

Children need to have a way to share their scary feelings and it often helps to write or draw them. However, it is hard to leave them in this fearful state. We can anchor a positive visualization by asking them to draw or write about a positive and safe space they can go to. This peaceful place can include people, animals, nature, and any other props. In the following examples Jonathan, age 11, chose to draw his nightmare as a very terrifying place. He then created a peaceful visualization with nature and animals that he could revisit when he felt afraid.

My Scariest Place by _____

Draw a place that is so scary for you it seems like a nightmare.

Tell me about it. _____

"This is a big, dark castle in my dream. My dad is there. There are scary monsters. I ran away. I woke up crying, and sweating and scared."

My Peaceful Place by_____

Draw a picture of a place where you feel safe, happy and peaceful. Put people or pets in if you want to.

Tell me about it. _____

(ARTWORK BY JON GOLDMAN, AGE 11)

"This is my peaceful place. There are animals I love and lots of trees, sky, and water that I like to look at."
Jonathan, age 11

A Scary and Peaceful Feeling

Myles is a seven-year-old who can see the New York skyline from his home. Many of his friends and family knew people who were hurt or killed by the terrorist bombings in New York. This picture was his way of showing the very scary airplane bombing of the World Trade Centers, expressing his sad feelings, and combining it with his hopes for peace.

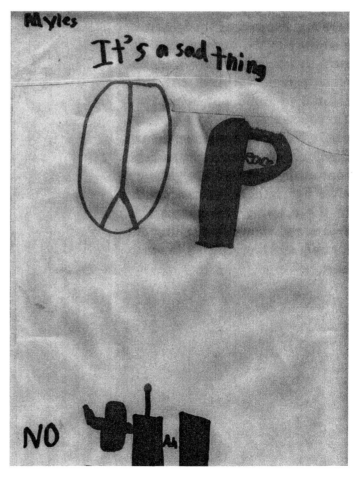

A PEACEFUL BOX

A peaceful box can contain comforting objects that create peaceful feelings and thoughts for children. They can choose items that bring positive feelings of quiet and protection. When fearful or angry thoughts and feelings emerge, this box can bring calm and comfort to the children.

After an earthquake, 6-year-old Chang made a peaceful box with his mom. Two of his friends had died and his school was demolished. Inside the box he put pictures of his friends that died, his dog, his favorite little stuffed toy (an angel bear), and a toy figure. He said he felt safe and protected when he opened it.

DREAM WORK

So often children feel "survivor guilt" after a sudden trauma. Sadness and depressing thoughts and feelings surface, accompanied by guilt that they have survived, another person has died, and they did not or could not help them. The following dream by a traumatized child shows a common theme. Eight-year-old Mary explained she continually revisited a nightmare after her father's sudden death. In the drawing, she shares this dream and shows Dad calling out for help and her inability to reach him.

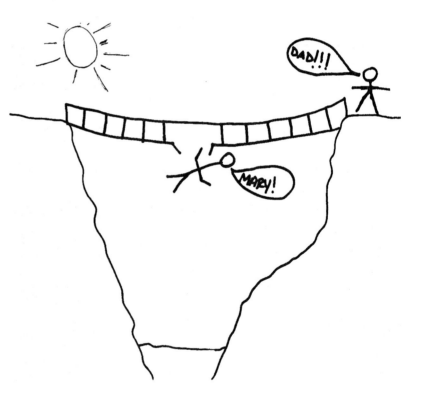

Five-year-old Sam witnessed a trauma. It was hard for him to talk about it. He began having nightmares. He tried to explain his trauma through his dream and by drawing and writing about it.

This is me. I'm hiding under a coat because I don't want to see something.

Here's step Like in a cabin. Hiding under coat because you didn't want to see what happened. You saw a man with a gun and he said, "Hey Brig." I heard a big "POW." This is too scarey to tell you. I saw a window that was smashed with blood on it. A white hand sticking in from outside. The dream was ended.

SAM

Brandon was on the school bus when his bus driver got killed. His counselor set up a toy bus and figures and he began to re-create what happened. "This is where I was sitting, this is what I heard, and this is how I got thrown out of my seat."

To recreate a hospital or medical setting, kids could retell their story through doctor and nurse figures, or medical props.

Stuffed animals and puppets can be a safe way for children to speak of the trauma. Statements like "I wonder what Bart (a puppet) would say if he had witnessed the school bus accident the way that you did?" or "Let's let Bart tell his story about the crash" can help promote discussion of feelings in a noninvasive way, and give options to children as well as model feelings.

Brandon loved music. His counselor told him to listen for music that gives him energy, relaxes him, makes him feel happy, and makes him feel sad. He brought in several CDs to share with her, and they listened together and shared feelings. Then she took out some musical instruments (a drum, sticks, a tambourine, and a harmonica). "Can I hear what your grief sounds like?" Brandon began to bang on the drums as hard as he could, then he switched to a soft sad sound on the harmonica. He shook the tambourine very loudly and explained "This is how it shook when the school bus crashed."

WHAT CAN WE DO FOR THE CHILDREN?

- Talk with and listen to them so that they can go forward.
- Stress to them that they are survivors of an incredibly hard experience.
- Find out what still "sticks" inside them after the trauma.
- Support them in creating the mental ability and emotional stamina to work with what life has given them.
- Ask them: "How are you now more wise, more strong, more prepared if another trauma occurs?"
- Ask them: "How would you take care of yourself if another emergency situation occurred?"

Other Resources

FOR ADULTS

Doka, K. (1996). *Living with Grief after Sudden Loss*. Bristol, PA: Taylor & Francis. This book discusses topics such as treatment implications for traumatic death, social psychological aspects of disaster death, and grief counseling for traumatic loss.

Jones, R. (1995). *Where Was God at 9:02 A. M.?* Nashville, TN: Thomas Nelson, Inc. This book presents miraculous stories of faith and love from the Oklahoma City bombing.

Pudney, W. & Whitehouse, E. *A Volcano in My Tummy*. BC, Canada: New Society Publishers. This is a resource book for adults to help children handle anger.

Stevenson, Robert. *What Will we Do?* (1994) Amityville, NY: Baywood Publishing Co. A book that prepares a school community to cope with crisis.

Taichung County Government. (2000). *Trauma of the Century*. Taichung County, Taiwan. The story of the Taiwan earthquake told through pictures and words.

Zinner, E., &Williams, M. B. (1999). *When a Community Weeps*. Bristol, PA: Taylor & Francis. This book presents case studies in group survivorship in trauma and loss.

FOR CHILDREN

Holmes, M. *A Terrible Thing Happened*. (2000). Washington, DC: Magination Press. Sherman is anxious and angry after he experiences something terrible. He learns to talk about it.

Jordan, M. K. *The Weather Kids*. (1993). Omaha, NE: Centering Corporation. This is a book for children who have experienced devastation caused by weather and earthquakes.

Mills, J. *Little Tree*. (1993). Washington, DC: Magination Press. This is a story for children with serious medical problems.

Salloum, A. *Reactions*. (1998). Omaha, NE: Centering Corporation. This workbook helps young people who are experiencing trauma and grief.

Sheppard, C. *Brave Bart*. (1998). Grosse Pointe Woods, MI: TLC. This is a story for traumatized and grieving children.

Just for Kids: Terrorism and Trauma. www.erols.com/ kids.info. An interactive website where children can read about terrorism and trauma, get ideas about things they can do, and share feelings with other kids.

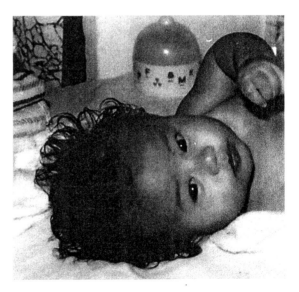

P A R T   I V

Resources

CHAPTER 11

National Resources
Bridge the Gap

NETWORKING • RESEARCH • HOTLINES
INFORMATION • ORGANIZATIONS

Children's Grief and Loss Resources

Mental health agencies

Child advocacy programs

Hospice programs

Hospital bereavement programs

Funeral service professionals

Pediatricians

Clergy

School counselors

School psychologists

Pupil personnel workers

Nurses

Agencies or programs dealing with specific losses

Hotlines

Hotlines

CHILD ABUSE HOTLINE

1-800-4ACHILD
1-800-2ACHILD (TDD for Hearing Impaired)

FRIENDS FOR SURVIVAL, INC.

Suicide Loss Helpline
1-800-646-7322

GRIEF RECOVERY HOTLINE

1-800-445-4808

MARYLAND YOUTH CRISIS HOTLINE

1-800-422-0009

NATIONAL AIDS HOTLINE

1-800-342-AIDS

NATIONAL CENTER FOR MISSING AND EXPLOITED CHILDREN

1-800-843-5678

NATIONAL COALITION AGAINST DOMESTIC VIOLENCE

1-800-333-7233

PARENT'S ANONYMOUS

1-800-421-0352

Crisis Intervention for Children and Teenagers

BOY'S TOWN CRISIS HOTLINE

1-800-448-3000

COVENANT HOUSE HOTLINE

1-800-999-9999

KID SAVE

1-800-543-7283

NATIONAL AIDS HOTLINE

English: 1-800-342-AIDS
Spanish: 1-800-344-SIDA
Hearing impaired: TDD-1-800-243-7899

NATIONAL DOMESTIC VIOLENCE HOTLINE

1-800-799-7233

NATIONAL RUNAWAY AND SUICIDE HOTLINE

1-800-621-4000

Resources for Suicide

AMERICAN ASSOCIATION OF SUICIDOLOGY

4201 Connecticut Avenue, Suite 310
Washington, DC 20008
202-237-2280

AMERICAN FOUNDATION FOR SUICIDE PREVENTION

120 Wall Street, 22nd Floor
New York, NY 10005
888-333-AFSP

SAMARITANS (SUICIDE)

500 Commonwealth Avenue
Boston, MA 02215
617-247-0220 (24 hours)
617-247-8050 (teens)

SPEAK (SUICIDE PREVENTION, EDUCATION, AWARENESS FOR KIDS)

423 Dumbarton Road
Baltimore, MD 21212
410-377-4004

SUICIDE AWARENESS/VOICE OF EDUCATION SA/VE

P.O. Box 24507
Minneapolis, MN 55424-0507
612-946-7998

SUICIDE EDUCATION AND INFORMATION CENTER

723 Fourteenth Street NW #102
Calgary, Alberta
Canada T2N 2A4
403-283-3031

SUICIDE INFORMATION AND EDUCATION CENTRE (SIEC)

201,16165 - 10th Avenue S.W.
Calgary, Alberta
Canada T3C OJ7
403-245-3900

SUICIDE PREVENTION CENTER, INC.

P.O. Box 1393
Dayton, OH 45401-1393
513-297-9096

SUICIDE PREVENTION AND CRISIS SERVICE OF TOMPKINS COUNTY, INC.

P.O. Box 312
Ithaca, NY 14851
607-272-1505

YOUTH RESOURCE SERVICES

P.O. Box 2100
Manhasset, NY 11030

YOUTH SUICIDE NATIONAL CENTER

1825 Eye Street NW #400
Washington, DC 20006
202-429-2016

Resources for Violence and Homicide

AMERICAN BAR ASSOCIATION VICTIM/ WITNESS PROGRAM

c/o Susan Hillenbrand
1800 M Street NW
Washington, DC 20036
202-331-2260

AMERICAN TRAUMA SOCIETY

1400 Mercantile Lane, Suite 188
Landover, MD 20785
1-800-556-7890

CHILDREN'S DEFENSE FUND

25 E. Street NW
Washington, DC 20001-0500
202-628-8787

CONCERNS OF POLICE SURVIVORS (COPS)

9423 A Marlborouth Pike
Upper Marlborouth, MD 20772
301-599-0445

CRIME VICTIMS LITIGATION PROJECT

c/o National Victim Center
4530 Ocean Front
Virginia Beach, VA 23451
804-422-2692

MOTHER'S AGAINST DRUNK DRIVING

669 Airport Freeway, Suite 310
Hurst, TX 76053
800-633-6233

NATIONAL ORGANIZATION FOR VICTIM ASSISTANCE (NOVA)

717 D Street NW
Washington, DC 20004
202-393-NOVA

NATIONAL SHERIFF'S ASSOCIATION VICTIM PROGRAM

1450 Duke Street
Alexandria, VA 22314
703-836-7837 or 1-800-424-7827

NATIONAL VICTIM CENTER

307 W 7th Street, Suite 1001
Fort Worth, TX 76102
817-877-3355

NATIONAL VICTIM'S RESOURCE CENTER

P.O. Box 6000 AIQ
Rockville, MD 20850
1-800-627-NVRC

OFFICE FOR VICTIMS OF CRIME

633 Indiana Avenue NW
Washington, DC 20531
202-724-5947

PARENTS OF MURDERED CHILDREN

1739 Bella Vista
Cincinnati, OH 45237
513-721-LOVE

TRAGEDY ASSISTANCE PROGRAM FOR SURVIVORS, INC. (TAPS)

2001 S Street, NW
Ste. 300
Washington, DC 20009
800-959-TAPS

VICTIMS OF CRIME RESOURCE CENTER

McGeorge School Of Law
University of the Pacific
3200 Fifth Ave.
Sacramento, CA 95817
1-800-VIC-TIMS

Resources for AIDS

AIDS ATLANTA

1132 W. Peachtree Street, NW, Suite 102
Atlanta, GA 30309
800-342-2437

AIDS ACTION COMMITTEE

131 Clarendon Street
Boston, MA 02116
617-536-7733 (Hotline)
617-437-6200

AIDS RESOURCE CENTER

National PTA
700 North Rush Street
Chicago, IL 60611
415-476-6430

AMERICA FOR A SOUND AIDS POLICY (ASAP)

P.O. Box 17433
Washington, DC 20041
703-471-7350

AMERICAN ACADEMY OF CHILD AND ADOLESCENT PSYCHIATRY

Commitee on HIV Issues
3615 Wisconsin Avenue, NW
Washington, DC 20016
202-966-7300

AMERICAN ACADEMY OF PEDIATRICS

Committee on School Health
141 NW Point Boulevard
P.O. Box 297
Elk Grove Village, IL 60009-0927
800-433-9016

AMERICAN FOUNDATION FOR AIDS RESEARCH

1515 Broadway, Suite 3601
New York, NY 10032
212-719-0033

AMERICAN RED CROSS

AIDS Education Office
1709 New York Avenue, NW
Washington, DC 20006
202-434-4074

ASSOCIATION FOR THE CARE OF CHILDREN'S HEALTH

3615 Wisconsin Avenue, NW
Washington, DC 20016
301-654-6549

HEALTH EDUCATION RESOURCE ORGANIZATION (HERO)

101 West Read Street, Suite 812
Baltimore, MD 21203
301-685-1180

MARCH OF DIMES

Birth Defect Foundation
1275 Mamaroneck Avenue
White Plains, NY 10805
914-428-7100

NATIONAL AIDS INFORMATION CLEARINGHOUSE

P.O. Box 6003
Rockville, MD 20850
800-458-5231

NATIONAL ASSOCIATION FOR CHILDREN WITH AIDS

P.O. Box 15485
Durham, NC 27704
919-477-5288

PAN AMERICAN HEALTH ORGANIZATION/WHO

AIDS Program
525 23rd Street, NW
Washington, DC 20037
202-861-4346

PEDIATRIC AIDS NETWORK

Children's Hospital of Los Angeles
4650 Sunset Boulevard, Box 55
Los Angeles, CA 90027
213-669-5616

SAN FRANCISCO AIDS FOUNDATION

P.O. Box 6182
San Francisco, CA 94101
415-861-3397

SEX INFORMATION AND EDUCATION COUNCIL OF THE US (SIECUS)

130 West 42nd Street, Suite 2500
New York, NY 10036
212-819-9770

THE AIDS HEALTH PROJECT

Box 0884
San Francisco, CA 94143
415-476-6430

Resources for Abuse

AMERICAN ASSOCIATION FOR PROTECTING CHILDREN

c/o American Humane Society
63 Inverness Drive East
Englewood, CO 80112-5117
303-792-9900

CHILD ASSAULT PREVENTION (CAP)

National Office
P.O. Box 02084
Columbus, OH 43202
614-291-2540

CHILDHELP IOS FORESTERS

P.O. Box 630
Hollywood, CA 90028
Hotline 1-800-4ACHILD
TDD for hearing impaired: 1-800-2ACHILD

INTERNATIONAL SOCIETY OF PREVENTION OF CHILD ABUSE AND NEGLECT

1205 Oneida Street
Denver, CO 80220
303-321-3963

NATIONAL RESOURCE CENTER ON CHILD SEXUAL ABUSE

107 Lincoln Street
Huntsville, AL 35801
205-534-6868

PARENTS' ANONYMOUS

National Headquarters
22330 Hawthorne Boulevard, Suite 208
Torrance, CA 90505
1-800-421-1325

National Resources and Organizations

ADVOCATES FOR CHILDREN AND YOUTH, INC.

300 Cathedral Street, Suite 500
Baltimore, MD 21201
410-547-9200

ASSOCIATION FOR THE CARE OF CHILDREN'S HEALTH

7910 Woodmont Avenue
Bethesda, MD 20814
301-654-6549

ASSOCIATION FOR DEATH EDUCATION AND COUNSELING (ADEC)

639 Prospect Avenue
Hartford, CT 06105
203-232-4285

BATON ROUGE CRISIS INTERVENTION CENTER

4837 Revere Avenue
Baton Rouge, LA 70808
504-924-1431

THE CANDLELIGHTERS

1312 18th Street, NW
Washington, DC 20036
202-659-5136

CENTER FOR LOSS AND GRIEF THERAPY

7801 Connecticut Avenue
Chevy Chase, MD 20895
301-657-1151

CENTER FOR LOSS AND LIFE TRANSITIONS

3735 Broken Arrow Road
Fort Collins, CO 80526
303-226-6050

CHILDREN OF SEPARATION AND DIVORCE (COSD)

2000 Century Plaza #121
Columbia, MD 21044
410-740-9553

CHILDREN'S DEFENSE FUND

25 E. Street, NW
Washington, DC 20001-0500
202-628-8787

CHILDREN'S HOSPICE INTERNATIONAL

11011 King Street, Suite 131
Alexandria, VA 22314
800-2-4-CHILD

COMPASSIONATE FRIENDS, INC. NATIONAL HEADQUARTERS

P.O. Box 1347
Oak Brook, IL 60521
312-323-5010

COVE: A SUPPORT PROGRAM FOR GRIEVING CHILDREN AND FAMILIES

New England Center For Loss and Transition
P.O. Box 292
Guilford, CT 06437
203-456-1734

D'ESOPO RESOURCE CENTER

280 Main Street
Wethersfield, CT 06109
860-563-5677

DOUGY CENTER

P.O. Box 97286
Portland, OR
503-775-5683

FERNSIDE, A CENTER FOR GRIEVING CHILDREN

2303 Indian Mound Avenue
Cincinnati, OH 45212
513-841-1012

GRIEFWORK CENTER, INC.

P.O. Box 5014
Kendall Park, NJ 08824
732-422-0400

GOOD GRIEF PROGRAM

Judge Baker Guidance Center
295 Longwood Avenue
Boston, MA 02115
617-232-8390

HOSPICE EDUCATION INSTITUTE

P.O. Box 713
Essex, CT 06426-0713
800-331-1620: Computerized "Hospice Link"

INNER SOURCE

980 Awald Drive
Annapolis, MD 21403
410-269-6298

INSTITUTE FOR THE ADVANCEMENT OF SERVICE

P.O. Box 19222
Alexandria, VA 22320
703-706-5333

KID'S PLACE

P.O. Box 258
Edmund, OK 73083
405-844-5437

KINDER-MOURN

1320 Harding Place
Charlotte, NC 28204
704-376-2580

MEN AGAINST BREAST CANCER

2379 Lewis Avenue
Rockville, MD 20851-2335
301-770-5333

NATIONAL HOSPICE ORGANIZATION

1901 N. Fort Myer Drive
Arlington, VA 22209
703-243-5900

NATIONAL SUDDEN INFANT DEATH SYNDROME FOUNDATION

105000 Little Patuxent Parkway, Suite 420
Columbia, MD 21044
800-221-SIDS

NEW ENGLAND CENTER FOR LOSS AND TRANSITION

P.O. Box 292
Guilford, CT 06437-0292
800-887-5677

PARENT ENCOURAGEMENT CENTER (PEP)

10100 Connecticut Avenue
Kensington, MD 20895
301-929-8824

PARENTS WITHOUT PARTNERS

7910 Woodmont Avenue, Suite 1000
Bethesda, MD 20814
800-638-8078

PARTNERS CAMPAIGN FOR HANDICAPPED CHILDREN AND YOUTH CLOSER LOOK

P.O. Box 1492
Washington, DC 20013
202-822-7900

PREGNANCY AND INFANT LOSS CENTER

1421 E Wayzata Boulevard, Suite 30
Wayzata, MN 55391
612-473-9372

RESOLVE THRU SHARING

Lacrosse Lutheran Hospital/Gunderson Clinic, LTD
1910 South Avenue
Lacrosse, WI 54601
608-791-4747

RONALD MCDONALD HOUSE

419 East 86th Street
New York, NY 10028
212-876-1590

SHARE PERINATAL NETWORK

St. Elizabeth's Hospital
211 S. Third Street
Belleville, IL 622
314-947-6164

SIBLING SUPPORT CENTER

4800 Sand Point Way, NE
P.O. Box C5371
Seattle, WA 98105

TEEN AGE GRIEF, INC.

P.O. Box 220034
Newhall, CA 91322-0034
661-253-1932

WILLIAM WENDT CENTER

730 Eleventh Street, NW, 3rd Floor
Washington, DC 20001
202-624-0010

WORLD PASTORAL CENTER

1504 N. Campbell Street
Valparaiso, IN 46385
219-531-2230

Materials to Explore and Annotated Bibliography: There is Hope

BOOKS • BOOK RESOURCES • VIDEOS • MANUALS
CD-ROMS • GUIDES • CURRICULUMS • WEBSITES

Adult Resources that Help: An Annotated Bibliography

BOOKS FOR ADULTS

Bolton, I. (1983). *My Son . . . My Son . . .* Atlanta, GA: Bolton Press. Iris Bolton's personal story of her son's suicide is deeply moving and revealing.

Bothum, L. (1988). *When Friends Ask about Adoption.* Chevy Chase, MD: Swan Publications. A useful question-and-answer guide on adoption for caring adults and nonadoptive parents.

Bradshaw, J. (1988). *The Family: A Revolutionary Way of Self-Discovery.* Deerfield Beach, FL: Health Communications, Inc. An introspective view of family systems and inner child work.

Brett, D. (1986). *Annie Stories.* New York, NY: Workman Publishing. A series of stories that can be read to children under 10 who are dealing with childhood issues, such as death and divorce. The author provides advice for caring adults on how to use these stories.

Capacchione, L. (1989). *The Creative Journal for Children.* Boston, MA: Shambhala. This is a creative journal that provides ways for caring adults to help children express their thoughts and feelings.

Cassini, K., & Rogers, J. (1990). *Death and the Classroom.* Cincinnati, OH: Griefwork of Cincinnati. A text that confronts death in the classroom.

Celotta, B. (1991). *Generic Crisis Intervention Procedures*. Gaithersburg, MD: Beverly Celotta Publisher. A guide for youth suicide crisis intervention in school settings.

Coles, R. (1991). *The Spiritual Life Of Children*. Boston, MA: Houghton Mifflin Co. A book sharing thoughts, drawings, and dreams that reflect the inner world of children.

Douglas, G. (1995). *Dead Opposite*. New York, NY: Henry Holt and Co. A compelling account of the murder of a well loved Yale student and the 16-year-old gang member accused of the murder.

DuPrau, J. (1981). *Adoption*. New York, NY: Julian Mesner. A series of stories for young adults about facts and feelings related to adoption. It includes a list of helpful agencies.

Fitzgerald, H. (1992). *The Grieving Child*. New York, NY: Simon and Schuster. A wonderful guide for parents to help children work with their grief.

Fitzgerald, H. (1994). *The Mourning Handbook*. New York, NY: Simon and Schuster. This is a comprehensive and compassionate resource to help families cope with death and dying. It explores complicated grief, murder, and suicide.

Fox, S. (1988). *Good Grief: Helping Groups of Children When a Friend Dies*. Boston, MA: New England Association for the Education of Young Children. An excellent source of information for adults working with children whose friends have died.

Frankl, V. (1984). *Man's Search for Meaning*. New York, NY: Simon and Schuster. A powerful account of the author's imprisonment in Nazi Germany and the love that helped him survive his losses.

Fried, S., & Fried, P. (1996). *Bullies and Victims*. New York, NY: M. Evans & Co., Inc. A book for parents to help their children deal with bullies.

Furth, G. (1988). *The Secret World of Drawings*. Boston, MA: Sigo Press. A comprehensive look at children's artwork and ways of understanding it.

Galinsky, E., & David, J. (1988). *The Preschool Years*. New York, NY: Ballantine Books. This book contains a wealth of knowledge for parents and educators of children ages 2–5.

Gardner, S. (1990). *Teenage Suicide*. Englewood Cliffs, NJ: Julian Mesner Pub. This book examines some of the reasons and causes of teenage suicide and offers some solutions.

Gibran, K. (1969). *The Prophet*. New York, NY: Alfred A. Knopf. A beautiful book of poetry expressing timeless feelings of life and death, pleasure and pain, and joy and sorrow.

Gil, E. (1991). *The Healing Power of Play*. New York, NY: Guilford. This book gives a history of play therapy and specific considerations for working with abused and neglected children.

Ginsberg, H., & Opper, S. (1976). *Piaget's Theory of Intellectual Development.* Englewood Cliffs, NJ: Prentice-Hall. A thorough look at Piaget's theory of development.

Gliko-Braden, M. (1992). *Grief Comes to Class.* Omaha, NE: Centering Corporation. This book is meant to help teachers and parents assist bereaved children.

Golden, T. (1994). *Swallowed by a Snake.* Gaithersburg, MD: Golden Healing. Tom Golden has written a valuable resource on men and grief. They define grief for men, describe gender differences of grieving, and offer ways men can work with their grief.

Goldman, L. (2000). *Helping the Grieving Child in the School.* Bloomington, IN: Phi Delta Kappa Pub. A fastback for educators to help the grieving child in the schools.

Goldman, L. (2000). *Life and Loss: A Guide to Help Grieving Children.* Philadelphia, PA: Taylor & Francis. A book that clearly and simply explains children's loss and grief issues and ways that caring adults can help.

Goldstein, A. (1999). *Low-Level Aggression.* Champagne, IL: Research Press. A study of low-level aggresion in kids as the first step towards violence.

Goldstein, A., Glick, B., & Gibbs. J. (1998). Champagne, IL: Research Press. A comprehensive intervention for aggressive youth.

Grollman, E. (1967). *Explaining Death to Children.* Boston, MA: Beacon Press. A book geared to adults who want to ease a child's first confrontation with the death of a loved one.

Hazler, R. (1996). *Breaking the Cycle of Violence.* Bristol, PA: Taylor & Francis. This book offers good interventions for bullying and victimization.

Heavilin, M. (1986). *Roses in December.* San Bernardino, CA: Here's Life Publishers. The author expresses a deep understanding of the grieving process, having experienced the death of three children.

Hendriks, J., Black, D., & Kaplan, T. (1993). *When Father Kills Mother.* New York, NY: Routledge. The authors combine their knowledge of bereavement and posttraumatic stress disorder to help children who have witnessed extreme violence.

Huntley, T. (1991). *Helping Children Grieve When Someone They Love Dies,* Minneapolis, MN: Augsburg Fortress. An easy to read resource for caring adults that honestly addresses children's grief.

Ilse, S. (1982). *Empty Arms.* Maple Plain, MN: Wintergreen Press. This is a practical book for anyone who has experienced infant death or miscarriage. It offers suggestions and support for decision making at both the time of loss and in the future.

Jenkins, B. (1999). *What to Do When the Police Leave.* Richmond, VA: WPJ Press. This book is a guide to the first days of traumatic loss after a homicide.

Johnson, S. (1987). *After a Child Dies: Counseling Bereaved.* New York, NY: Springer Publishing, Inc. A comprehensive text that offers information on counseling bereaved families when a child dies.

Kagan, H. (1998). *Gili's Book.* Columbia University, NY: Teacher's College Press. An excellent book telling of a mother's grief after the sudden death of her daughter, Gili.

Kubler-Ross, E. (1975). *On Death and Dying.* Englewood, NJ: Prentice-Hall. A pioneering book on the subject of death and dying, using real life situations to create true understanding.

Kubler-Ross, E. (1985). *On Children and Dying.* New York, NY: Macmillan. Elisabeth Kubler-Ross offers the families of dead and dying children honest information, helpful ideas, and strength to cope.

Kushner, H. (1981). *When Bad Things Happen to Good People.* New York, NY: Avon Books. Rabbi Kushner shares his thoughts and feelings of why we suffer. The book was written following his son's illness and subsequent death.

Leenaars, A., & Wenckstern, S. (1990). *Suicide Prevention in Schools.* New York, NY: Hemisphere Publishing Corporation. The authors attempt to outline the state of the art of suicide prevention in schools.

Leon, I. (1990). *When a Baby Dies.* New Haven, CT: Yale University Press. The first book to therapeutically explore the loss of a baby during pregnancy or as a newborn. It addresses the subject of surviving siblings.

Levine, S. (1987). *Healing into Life and Death.* New York, NY: Anchor Press. Stephen Levine explores ways to open our hearts to healing.

Linn, E. (1990). *150 Facts about Grieving Children.* Incline Village, NV: The Publisher's Mark. A series of 150 facts discussing important information and understandings about the grieving child.

Livingston, G. (1995). *Only Spring: On Mourning the Death of my Son.* New York: HarperCollins. An inspiring story of a father's love for his 6-year-old son, Lucas, and his deeply moving journey through his child's illness and death.

Lord, J. (1993). *No Time for Goodbyes.* Ventura, CA: Pathfinder Publishing. This book provides important suggestions for survivors grieving a loved one who has been killed.

MacLean, G. (1990). *Suicide in Children and Adolescents.* Lewiston, NY: Hogrefe & Huber Publishers. A practical and hands-on guide to work with children and young people at risk of killing themselves.

McEvoy, M., & McEvoy, A. (1994). *Preventing Youth Suicide.* Holmes Beach, FL: Learning Publications, Inc. This is a powerful handbook for educators and human service professionals to help prevent youth suicide.

Middelton-Moz, J. (1989). *Children of Trauma.* Deerfield Beach, FL: Health Communications, Inc. This book helps the reader discover his or her discarded self by coming face-to-face with emotional fears that may be the result of traumatic childhoods.

Middleton-Moz, J., & Swinell, L. (1986). *After the Tears*. Deerfield Beach, FL: Health Communications, Inc. This book helps adults come to terms with childhood trauma involving alcoholism.

Miller, A. (1984). *For your Own Good*. New York, NY: Farrar, Straus, and Giroux. Alice Miller deeply explores the repercussions of adults taking over a child's will.

Mills, G., Reisler R., Robinson, A., & Vermilye, G. (1976). *Discussing Death*. Palm Springs, CA: ETC Publication. A guide for death education giving practical suggestions and resources for many age levels.

Moustakas, C. (1992). *Psychotherapy with Children*. Greeley, CO: Carron Publishers. A classic text in understanding the therapeutic environment. This book creates guidelines and practical techniques to use when working with psychotherapy and children.

Oaklander, V. (1969). *Windows to our Children: Gestalt Therapy for Children*. New York, NY: Center For Gestalt Development. A gestalt therapy approach to children's loss and grief work with stories and practical suggestions for play therapy.

Parkes, C. M. (1996). *Bereavement* (3rd ed.). New York, NY: Routledge. Studies of grief in adult life.

Peck, S. (1978). *The Road Less Traveled*. New York, NY: Simon and Schuster, Inc. Scott Peck explores traditional values and spiritual growth through a new psychology of love.

Quackenbush, J. and Graveline, D. (1985). *When Your Pet Dies*. New York, NY: Pocket Books. A book for pet owners to help understand feelings when a pet dies.

Rando, T. (1988). *How to go on Living when Someone you Love Dies*. New York, NY: Lexington Books. A helpful and informative book addressing grief and how to work with it.

Rando, T. (1993). *Treatment of Complicated Grief*. Research Press. This is a thorough and informative book on issues relating to complicated mourning.

Redmond, L. (1990). *Surviving When Someone you Love was Murdered*. Clearwater, FL: Psychological Consultation and Educational Services, Inc. This is a professional's guide to group therapy for families and friends of murder victims.

Roberts, J., & Johnson, J. (1994). *Thank You for Coming to Say Goodbye*. Omaha, NE: Centering Corporation. For parents, funeral directors, and other caring professionals to help suggest ways to involve children in funeral services.

Rosenthal, H. (1998) *Favorite Counseling and Therapy Techniques*. Bristol, PA: Taylor & Francis. Fifty-one therapists share their most creative strategies.

Rosenthal, H. (2001). *Favorite Counseling and Therapy Homework Assignments*. Bristol, PA: Taylor & Francis. Leading therapists share their therapeutic homework assignments.

Ross, D. (1996). *Bullying and Teasing*. Alexandria, VA: ACA Publishers. A book on childhood bullying and teasing and what educators and parents can do.

Rubel, B. (1999). *But I Didn't Say Goodbye*. Kendall Park, NJ: Griefwork Center. This is a book for parents and professionals to help child suicide survivors.

Sandefer, K. (1990). *Mom, I'm All Right*. Garretson, SD: Sanders Printing Company. This is a book for parents and caring professionals addressing teen suicide. It's a mother's own story about her child's suicide and gives advice and helpful warnings.

Sanders, C. (1992). *How to Survive the Loss of a Child*. Rocklin, CA: Prima Publishing Company. This book helps explain the phases of grief for the bereaved parent and offers help in understanding the process of healing through grief.

Shamos, T. & Patros, P. (1990). *I Want To Kill Myself*. Lexington, MA: Lexington Books. This book talks frankly about children who are seriously depressed, the signs to watch for, and ways to help.

Siegel, B. (1986). *Love, Medicine and Miracles*. New York, NY: Harper and Row Publishers. This book emphasizes recognizing how our mind influences our body and how to use that knowledge for healing.

Silverman, P. (2000). *Never Too Young to Know*. New York, NY: Oxford University Press. A book combining important research and historical data to broaden the understandings involved with grieving children.

Smilansky, S. (1987). *On Death (Helping Children Understand and Cope)*. New York, NY: Peter Lang. The author bases her studies on children and their grief process in Tel Aviv.

Stillion, J., & McDowell, E. (1996). *Suicide Across the Lifespan–Premature Exits* (2nd ed.). Washington, DC: Taylor & Francis. This book is designed for graduate and undergraduate college students to help them examine developmental principles applying to suicide.

The Dougy Center. (1999). *What About the Kids? Understanding their Needs in Funeral Planning and Services*. Portland, OR: The Dougy Center. A practical guide for including children in funerals and services.

The Dougy Center. (1999). *Helping Teens Cope with Death*. Portland, OR: The Dougy Center. A guide to help caring adults understand and work with teens.

The Dougy Center (1999). *35 Ways to Help a Grieving Child*. Portland, OR: The Dougy Center. A practical guide book that speaks about children's grief and ways to help.

Trout, S. (1990). *To See Differently*. Washington DC: Three Roses Press. This is an excellent book to help readers heal their minds after experiencing many life issues. A chapter on working with feelings about death is included.

Webb, N. (1993). *Helping Bereaved Children*. New York, NY: The Guilford Press. This text contains theory, illustrative cases, and practical examples that professionals can use when working with bereaved children.

Wolfelt, A. (1983). *Helping Children Cope with Grief*. Muncie, IN: Accelerated Development, Inc. An infor-

mative resource for caring adults working with bereaved children. Includes ideas for leading discussions.

Wolfelt, A. (1992). *Sarah's Journey.* Fort Collins, CO: Center for Loss and Life Transition. Eight-year-old Sarah's father suddenly dies. Dr. Wolfelt presents three years of Sarah's grief experience and provides counseling perspectives and guidelines for caring adults.

Worden, J. W. (1991). *Grief Counseling and Grief Therapy.* New York, NY: Springer Publishers. A comprehensive handbook for grief counseling.

VIDEOS FOR ADULTS

Braza, K. (1994). *To Touch a Grieving Heart.* Salt Lake City, UT: Panacom Video Publishing. This film has sensitive and practical insights into helping families with grief.

Dougy Center. (1992). *Dougy's Place: A 20-20 Video.* Portland, OR: The Dougy Center. A candid look at the kids participating in The Dougy Center's program.

Ebeling, C., & Ebeling, D. (1991). *When Grief Comes to School.* (1991). Bloomington, IN: Blooming Educational Enterprises. A film and manual showing families and school personnel discussing grief issues.

Kussman, L. (1992). *What Do I Tell My Children?* Wellesley, MA: Aquarian Productions. A film narrated by Joanne Woodward showing experts, adults, and children exploring their thoughts and feelings regarding death.

Research Press. (1989). *A Family in Grief: The Ameche Story.* Champagne, IL: A real family story of bereavement, with guide included.

Wolfelt, A. (1991). *A Child's View of Grief.* Fort Collins, CO: Center For Loss and Life Transition. A 20-minute video with real children and parents sharing stories and emotions.

VIDEOS FOR CHILDREN

O'Toole, D. *(1994). Aarvy Aardvark Finds Hope.* Burnsville, NC: Compassion Books. The incredible journey of Aarvy Aardvark and the grief he experiences is presented through puppets and music for young children to relate to and learn from.

Rogers, F. (1993). *Mr. Rogers Talks About Living and Dying.* Pittsburgh, PA: Family Communications, Inc. This is a warm and comforting video that presents answers to questions about living and dying.

CURRICULUMS AND MANUALS

Beane, A. (1999). *Bully Free Classroom.* Minneapolis, MN: Free Spirit Publishing. This is a book that contains many strategies for teachers.

Beckman, R. (2000). *Children who Grieve.* Holmes Beach, FL: Learning Publications. A resource manual for conducting support groups for grieving children.

Britney, J. (1996). *No-Bullying Curriculum.* Minneapolis, MN: Johnson Institute. This is a manual for preventing bully–victim violence in schools.

Carlsson-Paige, N., & Levin, D. (1998). *Before Push Comes to Shove.* St. Paul, MN: Redleaf Press. A conflict resolution curriculum for teachers to guide young children to nonviolent behavior.

Celotta, B. (1991). *Generic Crisis Intervention Procedures.* Gaithersburg, MD: Celotta. A practical manual for youth suicide crisis intervention in the schools.

Davis, N. (1990). *Once Upon a Time.* Oxon Hill, MD: Psychological Associates of Oxon Hill. One of the best manuals I've seen, which provides therapeutic stories for children with a guide for each story. Covers a wide range of topics including all abuses and death.

Garon, R., DeLeonardis, G., & Mandell, B. (1993). *Guidelines for Child Focused Decision Making.* Columbia, MD: The Children of Separation and Divorce, Inc. An exceptional manual for judges, attorneys, mediators, and mental health professionals concerning children and divorce.

Garrity, C. E., Jens, K., Porter, W., Sager, N. E., & Short-Camilli, C. (2000). *Bully-Proofing your School* (2nd ed.). Longmont, CO: Sopris West. This is a comprehensive book for school interventions against bullying.

Kirsh, A., Cobb, S., & Curley, S. (1991). *Plan of Action for Helping Schools Deal with Death and Dying*. Center Line, MI: The Kids in Crisis Program. An excellent protocol for schools working with kids in crisis when there is death or dying.

Klicker, R. (2000). *A Student Dies, a School Mourns*. Buffalo, NY: Thanos Institute. This manual guides the school community in reducing the effects of personal loss and suffering when death occurs.

Lagorio, J. (1991). *Life Cycle Education Manual*. Solana Beach, CA: Empowerment in Action. A teacher's guide to help with loss issues including specific lesson plans and guided book activities.

O'Toole, D. (1989). *Growing through Grief*. Burnsville, NC: Compassion Books. A K–12 curriculum to help children through loss.

Smith, C. (1993). *The peaceful classroom*. Beltsville, MD: Gryphon House Publishers. Provides activities to teach preschoolers compassion and cooperation.

Smith, J. (1989). *Suicide Prevention*. Homes Beach, FL: Learning Publications, Inc. A crisis intervention curriculum that provides a school-based program for teenagers and on suicide prevention.

Star (1998). *No-Bullying Curriculum*. Chattanooga, TN: Star Publishers. This curriculum gives classroom teachers tools to deal with bullying.

Star (1998). *No Putdowns Character Building Violence Prevention Curriculum*. Chattanooga, TN: Star Publishers. A school-based curriculum for violence prevention.

Whitehouse, E., & Pudney, W. (1996). *A Volcano in My Tummy*. Gabriola Island, Canada: New Society Publishers. A curriculum for children in conflict that provides anger management plans.

GUIDES FOR GRIEF SUPPORT GROUPS FOR CHILDREN AND TEENS

Burrell, R., Coe, B., & Hamm, G. (1994). *Fernside: A Center for Grieving Children*. Cincinnati, OH: Fernside Publishers. A guidebook for grief support groups for facilitators.

Cunningham, L. (1990). *Teen Age Grief (TAG)*. Panarama City, CA. An excellent training manual for initiating grief support groups for teens.

Haasl, B., & Marnocha, J. (2000). *Bereavement Support Group Program for Children* (2nd ed.). Philadelphia, PA: Taylor & Francis Publishers. An excellent children's workbook and leader's manual for children's grief support groups.

Harris, E. S., & Harris, L. (1999). *Death of the Forest Queen.* Wilmore, KY: Words on the Wind Publishing, Inc. A grief dramatics script for groups, camps, and counseling.

Perschy, M. (1997). *Helping Teens Work Through Grief.* Bristol, PA: Taylor & Francis. This guide contains ways to create a grief support group for teens and provides activities to use.

BOOK SERVICES

Centering Corporation, Omaha, NE. A comprehensive grief resource center created by Marv and Joy Johnson offering publications, workshops, and membership programs on all aspects of loss and grief. 402-553-1200.

Childs work Childs play, King of Prussia, PA. This services provides a catalogue that addresses the mental health needs of children, parents, and counselors. 1-800-962-1886.

Compassion Book Service, Burnesville, NC. A wealth of resources and training tools that include books, videos, and cassettes dealing with loss, death, dying, and bereavement. 704-675-9687.

Mar*co Products, Inc., Warminster, PA. A resource made for and by educators that provides materials for professionals working with elementary, middle school, and high school age children. 1-800-448-2197.

Mental Health Resources, Saugerties, NY. A complete grief resource for children and families. 914-247-0116.

Waterfront Books Publishing, Burlington, VT. A service offering books that support children and the adults in their lives.

Western Psychological Services (WPS), Los Angeles, CA. An excellent service for therapists and counselors providing therapeutic tools. 800-251-8336

Wintergreen Press, Maple Plain, MN. A resource for materials relating to grief associated with miscarriage, stillborn, and infant death.

TAPES FOR CHILDREN AND TEENAGERS

Cunningham, L. (1993). *Teen Grief.* Newhall, CA: Teen Age Grief. Teenagers give personal interviews about their grief and loss experiences. For teens.

Hoffman, J. (1985). *Children's Meditation Tape.* Shawnee Mission, KS: Rythmic Mission. A child's tape of relaxation games and guided imagery. Ages 2–11.

WEBSITES FOR ADULTS ABOUT GRIEVING CHILDREN

Association for Death Education and Counseling (ADEC)	www.adec.org
Center for Loss and Grief Therapy	www.erols.com/lgold
Children of Separation and Divorce Center (COSD)	http://aspen.newc.com/cosd
Children's Defense Fund	www.childrensdefense.org
Compassionate Friends	www.compassionatefriends.org
Crisis, Grief, and Healing	www.webhealing.com
Death Education Resource	www.death.ed.com
D'Esopo Pratt Resource Center	www.safeplacetogrieve.com
Dougy Center for Grieving Children	www.dougy.org
Funeral Directory	www.the funeraldirectory.com
Kids' Place	www.kidsplace.org
Kinder-Mourn	www.kindermourn.com
Parents of Murdered Children	www.pomc.com
WINGS	www.wingsgrief.org

WEBSITES FOR GRIEVING CHILDREN

Barklay and Eve	www.BarklayandEve.com
Julie's Place	www.juliesplace.com
Kids Only: Terrorism and Trauma	www.erols.com/lgold/kidsinfo
KIDSAID-AIDS	www.thekidsaid.org
The Waterbug Story	www.hospicecares.org
Teenage Grief (TAG)	www.smartlink.net/~tag
Teens Helping Teens	www.bigteens.com/links/survivors.html
Where You Are Not Alone	www.bullying.org

CD-ROMS

A Look at Children's Grief presented by Linda Goldman. (2001). Association for Death Education and Counseling. A distance learning training CD on children and grief. CEU's (Continuing Education Units) available. 860-586-7703. E-mail: info@adec.org.

Team Up to Save Lives: What Every School Should Know About Suicide. (1996). Institute for Juvenile Resources. A CD for schools on suicide. 800-627-7646.

Children's Resources that Help: An Annotated Bibliography

BOOKS FOR CHILDREN ABOUT DEATH

Brown, L., & Brown M. (1996). *When Dinosaurs Die.* New York, NY: Little, Brown & Co. This is a wonderful and practical guide for children in helping them understand and deal with real concerns and feelings about death. Ages 5–11.

Brown, M. W. (1979). *The Dead Bird.* New York, NY: Dell Publishing. A story of four children who found a dead bird, bury it, and hold a funeral service. Ages 4–8.

Campbell, J. A. (1992). *The Secret Places.* Omaha, NE: Centering Corporation. This story of Ryan and his journey through grief is for children and adults to gain an in-depth look at childhood grief. Ages 6–12.

Dodge, N. (1984). *Thumpy's Story: The Story of Grief and Loss, Shared by Thumpy the Bunny.* Springfield, IL: Prairie Lark Press. The story of the death of Thumpy's sister, who was not strong enough to keep living. Ages 5–12.

Ferguson, D. (1992). *A Bunch of Balloons.* Omaha, NE: Centering Corporation. A resource to help grieving children understand loss and remember what they have left after someone dies. Ages 5–8.

Oehler, J. (1978). *The Frog Family's Baby Dies.* Durham, NC: Duke University Medical Center. A coloring story book for very young children discussing sibling loss. Ages 3–6.

O'Toole, D. (1988). *Aarvy Aardvark Finds Hope.* (Adult manual available) Burnsville: NC: Compassion Books. The story of animals that present the pain, sadness, and eventual hope after death. Ages 5–8.

Scravani, M. *Love, Mark.* Syracuse, NY: Hope For Bereaved. Letters written by grieving children to help them express feelings. Ages 7–12.

Stein, S. (1974). *About Dying.* New York, NY: Walker and Company. Simple text and photographs to help young children understand death. It includes a discussion about children's feelings for adults. Ages 3–6.

Varley, S. (1984). *Badger's Parting Gifts.* New York, NY: Morrow and Company. Badger was a special friend to all the animals. After his death, each friend recalls a special memory of Badger. All ages.

White, E. B. (1952). *Charlotte's Web.* New York, NY: Harper and Row. Through the eyes of the farm animals, life and death are sweetly portrayed. Ages 8–13.

BOOKS FOR TEENAGERS ABOUT DEATH

Bode, J. (1993). *Death is Hard to Live With.* New York, NY: Bantam Doubleday Dell Publishing. Teenagers talk frankly about how they cope with loss.

Dorfman, E. (1994). *The C-Word.* Portland, OR: New Sage Press. This author battled her own cancer at 16 and her mother's death due to breast cancer. She interviews five teenagers and their families sharing their cancer experience.

Fitzgerald, H. (2000). *The Grieving Teen.* New York, NY: Fireside Books. A guide for teens to help them through their experience of grief.

Gootman, M. (1994). *When a Friend Dies.* Minneapolis, MN: Free Spirit Publishing, Inc. This book was inspired by a mom who watched her teenage children suffer over the loss of a friend. It helps teens recognize and validate their feelings and provides good suggestions for healing.

Kolf, J. (1990). *Teenagers Talk about Grief.* Grand Rapids, MI: Baker Book House. A book written especially for and about teenage grief with firsthand accounts of experiences.

BOOKS ABOUT GRIEVING

Mundy, M. (1998). *Sad isn't Bad.* St. Meinrad, IN: Abbey Press. A guidebook for kids dealing with loss. Ages 5-8.

Spies, K. (1993). *Everything You Need to Know about Grieving.* New York, NY: The Rosen Publishing Company. This book helps explain how kids can talk to other kids that are going through a grief process. Ages 7–12.

BOOKS ABOUT A PARENT DYING

Jonah, S. (1999). *Transitions Along the Way.* Fairfield, CA: Visions. A guide to the dying process for children and young adults.

Levine, J. (1992). *Forever in my Heart.* Burnsville, NC: Compassion Books. A story to help children participate in life as a parent dies.

McNamara, J. (1994). *My Mom Is Dying*. Minneapolis, MN: Augsburg Fortress. This book is a diary by Kristine, a young girl who learns her mom is dying. It includes a discussion section for parents. Ages 5–9.

BOOKS ABOUT THE DEATH OF A PARENT

Blume, J. (1981). *Tiger Eyes*. New York, NY: Macmillan Children's Group. Fifteen-year-old Davey works through the feelings of his father's murder in a store hold up. Ages 11 and up.

Brisson, P. (1999). *Sky Memories*. New York, NY: Delacorte Press. Emily is 10-years old when her mother is diagnosed with cancer and 11 when she dies. Ages 9–13.

Clifton, L. (1983). *Everett Anderson's Goodbye*. New York, NY: Henry Holt & Company. Everett struggles with his sadness after his father's death. Ages 5–9.

Douglas, E. (1990). *Rachel and the Upside Down Heart*. Los Angeles, CA: Price Stern Sloan. The true story of 4-year-old Rachel, and how her father's death affects her life. Ages 5–9.

Frost, D. (1991). *DAD! Why'd You Leave Me?* Scottdale, PA: Herald Press. This is a story about 10-year-old Ronnie who can't understand why his dad died. Ages 8–12.

Greenfield, E. (1993). *Nathanial Talking*. New York, NY: Black Butterfly Children's Group. Nathanial, an energetic 9-year-old, helps us understand a black child's world after his mom dies. He uses rap and rhyme to express his feelings. Ages 7–11.

Klein, L. (1995). The Best Gift for Mom. Mahwah, NJ: Paulist Press. A story about a boy and his feelings for his dad who had died when he was a baby. Ages 7–12.

Krementz, J. (1996*). How it Feels When a Parent Dies*. New York, NY: Knoph Publishing Company. Eighteen children (ages 7–16) speak openly about their feelings and experiences after the death of a parent.

Lanton, S. (1991). *Daddy's Chair*. Rockville, MD: Kar-Ben Copies Inc. Michael's dad died. The book follows the Shiva, the Jewish week of mourning when Michael doesn't want anyone to sit in his daddy's chair. Ages 5–10.

LeShan, E. (1975). *Learning to Say Goodbye When a Parent Dies*. New York, NY: Macmillan Publishing Company. Written directly to children about problems to be recognized and overcome when a parent dies. Ages 8 and up.

Lowden, S. (1993). *Emily's Sadhappy Season*. Omaha, NE: Centering Corporation. The story of a young girl's feelings after her father dies. Ages 6–10.

Powell, E. S. (1990). *Geranium Morning*. Minneapolis, MN: Carol Rhoda Books, Inc. A boy's dad is killed in a car accident and a girl's mom is dying. The children share their feelings. Ages 6 and up.

Robinson, A. (1994). *Sophie*. New York, NY: Voyager Books. Sophie's grandfather dies and she feels very alone. Ages 3–7.

Thaut, P. (1991). *Spike and Ben*. Deerfield Beach, FL: Health Communications, Inc. The story of a boy whose friend's mom dies. Ages 5–8.

Tiffault, B. (1992). *A Quilt for Elizabeth*. Omaha, NE: Centering Corporation, Inc. Elizabeth's grandmother helps her understand her feelings after her father dies. This is a good story to initiate an open dialogue with children. Ages 7 and up.

Vigna, Judith. (1991). *Saying Goodbye to Daddy*. Niles, IL: Albert Whitman and Company. A sensitive story about a dad's death and the healing that takes place in the weeks that follow. Ages 5–8.

Whelan, G. (1998). *Forgive the River, Forgive the Sky*. Grand Rapids, MI: Eerdmans Books. Twelve-year-old Lilly struggles with her dad's death in the river. Ages 9–13.

BOOKS ABOUT SIBLING DEATH

Alexander, S. (1983). *Nadia the Willful*. New York, NY: Pantheon Books. Nadia's older brother dies, and she helps her father heal his grief by willfully talking about her brother. Ages 6–10.

Erling, J. & Erling, S. (1986). *Our Baby Died. Why?* Maple Plain, MN: Pregnancy and Infant Loss Center. A little boy shares his feelings about the death of his stillborn brother and the eventual birth of sibling twins. Children can read, draw, and color with this book. Ages 4–10.

Gryte, M. (1991*). No New Baby*. Omaha, NE: Centering Corporation. Siblings express their feelings about mom's miscarriage. Ages 5–8.

Johnson, J., & Johnson M. (1982*). Where's Jess?* Omaha, NE: Centering Corporation. A book for young children that addresses the questions and feelings kids have when a sibling dies. Ages 4–7.

Linn, E. (1982*). Children are not Paperdolls*. Springfield, IL: Human Services Press. Kids who have had brothers and sisters die draw and comment on their experiences. Ages 8–12.

Richter, E. (1986). *Losing Someone You Love: When a Brother or Sister Dies*. New York, NY: Putnam. Adolescents share feelings and experiences about the death of a sibling. Ages 11 and up.

Romond, J. (1989). *Children Facing Grief*. St. Meinrad, IN: Abbey Press. Letters from bereaved brothers and sisters, telling of their experiences and offering hope. Ages 6–14.

Sims, A. (1986). *Am I Still a Sister*. Slidell, LA: Big A and Company. This story was written by an eleven-year-old who experienced her baby brother's death. Ages 8–12.

Temes, R. (1992). *The Empty Place*. Far Hills, NJ: Small Horizons. The story of a third grade boy whose older sister dies. Ages 5–9.

BOOKS ABOUT A FRIEND'S DEATH

Blackburn, L. (1987). *Timothy Duck*. Omaha, NE: Centering Corporation. Timothy Duck's friend John gets sick and dies. He shares his feelings. Ages 5–8.

Blackburn, L. (1991). *The Class in Room 44*. Omaha, NE: Centering Corporation. The children in Room 44 share their feelings of grief when their classmate Tony dies. Ages 6–10.

Cohen, J. (1987). *I Had a Friend Named Peter*. New York, NY: William Morrow and Company. Betsy's friend Peter dies suddenly. She learns through parents and teachers that Peter's memory can live on. Ages 5–10.

Gootman, M. (1994). *When a Friend Dies*. Minneapolis, MN: Free Spirit Press. This is a book about grieving and healing when a friend dies. For teens.

Kaldhol, M., & Wenche, O. (1987). *Goodbye Rune*. New York, NY: Kane-Miller. A story about the drowning death of a girl's best friend and how parents can help. 5–12 years.

Kubler-Ross, E. (1987). *Remember the Secret*. Berkeley, CA: Celestial Arts. The imaginative story of love and faith of two children, and their experience with death. Ages 5–10.

Park, B. (1995). *Mike Harte was Here*. New York, NY: Random House. Mike Harte dies in an accident; he wasn't wearing his bike helmet. His friends grieve. Ages 10–14.

BOOKS ABOUT THE DEATH OF A GRANDPARENT

Fassler, J. (1983). *My Grandpa Died Today*. Springfield, IL: Human Sciences Press. David did not fear death as much because Grandpa knew that David would have the courage to live. Ages preschool to 7.

Holden, L. D. (1989). *Gran-Gran's Best Trick*. New York, NY: Magination Press. This book deals directly with cancer. It follows the treatment, sickness, and death of a grandparent. Ages 6–12.

Liss-Levinson, N. (1995). *When A Grandparent Dies*. Woodstock, VT: Jewish Lights Publishing. This is a children's memory workbook dealing with shiva and the year beyond. Ages 8–12.

Pomerantz, B. (1983). *Bubby, Me, and Memories*. New York, NY: Union Of American Hebrew Congregations. A child's grandmother dies. His feelings are addressed and his questions answered. Good source to explain Jewish rituals. Ages 5–8.

Thomas, J. (1988). *Saying Goodbye to Grandma*. New York, NY: Clarion Books. A sensitively written book about a family's joining together for grandma's funeral. Ages 5–10.

Thornton, T. (1987). *Grandpa's Chair.* Portland, OR: Multnomah Press. The story of a small boy's love for his grandfather, his last visit to see him, and his grandfather's eventual death. Ages 4–8.

Yolen, J. (1994). *Grandad Bill's Song.* New York, NY: Philomel Books. A little boy asks "What do you do on the day your grandfather dies?" and family and friends talk about memories. Then he discovers his own feelings. Ages 5–9.

WORKBOOKS ABOUT DEATH

Boulden, J., & Boulden, J. (1991). *Saying Goodbye.* Santa Rosa, CA: Boulden Publishing. A bereavement workbook for young children. Ages 5–8.

Carney, K. (1997). *Together we'll get Through This! Learning to Cope with Loss and Transition.* (Barklay & Eve series book 1). Wethersfield, CT: Dragonfly Publishing. This is an excellent resource for young children to express feelings about death. Ages 4–8.

Goldman, L. (1998). *Bart Speaks Out on Suicide.* Los Angeles, CA: WPS. This is an interactive story and memory book for a special person that has died of suicide. Ages 4–9.

Haasl, B., & Marnocha, J. (2000). *Bereavement Support Group Program For Children* (2nd ed.). Muncie, IN: Accelerated Development. A step-by-step children's workbook and leader's manual to use in bereavement groups. Ages 8–13.

Hammond, J. (1980). *When My Mommy Died / When My Daddy Died.* Flint, MI: Cranbrook Publishing. Both workbooks are geared to young children's bereavement work and parent death. Ages 4–8.

Heegaard, M. (1988). *When Someone Very Special Dies.* Minneapolis, MN: Woodland Press. An excellent workbook that uses artwork and journaling to allow children to work through their grief. A facilitator's manual is available. Ages 5–12.

O'Toole, D. (1995). *Facing Change.* Burnsville, NC: Compassion Books. An excellent resource for preteens and teens. Ages 11 and up.

Rogers, F. (1991). *So Much to Think About.* Pittsburgh, PA: Family Communications, Inc. An activity book for young children when someone they love has died. Ages 5–8.

Traisman, E. S. (1992). *Fire In My Heart; Ice In My Veins.* Omaha, NE: Centering Corporation. A wonderful workbook for teenagers to explore thoughts and feelings and record grief memories. For teenagers.

SPECIAL MEMORY BOOK

Chimeric. (1991). *Illustory*. Denver, CO. Kids can write and illustrate their own books that can be sent away and made into hardcover bound books. Ages 5–10.

BOOKS ABOUT LIFE CYCLES

Buscaglia, L. (1982). *The Fall of Freddie the Leaf*. Thorofare, NJ: Charles B. Slack Company. The story of the changing seasons as a metaphor for life and death. Ages 4–8.

Gerstein, M. (1987). *The Mountains of Tibet*. New York, NY: Harper and Row. The story of a woodcutter's journey from the mountains of Tibet through the universe of endless choices and back home again. Ages 7 and up.

Mellonie, B., & Ingpen, R. (1983). *Lifetimes: The Beautiful Way to Explain Death to Children*. New York, NY: Bantam Books. This book explains the ongoing life cycle of plants, animals, and people. Ages 3–10.

Munsch, R. (1983). *Love You Forever*. Willowdale, Canada: A Firefly Book. A beautiful book for adults and children alike about the continuance of love throughout life. All ages.

Wood, D. (1992). *Old Turtle*. Duluth, MN: Pfeifer-Hamilton. A fable for children and adults that captures the message of peace on earth and oneness with nature. The illustrations are beautiful. Ages 5 and up.

BOOKS ABOUT A DEPRESSED PARENT

Hamilton, D. (1995). *Sad Days, Glad Days*. Morton Grove, IL: Albert Whitman & Company. A story about how it feels as a child to have a parent suffer from depression. Ages 6–11.

Sanford, D. (1993). *It Won't Last Forever*. Sisters, OR: Questar Publishers. This is the story of Kristen, a little girl who worries over her Mom's ongoing sadness. Explains depression to children. Ages 6–10.

BOOKS ABOUT SUICIDE

Cammarata, D. (2000). *Someone I Love Died by Suicide*. Palm Beach Gardens, FL: Grief Guidance, Inc. This is a story for child survivors and those who care for them. Ages 5–9.

Garland, S. (1994). *I Never Knew Your Name*. New York, NY: Ticknor & Fields. A young boy tells the story of a teenage boy's suicide whose name he did not know. Ages 5–11.

Goldman, L. (1998). *Bart Speaks Out on Suicide*. An interactive storybook for children on suicide. It serves as a memory book for their person that died and also gives words for the way the person died. Ages 5–10.

Grollman, E., & Malikow, M. (1999). *Living When a Young Friend Commits Suicide*. Boston, MA: Beacon Press. This book discusses why people may die of suicide, and how we can talk about it. Teens and young adults.

Harper, J. (1993). *Hurting Yourself*. Omaha, NE: Centering Corporation. A pamphlet for teenagers and young adults who have intentionally injured themselves. For teenagers.

Kuklin, S. (1994). *After A Suicide: Young People Speak Up*. New York, NY: G.P. Putnam's Sons. This book addresses young people who are survivors after a parent's suicide. For teens.

McDaniel, L. (1992). *When Happily Ever After Ends*. New York, NY: Bantam Books. Shannon is a teen who struggles with living with her father's violent death by suicide.

Nelson, R., & Galas, J. (1994). *The Power to Prevent Suicide*. Minneapolis, MN: Free Spirit Publishing. This book appears to be very useful in involving teenagers with suicide prevention. It provides practical suggestions and examples with which teenagers can identify.

Norton, Y. (1993). *Dear Uncle Dave*. Hanover, NH: Shirley Baldwin Waring. A story written by a fourth grade girl sharing memories about Uncle Dave and his death by suicide. Ages 5–10.

Rubel, B. (1999). *But I Didn't Say Goodbye*. Kendall Park, NJ: Griefwork Center, Inc. A practical approach for parents and professionals to help children discuss suicide. Ages 9–13.

The Dougy Center. (1990). *I Wish I Were In A Lonely Meadow: When a Parent Commits Suicide*. Portland, OR: Dougy Center. This book is a compilation of children's own writings about their experience with a parent's suicide. Ages 9–15.

BOOKS ABOUT HOMICIDE

Aub, K. (1995). *Children Are Survivors, Too*. Boca Raton, FL: Grief Education Enterprises. This book presents many stories by young children to teenagers on their journey as homicide survivors. Ages 6 through teens.

Constans, G. (1997). *Picking up the Pieces*. Warminster, PA: Mar*co products. A program about violent death for use with middle school students. Ages 10–13.

Henry-Jenkins, W. (1999). *Hard Work Journal*. Omaha, NE: Centering Corporation. This is a book for teenagers and young adults to help them understand and overcome homicidal loss and grief.

Loftis, C. (1997). *The Boy Who Sat by the Window*. Far Hills, NJ: New Horizon Press. This is an excellent book for young children about a boy who gets murdered and the cycle of violence that surrounds him. Ages 6-12.

Lorbiecki, M. (1996). *Just One Flick of the Finger*. New York: Dial Books. The story of a young boy who accidentally brings a gun to school and shoots a friend. Ages 5-10.

Mahon, K. L. (1992). *Just One Tear*. New York, NY: Lothrop, Lee, and Shepard Books. This book is an honest account written by a 14-year-old of the overwhelming emotions after a boy witnesses his father being shot and fatally wounded. It includes accounts of the trial and its outcome. Ages 8-14.

Schleifer, J. (1998). When *Someone You Know has been Killed*. New York, NY: Rosen Publishing Group. This book discusses the emotions felt when someone experiences a murder and provides strategies to cope. Ages 10 to teens.

Smith, I. (1991). *We Don't Like Remembering Them as a Field of Grass*. Portland, OR: The Dougy Center. A book by children of many ages telling of how they feel about a loved one being murdered. Ages 7-16.

BOOKS ABOUT AIDS

Balkwill, F. (1993). *Cell Wars*. London, England: William Collins & Sons. This story for young children uses words and pictures to thoroughly explain cells, viruses, and good and bad cells. Ages 5-9.

Fassler, D., & McQueen, K. (1990). *The Kids' Book About AIDS*. Burlington, VT: Waterfront Books. This book approaches the subject of AIDS in a sensitive manner to which young children can relate. Kids can use it as a workbook. Ages 4-8.

Girard, L. (1991). *Alex, the Kid with AIDS*. Morton Grove, IL: Albert Whitman & Company. This is a story about a fourth-grade boy who has AIDS and the friendships he creates. Ages 6-11.

Hausherr, R. (1989). *Children and the Aids Virus*. New York, NY: Clarion Books. An informative book for older and younger children that tells and shows through pictures the world of AIDS. Ages 5 and up.

ordan, M. (1989). *Losing Uncle Tim*. Niles, IL: A. Whitman Niles. Daniel's Uncle Tim dies of AIDS, and he struggles with many feelings about it.

redge, M. (1991). *Teens with AIDS Speak Out*. New York, NY: Simon & Schuster. Teenagers with DS talk about their experience. Teens.

McCauslin, M. (1995). *Update: AIDS*. Parsippany, NJ: Crestwood House. This book discusses AIDS in the U.S. and how the disease affects society. Ages 10–14.

McNaught, D. (1993). *The Gift of Good-Bye: A Workbook for Children Who Love Someone with AIDS*. New York, NY: Dell Publishing. This is an interactive book to help adults and children deal with the painful experience of loving someone with AIDS. Ages 5–10.

Merrifield, M. (1990*). Come Sit by Me*. Ontario, Canada: Women's Press. A great book for parents and teachers to educate young children on the facts about AIDS. Ages 4–8.

Moutoussamy-Ashe, J. (1993). *Daddy and Me*. New York, NY: Alfred A. Knopf. A wonderful photo story of Arthur Ashe and his daughter Camera and their journey with AIDS. Ages 4 to adulthood.

Sanford, D. (1991). *David has AIDS*. Portland, OR: Multnomah Press. David struggles with the disease of AIDS. Ages 7–11.

Verniero, J. (1995). *You can tell me, Willie*. New York, NY: Magination Press. A practical story for children about AIDS. Ages 5–10.

Wiener, L., & Pizzo, P. A. (1994). *Be a Friend*. Morton Grove, IL: Albert Whitman & Company. A wonderful book written by children with AIDS and presented by people whose daily work is helping these children. Ages 5 through adulthood.

Wolf, B. (1997). *HIV Positive*. New York, NY: Dutton Children's Books. An excellent resource for children that includes photographs and honest explanations about HIV and AIDS. Ages 8–13.

BOOKS ABOUT CHILD ABUSE

Loftis, C. (1995). *The Words Hurt*. Far Hills, NJ: New Horizon Press. A story for young children explaining how words can be hurtful and abusive and what they can do about it.

Naylor, P. R. (1990). *Shiloh*. New York, NY: Atheneum Children's Books. The story about Shiloh, an abused dog, and the boy that loved him. Ages 8–12.

Pall, M., & Streit, L. (1983). *Let's Talk about it. The Book for Children about Child Abuse*. Saratoga, CA: R & E Publishers. Simple book defining child abuse that uses cartoon illustrations. Ages 9–14.

Wright, L. (1991). *I Love My Dad But...* Toronto, Ontario: Is Five Press. This book deals with an abusive parent in a practical way. Ages 4–8.

BOOKS ABOUT SATANIC RITUAL ABUSE

Sanford, D. (1990). *Don't Make Me Go Back Mommy*. Portland, OR: Multnomah Press. A book explaining satanic rituals to children and ways for caring adults to work with kids that have experienced them. Ages 6–10.

BOOKS ABOUT FOSTER HOMES AND ABANDONMENT

Lowery, L. (1995). *Somebody Somewhere Knows My Name*. Minneapolis, MN: Carolrhoda Books. Grace describes what happened when she and her brother are abandoned by their mom.

Nasta, P. (1991). *Aaron Goes to the Shelter*. Tucson, AZ: Whole Child. A story and workbook about children that have experienced family chaos and may be placed in a shelter or foster care. Ages 6–12.

Simon, N. *I Wish I Had my Father*. Morton Grove, IL: Albert Whitman & Company. A boy tells his feelings about a dad who left a long time ago and never communicates. Ages 6–10.

Sanford, D. (1993). *For Your Own Good*. Sisters, OR: Questar Publishers. A book for children about foster care and ways that caregivers can help them. Ages 6–10.

BOOKS ABOUT HOMELESSNESS

Kroll, V. (1995). *Shelter Folks*. Wm.B.Eerdmans Publishing Co. Nine-year-old Joelle tells about her life in a shelter. Ages 6–10.

Powell, S. (1992). *A Chance to Grow*. Minneapolis, MN: Carolrhoda Books. Joe, his mom, and his sister Gracey are evicted from their apartment. They are left homeless and live on the streets and in shelters seeking a permanent home. Ages 6–11.

Trottier, M. (1997). *A Safe Place*. Morton grove, IL: Albert Whitman & Company. Emily and her mother come to a shelter to escape her father's abuse. Ages 5–9.

BOOKS ABOUT SEXUAL ABUSE

Girard, L. (1984). *My Body Is Private*. Morton Grove, IL: Albert Whitman & Company. A direct approach to help children distinguish between good touching and bad touching, including help for parents. Ages 5–10.

Lowery, L. (1994). *Laurie Tells*. Minneapolis, MN: Carolrhoda Books. Twelve-year-old Laura tells a supportive aunt that her father is sexually abusing her. Ages 10–14.

Russell, P., & Stone, S. (1986). *Do You Have a Secret?* Minneapolis, MN: CompCare Publishers. This book helps adults talk to children about sexual abuse and explains how they can seek help. Ages 4–8.

Sanford, D. (1986*). I Can't Talk About It.* Portland, OR: Multnomah Press. Annie talks to an abstract form, Love, about her sexual abuse and begins to heal and trust. Ages 8–13.

Sanford, D. (1993). *Something Must Be Wrong with Me.* Portland. OR: Multnomah Press. This is the story of Dino, a boy who is sexually abused. He finds the courage to talk about it. Ages 7–12.

BOOKS ABOUT VIOLENCE IN THE HOME

Bernstein, S. (1991) *A Family that Fights.* Morton Grove, IL: Albert Whitman & Company. A story about a family's domestic violence and ways children and adults can get help. Ages 5–9.

Cohen, J. (1994). *Why Did It Happen?* New York, NY: Morrow Junior Books. This is a story about a boy who witnesses a violent crime in his neighborhood. The author provides ways to cope. Ages 6–11.

Davis, D. (1984). *Something Is Wrong In My House.* Seattle, WA: Parenting Press. A book about parents fighting, ways to cope with violence, and how to break the cycle. Ages 8–12.

Hochban, T., & Krykorka, V. (1994). *Hear My Roar: A Story of Family Violence.* New York, NY: Annick Press Ltd. This book is the story of Lungin, a little boy bear whose Dad is violently abusive. He and his Mom choose to take action and go to a shelter as a first step. Ages 7–12. Can be read to younger children.

Lorbiecki, M. (1996). *Just One Flick of the Finger.* New York, NY: Dial Books. A young boy takes a gun to school, and the gun goes off in an argument. Ages 6–11.

Paris, S. (1986). *Mommy and Daddy are Fighting.* Seattle, WA: Seals Press. Honest discussion of parental fighting, with a guide for parents. Ages 5–8.

Sanford, D. (1989). *Lisa's Parents Fight.* Portland, OR: Multnomah. The story of 10-year-old Lisa, her siblings, and parents who interact with angry outbursts and occasional physical abuse. Ages 8–12.

Winston-Hiller, R. (1986). *Some Secrets are for Sharing.* Denver, CO: MAC Publishing. A story of a family secret of a boy being beaten by his mom. He finally tells and gets help for him and his mom. Ages 6–11.

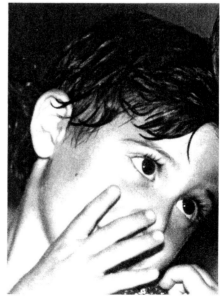

BOOKS ABOUT TRAUMA

Berry, J. (1990). *About Traumatic Experiences.* Chicago, IL: Children's Press. Answers to kid's questions about trauma and traumatic experiences. Ages 8–11.

Holmes, M. (2000). *A Terrible Thing Happened.* Washington, DC: Magination Press. Sherman becomes anxious and angry after something terrible happens to him. Talking to an adult helps him feel better. Ages 4–8.

Salloum, A. (1998). *Reactions.* Omaha, NE: Centering Corporation. This is a workbook to help children who are experiencing trauma and grief. Ages 6–11.

Sheppad, C. (1998). *Brave Bart.* Grosse Pointe Woods, MI: Institute for Trauma and Loss in Children. This is a book designed to help young children with trama and its connected grief reactions. Ages 4–8.

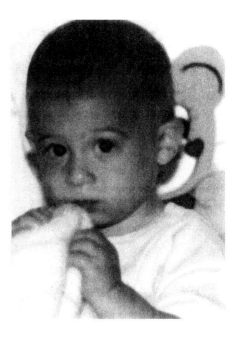

BOOKS ABOUT BULLIES

Boatwright, B., Mathis, T., & Smith, S. (1998). *Getting Equipped to Stop Bullying: A Kid's Survival Kit for Understanding and Coping with Violence in the Schools.* Minneapolis, MN: Educational Media Corporation. This book provides understandings of the dynamics of bullying and empowers children to recognize and deal with bullies.

Cohen-Posey, K. (1995). *How to Handle Bullies, Teasers and Other Meanies.* Highland City, FL: Rainbow Books. A practical resource for kids to help them with the issues of bullying. Ages 8–13.

Johnston, M. (1996). *Dealing with Bullying.* New York, NY: Rosen Publishers. This is a book that defines bullying, explains why bullies act the way they do, and discusses ways for change. Ages 4–8.

Kaufman, G., & Raphael, L. (1990). *Stick Up for Yourself.* Minneapolis, MN: Free Spirit Publishing. A guide to help kids feel personal power and self-esteem. Ages 8–12.

Romain, T. (1997). *Bullies are a Pain in the Brain.* Minneapolis, MN: Free Spirit Publishing. A good book to address the topic of bullying. Ages 7–11.

BOOKS ABOUT WEIGHT DISORDERS AND EATING PROBLEMS

Berry, J. (1990). *About Weight Problems and Eating Disorders.* Chicago, IL: Children's Press. An interesting book that explains the realities of eating disorders and weight problems. Ages 7–13.

BOOKS ABOUT STRANGER ANXIETY

Girard, L. (1985). *Who is a Stranger and What Should I Do?* Morton Grove, IL: Albert Whitman & Company. This book explains in simple language what a stranger is and what kids can do in different situations. Ages 6–10.

Schaefer, C. (1992). *Cat's Got Your Tongue.* New York, NY: Magination Press. This is the story of Anna, a kindergartener diagnosed as an electively mute child. Children with stranger anxieties can relate to Anna's behaviors. Ages 3–7.

BOOKS ABOUT ADULT ILLNESS

Carney, K. (1997). *Barklay and Eve: What is Cancer, Anyway?* Wethersfield, CT: Dragonfly Publishing. This book gives words to use for young children to talk about cancer. Ages 3–7.

Dorfman, E. (1994). *The C-Word.* Portland, OR: New Sage Press. This book presents family interviews and photographs about their cancer experience. For teens.

Goodman, M. B. (1991). *Vanishing Cookies.* Mississauga, Canada: Arthur Jones Lithographing Ltd. A book that talks honestly about a parent's cancer treatment. Ages 6–13.

Heegaard, M. (1991). *When Someone Has a Very Special Illness.* Minneapolis, MN: Woodland Press. A practical and interactive workbook that addresses feelings when a loved one is very sick. Ages 6–12.

LeShan, E. (1986). *When a Parent is Very Sick.* Boston, MA: Joy Street Books. A helpful book for children and parents that talks openly about the stress of having a parent with a serious illness. Ages 8–13.

Nystrom, C. (1990). *Emma Says Goodbye.* Batavia, IL: Lion Publishers. Emma's aunt has a terminal illness, and she comes to live with Emma. Ages 8–14.

Parkinson, C. (1991). *My Mommy has Cancer.* Rochester, NY: Park Press. This book helps young children learn about cancer, its treatment, and its emotional impact. Ages 4–8.

Strauss, L. (1988). *Coping When a Parent has Cancer.* New York, NY: Rosen Publishing. A book for teenagers who are coping with a parent with cancer. For teenagers.

BOOKS ABOUT ORGAN DONORS

Carney, K. (1999). *Precious Gifts: Katie Coolican's Story* (Barklay and Eve Explain Organ and Tissue Donation). Wethersfield, CT: Dragonfly Publishing. This is an excellent resource for young children on organ and tissue donation. Ages 3–7.

BOOKS ABOUT CHILDREN'S ILLNESS

Baznik, D. (1981). *Becky's Story.* Bethesda, MD: Association for the Care of Children's Health. Becky, a 6-year-old, feels confused and left out when her brother is in a bad accident and is given all the attention. Ages 4–7.

Foss, K. (1996). *The Problem with Hair.* Omaha, NE: Centering Corporation. This is a story about a little girl that has cancer and has lost her hair through chemotherapy. Ages 5–10.

Gaes, J. (1989) *My Book for Kids With Cansur.* Pierre, SD: Melius-Peterson. The story of 8-year-old Jason who successfully battles cancer. Jason's brothers illustrate the book. Ages 7–12.

Lawrence, M. (1987). *My Life: Melinda's Story.* Alexandria, VA: Children's Hospice International. A story by Melinda and her journey through illness. Ages 5 and up.

Maple, M. (1992). *On the Wings of a Butterfly.* Seattle, WA: Parenting Press. A butterfly becomes a friend to Lisa, a child dying of cancer. She shares her fears of dying. Ages 5–10.

Sanford, D. (1992). *No Longer Afraid.* Sisters, OR: Multnomah Press. A story about Jaimie, a young girl with cancer, and her journey with this critical illness. Ages 7–11.

Schultz, C. M. (1990). *Why, Charlie Brown, Why?* New York, NY: Topper Books. The story about Charlie's friend Janice, who has leukemia, and what happens when a friend is very ill. Ages 5–10.

Stolp, H. (1990). *The Golden Bird.* New York, NY: Dial Books. An 11-year-old boy is terminally ill and explores his thoughts and feelings about death.

Tartakoff, K. (1994). *My Stupid Illness.* Denver, CO: The Children's Legacy. This interactive book enables children and their families to tell their story. Ages 4–9.

Warner, S. (1998). *Sort of Forever.* New York, NY: Knopf, Inc. Twelve-year-olds explore their feelings as they live with their friend having cancer. Ages 10–13.

BOOKS ABOUT HOSPICE

Carney, K. (1999). *Everything Changes, but Love Endures*. Wethersfield, CT: Dragonfly Publishing. This book gives excellent explanations of hospice for young children. Ages 3–7.

Flynn, J. (1996). *Hospice Hugs*. Accord Aftercare Services. This book speaks to young children about hospice. Ages 3–7.

BOOKS ABOUT WAR/DEATH

Bunting, E. (1990). *The Wall*. New York, NY: Clarion Books. Illustrations and story about a father and son that visit the Vietnam Veterans Memorial and the impact of three generations of war. Ages 5–8.

Coerr, E. (1993). *Sadako and the Thousand Paper Cranes*. New York, NY: Putnam. This is a true story about a Japanese girl who is dying from her exposure to radiation from the bomb at Hiroshima. Her hope for peace and life is symbolized in her paper cranes. Ages 8–13.

Finkelstein, N. (1985). *Remember Not to Forget*. New York, NY: Mulberry Book. This book clearly describes for young children the history and origins of the holocaust in Nazi Germany. Ages 6–10.

BOOKS ABOUT DRUGS

Sanford, D. (1987). *I Can Say No*. Portland, OR: Multnomah Press. David's story about his feelings concerning his older brother's involvement with drugs. Ages 6–10.

Taylor, C. (1992). *The House that Crack Built*. San Francisco, CA: Chronicle Books. A poetic story for young children that explores today's drug problems. Ages 7–12.

BOOKS ABOUT FAMILIES WITH ALCOHOLICS

Black, C. (1982). *My Dad Loves Me, My Dad has a Disease.* Denver, CO: MAC Publishing. This is a workbook for children of alcoholics to help them better understand alcoholism and their feelings about it. Ages 6–14.

Carbone, E. L. (1992). *My Dad's Definitely not a Drunk.* Burlington, VT: Waterfront Books. Corey is a 12-year-old boy who struggles with a secret that his dad drinks too much. Corey and his mom discover a way to get help. Ages 9–14.

Hastings, J., & Typpo, M. (1984). *An Elephant in the Living Room.* Minneapolis, MN: CompCare Publishers. A workbook about alcoholism that allows children to express their feelings. Ages 8–12.

Sanford, D. (1984). *I Know the World's Worst Secret.* Portland, OR: Multnomah Press. A girl talks about her alcoholic mom. Ages 8–13.

Vigna, J. (1988). *I Wish Daddy Didn't Drink So Much.* Morton Grove, IL: Albert Whitman & Company. The story of a little girl who is constantly disappointed by her Dad's drinking. With help from caring adults, she gains new hope in her situation. Ages 4–8.

BOOKS ABOUT DAD'S LEAVING

Cochran, Vicki. (1992). *My Daddy is a Stranger.* Omaha, NE: Centering Corporation. The story of a little girl whose dad left home when she was a baby and how she feels about and explains his absence. Ages 5–8.

Hickman, M. (1990). *When Andy's Father Went to Prison.* Niles: IL: Albert Whitman & Company. Andy's dad was arrested for stealing and put into prison. He copes with his feelings of shame and abandonment while his dad is away. Ages 5–9.

Lindsay, J. (1993). *Do I Have a Daddy?* Buena Park, CA: Morning Glory Press. The story of a single-parent child whose parents had never married and father is totally absent. It contains a special section for single parents. Ages 5–8.

BOOKS ABOUT MOVING

Blume, J. (1986). *Are You There God? It's Me Margaret.* New York, NY: Dell Publishing. Margaret has to face moving and a new life. Ages 9–12.

McKend, H. (1988). *Moving Gives Me a Stomachache.* Ontario, Canada: Black Moss Press. The story of a child's anxiety and fear of moving. Ages 5–8.

Viorst, J. (1998). *Alexander, Who's Not (Do you hear me? I mean it!) Going to Move.* New York, NY: Aladdin Paperbacks. A story about Alexander's overwhelming feelings about moving. Ages 4–10.

BOOKS ABOUT DIVORCE

Boulden, J., & Boulden J. (1991). *Let's Talk.* Santa Rosa, CA: Boulden Publishing. A kid's activity book for separation and divorce. Ages 5–8.

Evans, M. D. (1989). *This is Me and My Single Parent.* New York, NY: Magination Press. A discovery workbook for children and single parents. Ages 8–13.

Fassler, D., Lash, M., & Ives, S. (1988). *Changing Families.* Burlington, VT: Waterfront Books. Advice for kids in coping with divorce and remarriage. Ages 4–12.

Heegaard, M. (1990). *When Mom and Dad Separate.* Minneapolis, MN: Woodland Press. A workbook for children exploring thoughts and feelings about separation and divorce. Ages 6–12.

Krementz, J. (1988*). How It Feels When Parents Divorce.* New York, NY: Knopf. Children describe how divorce has affected them. Ages 8–13.

Sanford, D. (1985). *Please Come Home.* Portland, OR: Multnomah Press. Jenny's thoughts and feelings are expressed to her teddy bear about her parents divorce. Ages 7–12.

Stern, E. S. (1997). *Divorce is not the End of the World.* Singapore, China: Tricycle Press. A teenage brother and sister discuss topics related to divorce. Teens.

Swan-Jackson, A. (1997). *When Your Parents Split Up . . .* New York, NY: Price Stern Sloan, Inc. This book focuses on various aspects of divorce and provides practical advice. Teens.

BOOKS ABOUT ADOPTION

Banish, R., & Jordan-Wong, J. (1992). *A Forever Family.* New York, NY: Harper Collins. Eight-year-old Jennifer was in many foster homes before being adopted as a part of her forever family. Ages 5–8.

Girard, L. (1989). *We Adopted You Benjamin Koo.* Niles, IL: Alfred Whitman & Company. Benjamin is a 9-year-old boy from another country. He tells of how he adjusted to adoption and a culturally blended family.

Sanford, D. (1989*). Brian Was Adopted.* Portland, OR: Multnomah Press. Brian questions many parts of adoption and talks to God about it. Ages 7–11.

Stinson, K. (1992). *Steven's Baseball Mitt.* Ontario, Canada: Annick Press Ltd. This book describes the thoughts and feelings that go through an adopted child's mind about his birth mother. Ages 5–8.

BOOKS ABOUT NATURAL DISASTERS

Jordon, M. (1993). *The Weather Kids*. Omaha, NE: Centering Corporation. Stories about kids that have experienced devastation through tornados, earthquakes, and floods. Ages 8–11.

Williams, V. (1992). *A Chair for My Mother*. New York, NY: Mulberry Books. After a fire destroys their home, Rosa, her mom, and grandmother save their money for a big chair to share. Ages 5–10.

BOOKS ABOUT MAGICAL THINKING

Blackburn, L. (1991). *I Know I Made it Happen*. Omaha, NE: Centering Corporation. This book presents different circumstances where children find themselves feeling guilty and responsible for making things happen. Ages 5–8.

Rappaport, D. (1995). *The New King*. New York, NY: Penguin Books. A boy becomes king after his father dies and commands his court to bring his father back from the dead. Ages 6–11.

BOOKS ABOUT FEELINGS

Crary, E. (1992). *I'm Mad*. Seattle, WA: Parenting Press. A children's book that identifies feelings and gives options on what to do with them. Ages 3–8.

Crary, E., & Steelsmith, S. (1996). *When You're Mad and You Know it*. Singapore: Parenting Press. One of a series of board books for toddlers to learn about expressing feelings. Ages 2–5.

Doleski, T. (1983). *The Hurt*. Mahwah, NJ: Paulest Press. The wonderful story about a little boy who keeps all of his hurts inside, until the hurt grows so big it fills his room. When he shares his feelings, the hurt begins to go away. All ages.

Hazen, B. (1992). *Even if I Did Something Awful*. New York, NY: Aladdin Books. The reassuring story of a little girl who realizes Mom will love her no matter what she does. Ages 5–8.

Jampolsky, G., & Cirincione, D. (1991). *"Me First" and the Gimme Gimmes*. Deerfield Beach, FL: Health Communication, Inc. A story that shows the transformation of selfishness into love. All ages.

Kaufman, G. & Raphael L. (1990). *Stick Up for Yourself*. Minneapolis, MN: Free Spirit Publishing Company. A guide to help kids feel personal power and self esteem. Ages 8-12.

Moser, A. (1988). *Don't Pop Your Cork On Monday*. Kansas City, MO: Landmark Editions. A handbook for children to explore the causes of stress and techniques to deal with it. Ages 5-8.

Moser, A. (1991). *Don't Feed the Monster on Tuesday*. Kansas City, MO: Landmark Editions. Dr. Moser offers children information on the importance of knowing their own self-worth and ways to improve self-esteem. Ages 5-8.

Munsch, R., & Martchenko, M. (1985). *Thomas's Snowsuit*. Ontario, Canada: Annick Press, Ltd. A story about a child who refuses to wear his snowsuit and will not be manipulated by adults. Ages 5-8.

Oram, H. (1982). *Angry Arthur*. New York, NY: E.P. Dutton. Arthur becomes enraged with his mom and creates havoc on the planet. Ages 5-8.

Sanford, D. (1986). *Don't Look at Me*. Portland, OR: Multnomah Press. The story of Patrick who feels very stupid and learns to feel special about himself. Ages 7-11.

Simon, N. (1989). *I Am Not a Crybaby*. New York, NY: Puffin Books. This book shows how children of different races and cultures share the commonality of feelings. Ages 5-8.

Seuss, Dr. (1990). *Oh, The Places You'll Go*. New York, NY: Random House. Dr. Seuss uses his magical creativity to inspire young and old to succeed in life, despite the many ups and downs they face. Ages 5 to adult.

Steig, W. (1988). *Spinky Sulks*. Singapore: Sunburst Books. Spinky is angry and begins to sulk. No one can make him stop until he is ready. Ages 5-8.

Voirst, J. (1972). *Alexander and the Terrible Horrible No Good Very Bad Day*. New York, NY: Aladdin Books. Alexander has a day where everything goes wrong. Everyone can relate to this. Ages 5-8.

Voirst, J. (1981). *If I Were in Charge of the World and other Worries.* New York, NY: Aladdin Books. A book of poems for children expressing how kids feel about a lot of things. Ages 5 and up.

BOOKS ABOUT NIGHTMARES

Devlin, W., & Devlin H. (1994). *Maggie Has A Nightmare.* New York, NY: Macmillan Publishing Company. Maggie's daytime fears appear in her dreams. Sharing them helped her fears disappear. Ages 4–7.

Lobby, T. (1990). *Jessica and the Wolf.* New York, NY: Magination Press. Jessica's parents help her solve the problem of her recurring nightmare. Ages 4–8.

Marcus, I., & Marcus P. (1990). *Scary Night Visitors.* New York, NY: Magination Press. Davey has fears at night and learns to feel safe through experiencing his feelings directly. Ages 4–7.

McGuire, L. (1994). *Nightmares in the Mist.* Palo Alto, CA: Enchante Publishing. Alicia has many fears since her mom went into the hospital. Magical paint helps her overcome them. Ages 5–9.

BOOKS ABOUT CREMATION

Carney, K. (1997). *Our Special Garden: Understanding Cremation* (Barklay & Eve Series Book 4). Wethersfield, CT: Dragonfly Publishing. This book is an excellent resource to explain cremation to young children. Ages 3–7.

Flynn, J. (1994). *What is Cremation?* Accord Aftercare Services. A book that helps young children understand cremation. Ages 3–7.

BOOKS ABOUT FUNERALS AND MEMORIAL SERVICES

Ancona, G. (1993). *Pablo Remembers.* New York, NY: Lothrop, Lee & Shepard Books. A beautiful book with wonderful photographs that explains the Mexican fiesta of The Day of the Dead which celebrates the life of loved ones each year. Ages 6–11.

Balter, L. (1991). *A Funeral for Whiskers.* Hauppauge, NY: Barron's Educational Series, Inc. Sandy's cat dies, and she finds useful ways to express her feelings and commemorate. Ages 5–9.

Carney, K. (1997). *Barkley and Eve: Sitting Shiva* (Barklay and Eve Series Book 3). Wethersfield, CT:

Dragonfly Publishing. This book explains the Jewish ritual of sitting Shiva after a funeral. Ages 3–7.

Carson, J. (1992). *You Hold Me and I'll Hold You.* New York, NY: Orchard Books. A soft story for young children about a little girl's feelings of wanting to hold and be held at a memorial service. Ages 5–9.

Grollman, E., & Johnson, J. (2001). *A Child's Book About Funerals and Cemetaries.* Omaha, NE: Century Corporation. This is a helpful, interactive guide for children to understand and express feelings about cemetaries and funerals. Ages 4–9.

Johnson, J., & Johnson, M. (1990). *Tell Me, Papa.* Omaha, NE: Centering Corporation. This book simply and clearly explains how kids feel about death, burial, and funerals. Ages 6–10.

Jukes, M. (1993). *I'll See You in my Dreams.* New York, NY: Alfred A. Knopf. A little girl prepares to visit a seriously ill uncle and imagines writing a farewell message across the sky. Ages 5–10.

Kloeppel, D. (1981). *Sam's Grandma.* College Park, GA: Darlene Kloeppel. A 7-year-old boy tells his story of his Grandma's death and subsequent funeral. Kids can color this book. Ages 4–8.

Techner, D., & Hirt-Manheimer, J. (1993). *A Candle for Grandpa: A Guide to the Jewish Funeral for Children and Parents.* New York, NY: UAHC Press. A book simply written for children to explain a Jewish funeral and burial practices. Ages 7–12.

Death and transformation are man's unchosen and unchangeable fate.

All that he can choose and change is consciousness. But to change this

is to change all.

Rodney Collin

Campbell, 1991

References

Adler, J. (1994, January 10). Kids growing up scared. *Newsweek*, 43–50.

Ancona, G. (1993). *Pablo remembers.* New York: Lothrop, Lee & Shepard Books.

Aub, K. (1995). *Children are survivors too.* Boca Raton, FL: Grief Education Enterprises, Inc.

Beane, A. (1999). *The bully-free classroom.* Minneapolis, MN: Free Spirit Publishing.

Bitney, J. (1996). *No-bullying program.* Minneapolis, MN: Johnson Institute.

Blackburn, L. (1991). *I know I made it happen: A book about children and guilt.* Omaha, NE: Centering Corporation.

Bode, J. (1993). *Death is hard to live with.* New York: Bantam Doubleday Dell.

Braza, K. (1988). *Memory book for bereaved children.* Salt Lake City, UT: Healing Resources.

Brown, T. (1993). *A broken toy.* Chattanooga, TN: STARS Production.

Brohl, K., & Corder, C. (1999). *It couldn't happen here.* Washington, DC: Child Welfare League of America.

Campbell, E. (Ed.). (1991). *A dancing star: Inspirations to guide and heal.* San Francisco, CA: Aquarian Press.

Carney, K. (1997). *Honoring our loved ones, going to a funeral.* Wethersfield, CT: Dragonfly Publishing.

Carney, K. (1997). *Together we'll get through this! Learning to cope with loss and transition.* Wethersfield, CT: Dragonfly Publishing.

Carney, K. (2001). *Barklay and Eve: Sitting Shiva.* Wethersfield, CT: Dragonfly Publishing.

Carson, J. (1992). *You hold me and I'll hold you.* New York: Orchard Books.

Cassini, K., & Rogers, J. (1990). *Death and the classroom.* Cincinnati, OH: Griefwork of Cincinnati.

Celotta, B., Jacobs, G., & Keys, S. (1987, January). Searching for suicidal precursors in the elementary school. *American Mental Health Journal.*

Centers for Disease Control and Prevention. (1995, June). *HIV/AIDS Surveillance Report,* 7(1), 12–14.

Children's Defense Fund. (2001, February). *Key facts on youth, crime, and violence.* http://www.childrensdefense.org/youthviolence/keyfacts.youthcrime.htm

Children's Defense Fund. (2001, February). *Every child deserves a safe start.* http://www.childrensdefense.org/youth/keyfacts_youthcrime.htm

Children's Defense Fund. (2001, February). *Key facts about children and families in crisis* http://www.childrensdefense.org/youth/keyfacts_family-crisis.htm

Cohen, J. (1994). *Why did it happen?* New York: Morrow Junior Books.

Columbia Broadcasting System (CBS). (1993, November). *There are no children here*. Harpo Productions.

Compassionate Friends. (1999–2000). Compassionate friends moves to change suicide language. *Surving Suicide: American Association of Suicidology, 11*(3).

Crary, E. (1992). *I'm mad*. Seattle, WA: Parenting Press.

Cunningham, L. (1990). *Teen age grief (TAG)*. Panorama, CA: Teen Age Grief.

Davis, N. (1990). *Once upon a time: Therapeutic stories*. Oxon Hill, MD: Psychological Associates of Oxon Hill.

Doka, K. (1996). *Living with grief after sudden loss*. Bristol, PA: Taylor & Francis.

Doleski, T. (1983). *The hurt*. Mahwah, NJ: Paulist Press.

Dorfman, E. (1994). *The C-word*. Portland, OR: New Sage Press.

Fanos, J., & Wiener, L. (1994, June). Tomorrow's survivors: Siblings of Human Immunodeficiency Virus infected children. *Developmental and Behavioral Pediatrics, 15*(3), 43.

Fassler, D. (1990). *What's a virus anyway?* Burlington, VT: Waterfront Books.

Fox, S. (1988). *Good grief: Helping groups of children when a friend dies*. Boston: New England Association for the Education of Young Children.

Fried, S., & Fried, P. (1996). *Bullies & victims*. New York: Evans and Co.

Garrity, C., Jens, K., Porter, W., Sager, N. E., & Short-Camilli, Cam. *Bully-proofing your school* (2nd ed.). Longmont, CO: Spris West.

Gil, E. (1991). *The healing power of play*. New York: Guilford Press.

Gliko-Bradon, M. (1992). *Grief comes to class*. Omaha, NE: Centering Corporation.

Goldman, L. (1998). *Bart speaks out on suicide*. Los Angeles: WPS Publishers.

Goldman, L. (1998, October). *How to make yourself bully-proof*. Current health magazine. Weekly Reader Publisher.

Goldman, L. (2000). *Life and loss: A guide to help grieving children*. New York: Taylor & Francis.

Gootman, M. (1994). *When a friend dies*. Minneapolis, MN: Free Spirit Publishing.

Grollman, & Johnson. (2001). *A child's book about funerals and cemetaries*. Omaha, NE: Centering Corporation.

Harper, J. (1993). *Hurting yourself*. Omaha, NE: Centering Corporation.

Harrison, & Dawson. (1999). *Death of the forest queen*. Wilmore, KY: Words on the Wind Publisher.

Heegaard, M. (1988). *When someone very special dies*. Minneapolis, MN: Woodland Press.

Henderson, R. (1995, January/February). Caught in the crossfire. *Common Boundary*, 28–35.

Henry-Jenkins, W. (1989). *Hard work journal*. Omaha, NE: Centering Corporation.

Hochban, T., & Krykorka, V. (1994). *Hear my roar: A story of family violence*. New York: Annick Press.

Holmes, M. (2000). *A terrible thing happened*. Washington, DC: Magination Press.

Hughes, L. (1994). *Collected poems*. New York: Alfred A. Knopf.

Johnson, J., & Johnson, M. (1990). *Tell me, Papa*. Omaha, NE: Centering Corporation.

Johnston, M. (1996). *Dealing with bullying*. New York: Rosen Publishing.

Jones, A. (1998). *Self-injurious behavior in children and adolescents: Part 21. What is SIB?* Healing Magazine, Kidspeace Pub. p. 35.

Jones, R. (1995). *Where was God at 9:02 a.m.?* Nashville, TN: Thomas Newson Pub.

Jordan, M. K. (1993). *The weather kids.* Omaha, NE: Centering Corporation.

Klicker, R. (1990). *A student dies, a school mourns . . . Are you prepared?* Buffalo, NY: Thanos Institute.

Lantieri, L., & Patti, J. (1996). *Waging peace in our schools.* Boston: Beacon Press.

Leenaars, A., & Wenckstern, S. (1991). *Suicide prevention in schools.* New York: Hemisphere.

Lobby, T. (1990). *Jessica and the wolf.* New York: Magination Press.

Loftis, C. (1991). *The boy who sat by the window.* Far Hills, NJ: New Horizon Press.

Loftis, C. (1995). *The words hurt.* Far Hills, NJ: New Horizon Press.

Lorbiecki, M. (1996). *Just one flick of the finger.* New York, NY: Dial Books.

MacLean, G. (1990). *Suicide in children and adolescents.* Lewiston, NY: Hogrefe & Huber Publishers.

Mahon, K. L. (1992). *Just one tear.* New York: Lothrop, Lee, and Shepard Books.

Merrifield, M. (1990). *Come sit by me.* Ontario, Canada: Women's Press.

Mills, J. (1993). *Little tree.* Washington, DC: Magination Press.

Mishara, B. (1999). Implications of death and suicide in children ages 6–12 and their implications for suicide prevention. *Suicide & Life Threatening Behavior, 29*(2), 105.

Morbidity and Mortality Weekly Report. (1994, August 26). p. 43.

Moser, A. (1988). *Don't pop your cork on Mondays.* Kansas City, MO: Landmark Editions.

Moutassamy-Ashe, J. (1993). *Daddy and me.* New York: Alfred A. Knopf.

National Committee for the Prevention of Child Abuse. (1994, January 10). In J. Adler, Kids group up scared. *Newsweek,* 43–50.

National Vital Statistics Report. (1999, June), Vol. 47, No. 19.

Naylor, P. R. (1991). *Shiloh.* New York: Atheneum Children's Books.

Oates, M. (1993). *Death in the school community.* Alexandria, VA: American Counseling Association.

Oliver, L. Y-K. (2000). *Trauma of the century* (pp. 15, 68, 187, 189). Taichung, Taiwan: Taichung County Governmment.

Olweus, D. (1993). *Bullying at school.* Maiden, MA: Blackwell Publishing.

O'Toole, D. (1988). *Aarvy Aardvark finds hope.* Burnsville, NC: Compassion Books.

O'Toole, D. (1989). Growing through grief: A K–12 curriculum to help young people through all kinds of grief. Burnsville, NC: Compassion Books.

O'Toole, D. (1994). *Aarvy Aardvark finds hope* (video). Burnsville, NC: Compassion Books.

O'Toole, D. (1995). *Facing change.* Burnesville, NC: Compassion Books.

Pall, M., & Streit, L. B. (1983). *Let's talk about it: The book for children about child abuse.* Saratoga, CA: R & E Publishers.

Peplar, D. (2000, October 22). Expert on bullying tells how it can be stopped. *The Province News.*

Pudney, W., & Whitehouse, E. (1996). BC, Canada: New Society Publishers.

Rigby, K., Slee, P. (1999). Suicidal ideation among adolescent school children: Involvement in bully-victim problems, and perceived social support. *Suicide and Life Threatening Behavior, 29,* 119–130.

Roberts, J., & Johnson, J. (1994). *Thank you for coming to say good-bye.* Omaha, NE: Centering Corporation.

Romoin, T. (1997). *Bullies are a pain in the brain.* Minneapolis, MN: Free Spirit Press.

Ross, D. (1996). *Childhood bullying and teasing.* Alexandria, VA: ACA Publishers.

Rubel, B. (1999). *But I didn't say goodbye.* Kendall Park, NJ: Griefwork Center, Inc.

Russell, P., & Stone, B. (1986). *Do you have a secret?* Minneapolis, MN: CompCare Publishers.

Ryan, M. (1994, October 9). What our children need is adults who care. *Parade Magazine.*

Sanford, D. (1986). *I can't talk about it.* Portland, OR: Multnomah Press.

Salloum, A. (1998). *Reactions.* Omaha, NE: Centering Corporation.

Schaefer, C. (1992). *Cat's got your tongue.* New York: Magination Press.

Sheppard, C. (1998). *Brave Bart.* Grosse Pointe Woods, MI: TLC.

SIEC (Suicide Information and Education Center). (2001, July). SIEC alert. Alberta, Canada: SIEC Publisher.

Smith, C. (1993). *The peaceful classroom.* Beltsville, MD: Gryphon Horse Publisher.

Smith, J. (1989). *Suicide prevention.* Holmes Beach, FL: Learning Publications.

Stein, S. (1984). *About dying.* New York: Walker and Company.

Stevenson, R. (1994). *What will we do?* Amityville, NY: Baywood Publishing.

Taichung County Government. (2000). Trauma of the century. Taichung County, Taiwan. Taichung County Government.

Techner, D., & Hirt-Manheimer, J. (1993). *A candle for Grandpa: A guide to the Jewish funeral for children and parents.* New York: UAHC Press.

The Dougy Center. (1991). *We don't like remembering them as a field of grass.* Portland, OR: The Dougy Center.

The Dougy Center. (1998). *Helping the grieving student: A guide for teachers.* Portland, OR: The Dougy Center.

The Dougy Center. (1999). *Helping teens cope with death.* Portland, OR: The Dougy Center.

The Dougy Center. (1999). *I wish I was in a lonely meadow.* Portland, OR: The Dougy Center.

The Dougy Center. (1999). *What about the kids? Understanding their needs in funeral planning and services.* Portland, OR: The Dougy Center.

The Dougy Center. (2000). *When death impacts your school: A guide for administrators.* Portland, OR: The Dougy Center.

Tongue, B. J. (1982). *The international book of family therapy.* New York: Brunner/Mazel.

Traisman, E. (1992). *Fire in my heart, ice in my veins.* Omaha, NE: Centering Corporation.

Traisman, E. (1994). *A child remembers.* Omaha, NE: Centering Corporation.

U.S. Advisory Board on Child Abuse and Neglect. (1995, April). *Nation's shame: Fatal child abuse and neglect in U.S.* Washington, DC: Author.

U.S. Agency for Institutional Development Compiled by U.S. Census. (1997, November). Orphans of worldwide AIDS. *Washington Post.*

U.S. Department of Health and Human Services. (1994, November 14). In D. Van Biema, Parents who kill. *Time,* p. 50.

Van Biema, D. (1994, November 14), Parents who kill, *Time,* 50–51.

Ward, B. (1993). *Good grief.* London: Jessica Kingsley.

Webb, N. B. (1993). *Helping bereaved children.* New York: Guilford Press.

Whitehouse, E., & Pudney, W. (1996). *A volcano in my tummy.* BC, Canada: New Society Publishers.

Wiener, L. S., Best, A., & Pizzo, P. A. (1994). *Be a friend: Children who live with HIV speak.* Morton Grove, IL: Albert Whitman & Company.

Wiener, L., Fair, C., & Pizzo, P. A. (1993). Care for the child with HIV infection and AIDS. In A. Armstrong-Dailey & S. Z. Goltzer (Eds.), *Hospice care for children* (pp. 85–104). New York: Oxford Press.

Yankelovich Youth Monitor. (1994, January 10). In J. Adler, Kids growing up scared. *Newsweek*, p. 50.

Zinner, E. & Williams, M. B. (1999). *When a community weeps.* Bristol, PA: Taylor & Francis.

About the Author

Linda Goldman is the author of *Life and Loss: A Guide To Help Grieving Children* (2nd ed.), *Bart Speaks Out on Suicide*, *Helping the Grieving Child in the School*, and a Chinese translation of *Breaking the Silence*. She has been an educator in the public school system for almost 20 years, in both teaching and counseling capacities.

Presently Linda is a certified grief therapist and certified death educator who practices near Washington, DC. A creative therapist, Linda began her private grief practice after the death of her stillborn daughter, Jennifer. Working with grieving children, teenagers, and adults, Linda finds gentle and innovative ways to work through the pain and confusion of loss and grief. She has developed special expertise in the area of prenatal loss, as well as an ability to identify and normalize complicated grief issues. She was acknowledged by *Washingtonian Magazine* as one of the top therapists in the Washington, DC, Virginia, and Maryland areas.

The success of her grief work has led her to educate other caring adults through training in school systems and universities, including Johns Hopkins Graduate School, University of Maryland School of Social Work/Advanced Certification Program for Children and Adolescents, and the National Changhua University of Education in Taiwan. She also teaches adults by sharing diverse ways to help grieving children, and was a panelist for the National Teleconference "When A Parent Dies: Helping the Child." She also serves on the board of the Association for Death Education and Counseling (ADEC). Linda lives in Chevy Chase, MD with her husband, Michael, and son, Jonathan.

Author Index

Subject Index

Abandonment, 9, 67, 83–84
  books about, 252, 258
  fear of, 9
Abuse, 9, 73–90, 184, 217–218, 224, 251–253
  activities, 82, 84–86
  case examples, 11, 78–81, 83–84
  definitions, 12, 19, 88–89
  educators helping children, 174–175
  emotional, 78–80
  Jill's story, 87
  physical, 83–84
  reporting, 77, 174
  resources, 88–90
  sexual, 81–82
  statistics, 75–76
  suicide and, 38
Accidents, 8
  case examples, 192–198
Acting out, 81
Activities
  after trauma, 201–210
  AIDS, 56
  facilitating meltdown process, 15
  for children, 15, 43, 56, 68–69, 201–210
  for teenagers, 15–17, 195–198
  handling bullying, 99–102
  physical abuse, 84–86
  sexual abuse, 82
  suicide, 43
  violent crimes, 68–69
  visualization, 15, 111, 119–121, 129
Adoption
  books about, 259
AIDS, 47–58
  activities for children, 56
  case examples, 52–53
  children's worries, 52–53
  definitions, 12, 49–51, 58
  facts and statistics, 49
  resources, 57, 218, 222–223, 250–251
  siblings' worries, 54–55
  social stigma, 8
Alcoholism
  books about, 258
Ambivalence, 9, 38
Anger, 82
  homicide, 65
  working with, 29–30, 122–124
Antidepressants, 31–32
Art therapy, 27, 43, 56, 68–69, 86, 117–119, 188, 202–209
At-risk children, 165
  gays, lesbians, and bisexuals, 169
  grieving children, 166
  self-injurious behaviors, 167–168
  suicide warning signs, 170

Balloon techniques, 7, 69, 155–156, 197
Bed wetting, 7, 9, 28–29, 67
Bisexuals
  at-risk students, 169
Books
  abandonment, 252, 258
  abuse, 88, 176, 251–253
  adoption, 259
  adult illness, 255
  AIDS, 57, 250–251
  alcoholism, 258
  bullying, 102–104, 254
  children's illness, 256
  cremation, 262
  death, 242–248
  depression, 248
  divorce, 259
  drug abuse, 257
  eating disorders, 255
  feelings, 260–262
  for adults, 103–104, 211, 230–236
  for children, 57, 102, 157, 211, 242–243
  for teens, 57, 243
  funerals, 262–263
  grief, 14, 18, 243
  homelessness, 252
  homicide, 249–250
  hospice, 257
  life cycles, 248
  magical thinking, 260
  memorial services, 157, 262–263
  memory, 43, 69, 126–127, 130, 248
  moving, 258–259
  natural disasters, 260
  nightmares, 262
  organ donation, 256
  services, 239
  stranger anxiety, 255
  suicide, 44, 249
  support group guides, 238–239
  trauma, 211, 254
  violence, 70, 253
  war, 257
  weight problems, 255
  workbooks, 247
Bubbles, 146, 155–156
Bullying, 91–104, 184
  activities for children, 101–102
  case examples, 97
  gays and bisexuals, 169
  parents helping, 100–103
  resources, 102–104, 254
  school shootings, 93–95
  statistics, 96
  talking about, 98–99

disease, 58
funerals, 19
grief, 12, 19–20, 44
guilt, 19, 44, 89
HIV, 58
homicide, 12, 19, 71
immune deficiency, 58
immune system, 58
infection, 58
judge, 71
jury, 71
justice, 71
legal system, 71
mourning, 6, 19
murder, 71
protection, 89
rage, 19, 89
revenge, 20
sentences, 71
shame, 20, 89
stigma, 20, 89
suicide, 12, 20, 35, 44
syndromes, 58
terror, 20, 89
violence, 12, 71, 89
virus, 58
white blood cells, 58
Denial, 10
suicide and, 39
Depression, 8–9, 165
books about, 248
defining for children, 19, 44
gays and bisexuals, 169
Disbelief, 8
Divorce
books about, 259
Doll play, 112, 210
Dream work, 114–116, 129
case examples, 114–115, 209
Drug abuse
books about, 257

Eating disorders, 7
books about, 255
Educators, 159–177
commemorating students, 164
dealing with homicide, 172–173
discussing suicide, 171–172
handling bullying, 100–103
helping abused children, 174–175
helping gays, lesbians, and bisexuals, 169
helping with self-injurious behaviors, 167–168
identifying grieving children, 166
recognizing suicide signs, 170
resources for, 176–177
signs of at-risk children, 165
supporting bereaved students, 160–164
Emotional abuse, 78–80

Family trees, 15
Fear, 7–8, 10, 67, 81, 185, 192
of abandonment, 9
of AIDS, 52–55
of bullying, 96–97
of ridicule, 8
Feelings
books about, 260–262
cards, 112

Flowers
at memorials, 155–156
planting, 7, 189
Frozen blocks of time, 8, 10
suicide and shame, 36–37
Funerals, 133–157
after the service, 136–149
children commemorating, 155
commemorating afterward, 149–152
opening to children, 134
planning, 138
preparing children, 139
preparing parents, 137–138
preparing the community, 135–136
preparing the school, 136–137
remembering special days, 153–154
resources, 157, 262–263
the service, 143–146
sharing memories, 139–142
summary, 155–156

Gangs, 184
Gays
at-risk students, 169
Geneograms, 15
Going on, 6–8
Grief, 6–7
after violent crime, 67
complicated, 1–20
defining for children, 19, 44
helping with, 190–191
normal, 6–7, 108
psychological tasks, 6–7
resources, 216, 243
signs of, 81
unexpressed, 184
Guilt, 8–9
defining for children, 19, 44, 89
gays and bisexuals, 169
homicide, 64, 69
magical thinking, 14
suicide and, 39–40

Headaches, 7, 29
Helping organizations, 217–228
abuse prevention, 177
HIV. See AIDS
Homelessness
books about, 252
Homicide, 8, 59–71, 184
activities, 68–69
case examples, 61, 66, 68
child's experience of, 64–65
dealing with at school, 172–173
definitions, 12, 19, 71
effect on children, 62–64
in America, 67
media images, 61
normal responses to, 66–67
resources, 70–71, 220–221, 249–250
social stigma, 8
Hospice
books about, 257
Hostility, 6–7, 165, 193
Hotlines, 217–218

Illnesses, 8
books about, 255–256

Journals, 17, 43

Kids' Place (Oklahoma), 199-201
Kinder-Mourn, 195-198

Legal processes, 65
  definitions for children, 71
Lesbians
  at-risk students, 169
Letter writing, 29, 33-34, 43, 69, 156, 189
  case examples, 109-110, 197
  preparing for memorials, 135-137
Life lines, 205
Linking objects, 128
Loss story, 204
Loss timelines, 15, 205

Magical thinking
  books about, 260
Manuals, 17
Media images, 9
  discussing, 101
  effects on children, 62-64
  of violence, 61
Meltdown process, 10-12
  case examples, 11
  facilitating, 12-20
  resources, 14-20
  working with anger, 29-30
Memorials, 133-157
  after the service, 136-149
  children commemorating, 155
  commemorating afterward, 149-152
  opening to children, 134
  planning, 138
  preparing children, 139
  preparing parents, 137-138
  preparing the community, 135-136
  preparing the school, 136-137
  remembering special days, 153-154
  resources, 157, 262-263
  the service, 143-146
  sharing memories, 139-142
  summary, 155-156
Memory bags, 147, 156
Memory books, 43, 69, 126, 130
  commercial, 127, 248
  for children, 127
  for teens, 127
Memory boxes, 127, 130
Memory work, 123-128, 130
  sharing memories, 139
  tools for, 126-128
Moving
  books about, 258-259
Multiple losses, 9
  case examples, 11, 199
  suicide and, 28-32
Murals, 43, 69, 155, 188
Murder. See Homicide
Music
  for children's memorial service, 146
  for teenagers, 17

Natural disasters (See also Taiwan earthquake; Traumatic events)
  books about, 260
Neglect, 9

Nightmares, 6-7, 9, 67, 81, 192
  books about, 262
Noncommunication, 12-13
Normal grief, 6-7
  symptoms of, 6
Normalcy
  creating, 108-110, 129

Oklahoma City bombing, 199-201
Organ donation
  books about, 256
Organizations. See Helping organizations
Over-responsibility
  homicide and, 64
  suicide and, 39-40

Parents
  death of, 243-245
  grief processes of, 9, 12, 25-27
  handling bullying, 100-103
  of schoolmates, 136-137
  preparing for memorials, 137-138
  suicide response, 33-34
  support group, 196
Peaceful box, 208
Peaceful place, 206-207
Play therapy, 210
  using dolls, 112, 210
  using puppets, 43, 69, 112, 121, 210
  using toys, 27, 43, 68-69, 112, 130, 210
Poetry, 7, 86
Post-traumatic stress disorder. See Traumatic events
Projective techniques, 27, 130
  clay modeling, 27, 29, 68-69, 121
  drawing, 27, 43, 56, 68-69, 86, 117-119, 188, 202-209
  sand play, 113, 121
  storytelling, 15, 27, 43, 117-119, 130, 175, 202-203
Puppets, 43, 69, 112, 121, 210

Rage, 8, 28-29
  definitions, 19, 89
  over homicide, 65
Reality checks, 105, 129
Resources, 213-269
  abandonment, 252, 258
  abuse, 8-90, 217-218, 224, 251-253
  adoption, 259
  adult illness, 255
  AIDS, 57, 222-223, 250-251
  alcoholism, 258
  book services, 239
  books, 230-236, 242-263
  bullying, 102-104, 254
  children's illness, 256
  cremation, 262
  crisis intervention, 218
  CS-ROMs, 241
  curricula, 237-238
  death, 242-248
  depression, 248
  divorce, 259
  drug abuse, 257
  facilitating meltdown process, 14-20
  feelings, 260-262
  for adults, 211, 230-237, 240
  for children, 211, 216, 237, 240, 242-243
  for educators, 176-177

for grief support groups, 238-239
for teens, 240, 243
funerals, 262-263
grief and loss, 216, 243
homelessness, 252
homicide, 220-221, 249-250
hospice, 257
hotlines, 217-218
magical thinking, 260
memorial services, 156-157, 262-263
moving, 258-259
natural disasters, 260
nightmares, 262
organ donation, 256
organizations, 217-228
stranger anxiety, 255
suicide, 44-45, 219, 249
tapes, 240
trauma, 211, 254
videos, 236-237
violence, 70-71, 220-221, 253
war, 257
Websites, 240
weight problems, 255
Revenge
defined, 20
fantasies, 8, 65
Rituals
creating, 131
defined, 6
Role play, 29, 101, 129, 174-175

Sand play, 113, 121
Scary place, 206
School problems, 6-7, 29, 67, 161-162
School shootings, 93-95
Secret jars, 56
"Secret Witchie," 43
Self-blame, 81
Self-defense, 99
Self-doubt, 9
Self-hatred, 8
Self-injurious behaviors, 167-168
Separating, 12, 36-37
Sexual abuse, 81-82
books about, 252-253
helping children, 82
Shame, 8-10
defining for children, 20, 89
suicide and, 36-37
Shock, 8-9, 64
Silence, 122, 131
Smith, Susan, 61
Special days, 153-154, 161, 163, 197-198
Statistics
AIDS, 49
bullying, 94, 96
child abuse, 75-76
homicide, 62-64
suicide, 25
violence, 62-64
Stigma, 8
definitions, 20, 89
suicide, 36-37
violent death, 64
Stomach aches, 6-7
Story boxes, 119

Storytelling, 15, 27, 43, 117-119, 130, 175, 202-203
case examples, 117-118
Stranger anxiety
books about, 255
Sudden death, 8
Suicide, 8, 23-46
abuse and, 38
activities for children, 43-44
case examples, 28-34, 36-40
children's thoughts, 40-40
complications of, 25-27
definitions, 12, 20, 35, 44
denial and, 39
discussing with children, 171-172
facts and statistics, 25
gays and bisexuals, 169
guilt and, 39-40
multiple loss and, 28-32
over-responsibility and, 39-40
parental grief process, 33-34
projective techniques, 27
resources, 44-45, 219, 249
shame and, 36-37
social stigma, 8, 36-37
summary, 46
talking about, 35
warning signs, 42, 170
Sunglasses, 113
Support groups. See Crisis support groups
Symbolic expressions, 111-113, 124, 210

Taiwan earthquake, 185-191
conference on grieving children, 191
creating safety, 187-190
fear, 185
helping with grief, 190-191
Tapes, 240
Teachers. See Educators
Techniques, 105-131
art therapy, 27, 43, 56, 68-69, 86, 117-119, 130, 188, 202-209
collages, 43, 69, 155, 204
commemorating, 111-113
creating normalcy, 108-110, 129
dealing with abuse, 82, 84-86
dream work, 114-116, 129, 209
for children, 15, 27, 29-30, 56, 68-69
for teens, 15-17
journals, 17, 43
letter writing, 29, 33-34, 43, 69, 109-110, 135-137, 156, 189, 197
life lines, 205
loss story, 204
loss timelines, 15, 205
memory books, 43, 69, 126-127, 130, 248
memory work, 123-128, 130, 139
peaceful box, 208
peaceful place, 206-207
play therapy, 27, 43, 68-69, 27, 112, 130, 210
projective, 27
role play, 29, 101, 129, 174-175
scary place, 206
secrecy work, 84-85
silence, 122, 131
storytelling, 15, 27, 43, 117-119, 130, 175, 202-203
summary, 129-131
symbolic expressions, 111-113, 129
visualization, 15, 111, 119-121, 129
working with anger, 29-30

writing activities, 55, 68–69, 202–208
Telephones, 112
Terror, 8–10, 83
  defining for children, 20, 89
Terrorism, 201
Tommy, 15–16
Toys in therapy, 27, 43, 68–69, 112, 130, 210
Trauma
  resources, 254
Traumatic events, 8, 179–211
  activities for children, 201–210
  children's reactions to, 192–194
  creating safety, 187–190
  grief workshop, 181
  helping children, 182–183, 190–191
  Oklahoma City bombing, 199–201
  resources, 211, 254
  school bus accident, 192–194
  student's death, 195–198
  Taiwan earthquake, 185–191
  unexpressed grief continuum, 184
Traumatic stress quiz, 193

Understanding, 6
Unexpressed grief, 184

Videos
  for adults, 236–237
  for children, 237

on bullying, 103
Violence, 59–71, 184
  activities, 68–69
  at school, 172–173
  bullying, 91–104
  child's experience of, 64–65
  definitions, 12, 71, 89
  effects on children, 62–64
  in America, 67
  media images, 61
  normal responses to, 66–67
  resources, 70–71, 220–221, 253
  school shootings, 93–95
Visualization, 15, 111, 119–121, 129
  case example, 121
  procedure for, 120

War
  books about, 257
Websites, 240
  for adults, 102, 240
  for children, 102, 240
Weight problems
  books about, 255
Workbooks, 247
Worry boxes, 43
Writing activities (*See also* Journals; Letter writing), 55, 68–69, 202–208